PRIMARY MATHEMATICS 5A Home Instructor's Guide

Authored by: Jennifer Hoerst
Printed by: Avyx, Inc.

Copyright © 2004 by Jennifer Hoerst
Published by Avyx, Inc.
Reprinted 2005
New edition 2006
Reprinted 2008

All Rights Reserved

The appendix pages may be reproduced for individual class use only. No other part of this publication may be reproduced, stored in a retrieval system, or transmitted in any form or by any means — electronic, mechanical, photocopy, recording, or any other — except for brief quotations embodied in critical articles or printed reviews, without prior written permission of the publisher.

Go to:
www.avyx.com

Or e-mail:
info@avyx.com

Or write:
Avyx, Inc.
8032 South Grant Way
Littleton, CO 80122-2705
USA
303-483-0140

ISBN 13: 978-1-887840-86-6

Printed in the United States of America

Avyx, in an effort to help purchasers of the Singapore Primary Mathematics 5A Textbook and Workbook is providing this Home Instructor's Guide. We welcome your feedback and input. If you find errors, we also welcome your pointing these out to us. To give us feedback or to note corrections, please send an email to info@avyx.com, or to the author at jenny@singmath.com, or you may send via the postal system to Avxy, Inc., 8032 South Grant Way, Littleton, CO, 80122-2705.

As errors are detected and corrected, you may find the error corrections posted online at the author's web site, http://www.singmath.com. Additional help may be obtained at the forum linked there. **NOTE:** This site is the sole property of Jennifer Hoerst and is not a site maintained by Avyx. This site is offered solely as a courtesy to help purchasers see corrections as Jennifer Hoerst posts them. All corrections captured will be included in updates to the manuals prior to their reprinting.

Contents

Workbook Answers and Solutions

Using this Guide

This guide is meant to help instructors using *Primary Mathematics 5A* when teaching one student or a small group of students. It should be used as a guide and adapted as needed.

The textbook is divided into units and parts. Within each part, there is a page for discussion, followed by *learning tasks*.

This guide further subdivides each textbook part into ***sessions*** (designated with (1), (2), (3),...) for a specific set of learning tasks. A session can take 1-2 days to teach. For each session, the guide provides

 objectives

 and background notes to the instructor. Following the notes, there are some

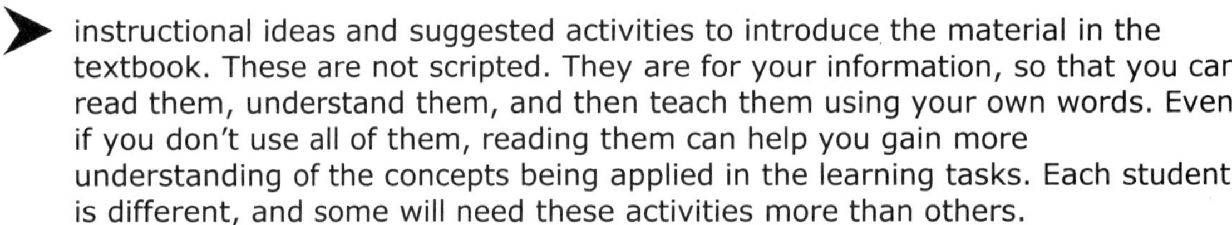

instructional ideas and suggested activities to introduce the material in the textbook. These are not scripted. They are for your information, so that you can read them, understand them, and then teach them using your own words. Even if you don't use all of them, reading them can help you gain more understanding of the concepts being applied in the learning tasks. Each student is different, and some will need these activities more than others.

After the introductory activities, the guide indicates

 corresponding textbook pages and learning tasks, along with answers and sometimes solutions, and sometimes with some additional notes to you and suggestions for discussion as you do the textbook pages with your student. Before doing the lesson with your student, you should read this material and study the textbook pages yourself. This will make the lesson go more smoothly.

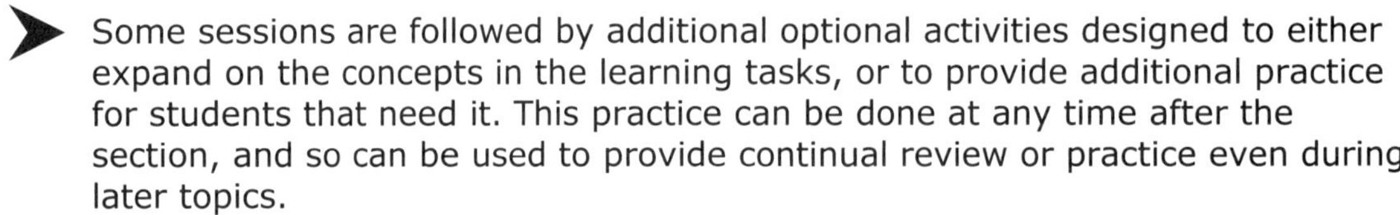

Some sessions are followed by additional optional activities designed to either expand on the concepts in the learning tasks, or to provide additional practice for students that need it. This practice can be done at any time after the section, and so can be used to provide continual review or practice even during later topics.

 At the end of the session, the corresponding workbook exercise is indicated.

 The textbook contains periodic **practices**. They can be done as encountered, or used for additional problems during a lesson. Generally they cover the material taught in the previous few pages, but can also bring in concepts from other previous units. They contain occasional challenging problems that can be used for discussion. In this guide, the practices are treated as separate sessions and sometimes include

 activities or games using cards or dice for more practice, if desired.

 The textbook also has periodic **reviews**. These reviews cover all previous material and can be lengthy. They are meant to be used as reviews; that is, a way to see if your student remembers previous material, and to re-teach if necessary. If your student has trouble with some of the problems, it may mean than you need to go back and review the concepts, provide additional practice from a supplementary book, or simply "remind" the student of a concept. The reviews not only provide more practice, but also include problems which combine earlier concepts with new concepts, or ask the student to apply a concept in a new way. So it is not always possible to go back to one place in the textbook and find a problem just like the one in the review. The review problems can therefore deepen a student's understanding, particularly through discussion. Textbook reviews are an important part of this curriculum.

There are answers and solutions to workbook problems at the back of the guide. You can use workbook reviews as assessments (after using the textbook review as review).

On the next page is a *suggested* weekly schedule.

This guide can be used with both the third edition and the U.S. edition of *Primary Mathematics 5A*.

3d› indicates portions pertaining only to the third edition, and
US› indicates portions pertaining only to the US edition (except for number words).

In writing out numbers, the US edition uses the word "and" only for the decimal place, not for whole numbers (e.g. four hundred one thousand, sixty-two). The 3rd edition uses "and" in more places (e.g. four hundred and one thousand and sixty-two). Answers in this guide for number words will only be given for the US edition — you can allow your student to use "and" as you wish according to the conventions in your country if you are using the 3d edition.

I wish to thank Suzanne Arganbright for her invaluable help in proofing this guide.

Suggested Weekly Schedule

Week	Unit	Part	Textbook	Workbook	Materials
1	1 Whole Numbers	1 Place Values	p. 6 p. 7, tasks 1-3	Ex. 1	Base-10 blocks
		2 Millions	p. 8 p. 9, tasks 1-3	Ex. 2	Number cards 0-9
		Practice	p. 10, Practice 1A		
		3 Approximation and Estimation	p. 11 pp. 12-13, tasks 1-7	Ex. 3	
			p. 13, tasks 8-12	Ex. 4	
2		Practice	p. 14, Practice 1B		
		4 Multiplying by Tens, Hundreds or Thousands	p. 15 p. 16, tasks 1-8	Ex. 5	
		5 Dividing by Tens, Hundreds or Thousands	p. 17 p. 18, tasks 1-6	Ex. 6	
		6 Order of Operations	p. 19 p. 20, tasks 1-3	Ex. 7	
			p. 20, tasks 4-6	Ex. 8	
3		Practice	p. 21, Practice 1C		
		7 Word Problems	p. 22 p. 23, tasks 1-2	Ex. 9	
			p. 24, tasks 3-4	Ex. 10	
		Practice	p. 25, Practice 1D		
4	2 Multiplication and Division by a 2-digit Whole Number	1 Multiplication	p. 26 p. 27, tasks 1-6	Ex. 11	
		2 Division	p. 28 pp. 29-30, tasks 1-11	Ex. 12	
5			p. 31, tasks 12-13	Ex. 13	
		Practice	p. 32, Practice 2A		
	Review			Review 1	
6	3 Fractions	1 Fractions and Division	p. 33 pp. 34-35, tasks 1-4	Ex. 14	
		Practice	p. 36, Practice 3A		
		2 Addition and Subtraction of Unlike Fractions	p. 37 p. 38, tasks 1-4	Ex. 15	Fraction circles or bars
			p. 39, tasks 5-8	Ex. 16	
7		Practice	p. 40, Practice 3B		
		3 Addition and Subtraction of Mixed Numbers	p. 41 p. 42, task 1	Ex. 17	
			p. 42, tasks 2-3	Ex. 18	
		Practice	p. 43, Practice 3C		
8		4 Product of a Fraction and a Whole Number	p. 44 pp. 45-46, tasks 1-6	Ex. 19	Fraction circles or bars
			p. 47, tasks 7-9	Ex. 20	
			p. 47, task 10	Ex. 21	
		Practice	p. 48, Practice 3D		
9		5 Product of Fractions	p. 49 pp. 50-51, tasks 1-7	Ex. 22 Ex. 23	
		Practice	p. 52, Practice 3E		
		6 Dividing a Fraction by a Whole Number	p. 53 p. 54, tasks 1-3	Ex. 24 Ex. 25	

Week	Unit	Part	Textbook	Workbook	Materials
10		Practice	p. 55, Practice 3F		
		7 Word Problems	p. 56 p. 57, tasks 1-3	Ex. 26 Ex. 27	
11			pp. 58-59, tasks 4-6	Ex. 28 Ex. 29	
		Practice	p. 60, Practice 3G		
	Review		pp. 61-64, Review A		
12	4 Area of a Triangle	1 Finding Area of a Triangle	p. 65-66 p. 67, task 1	Ex. 30	Square grid paper
			p. 68, tasks 2-3	Ex. 32 Ex. 33	
			p. 69, tasks 4-5	Ex. 33	
		Practice	p. 70, Practice 4A		
13	5 Ratio	1 Finding Ratio	p. 71 pp. 72-74	Ex. 34	Counters, 2 colors
		2 Equivalent Ratios	p. 75 p. 76, tasks 1-3	Ex. 35	
			pp. 77-78, tasks 4-7	Ex. 36	
		Practice	p. 79, Practice 5A		
14		3 Comparing Three Quantities	p. 80 p. 81, task 1	Ex. 37	Counters, 3 colors
			p. 81, task 2	Ex. 38	
		Practice	p. 82, Practice 5B		
	6 Angles	1 Measuring Angles	p. 83 p, 84, task 1	Ex. 39	Protractor Ruler Compass (directional – used to find north)
15			p. 84, tasks 2-3	Ex. 40	
		2 Finding Unknown Angles	pp. 85-86 pp. 87-88, tasks 1-7	Ex. 41	
	Review		pp. 89-92, Review B		
16			**US›** pp. 93-96, Review C	Review 2	

Additional Materials

Base-10 set. A set usually has 100 unit-cubes, 10 or more ten-rods, 10 hundred-flats, and 1 thousand-block.

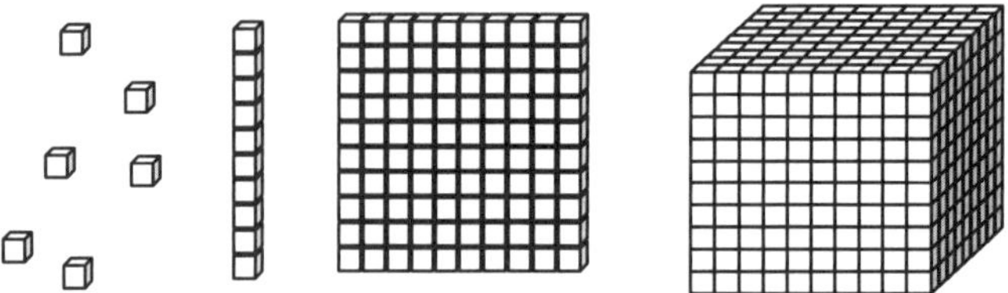

4 sets of number cards 0-10
Use two decks of **playing cards**. For one deck, remove the face cards and white out the 1 and the symbols on the tens card to make it into a 0. You can also white out the aces and draw a 1 in place of the A. Add in the tens from the other deck. Or just use the other deck without face cards for activities that involve numbers 1-10 only.

Fraction circles or bars
There are some fraction circles in the appendix that can be copied.

Counters
Plastic discs of different colors. Or use any other small objects, such as multi-link cubes.

Protractor, ruler

Square grid paper
There is one in the appendix that can be copied.

Compass to find north and other points of the compass.

Unit 1 – Whole Numbers

Part 1 – Place Values (pp. 6-7)

(1) Place Value

- Interpret numbers up to 1,000,000 in terms of place value.
- Read and write 6-digit numbers and corresponding number words.
- Compare and order numbers within 10,000,000.

In *Primary Mathematics* 4A students learned to relate 5-digit numbers to the place value concept and to order numbers within 100,000. This is extended here to 6-digit numbers and to ordering numbers within 10,000,000.

US› For numbers greater than one thousand, we use commas to separate each period of three digits. The comma is optional for 4-digit numbers (e.g. 4500 or 4,500). When writing number words we also write a comma where the comma would be in the numeral representation. For example, we write 456,021 as *four hundred fifty-six thousand, twenty-one*. We write 10,305,123 as *ten million, three hundred five thousand, one hundred twenty-three*. At this point in time, in the U.S. the word "and" is reserved for the decimal point, and decimal numbers are read as fractions: 4.143 is read as *one and one hundred forty-three thousandths*.

3d› The 3rd edition of Primary Mathematics follows the European convention of using spaces to separate all periods of three digits except for the first one. In much of the world, 1 234 567 is written as *one million, two hundred and thirty-four thousand, five hundred and sixty-seven*. Decimal numbers are not written out as fractions: 4.1432 is read as *four point one four three two*.

Discuss base-10 concepts through at least 1,000,000. Suggested discussion:

Write	Ask:
1 one 2 3 ... 9	How many digits are there? (10, if we include 0 which is a place-holder). We can write the digit 2 to show one more than 1, the digit 3 to show one more than 2, and so on to 9. How do we show one more than 9? (We need to write a 1 in the next place).

1 0 1 1 1 2 … 1 9 2 0	ten	Now we can write a 1 in the ones place to show one more than 10, then a 2 to show one more than 11, and so on. When we get to 9, to add one more we change the 1 in the tens place to 2 and put 0 in the ones place for the number 20.
2 1 … 2 9 3 0 … 9 9		Then we can show one more again from 20 by writing the digits from 1 to 9 in the ones place again. And so on, until we get to 99. What do we do to show one more after 99? We make another place, called the hundreds, and a digit we put there is ten times the digit in the tens place.
1 0 0 1 0 1 … 9 9 9	hundred	How many tens are in one hundred? (10) Now we can keep changing digits to count up to 999, starting with the ones place. Then what? We make another place value, called the thousands, to show ten times as much as the hundreds.
1, 0 0 0 … 9, 9 9 9	thousand	How many hundreds are in a thousand? (10) How many tens are in a thousand? (Ten times ten, or 100) After we get to nine thousand nine hundred ninety-nine, what do we do? We have to make another place.
1 0, 0 0 0 … 9 9, 9 9 9	ten thousand	This is called the ten thousands place. How many thousands are in ten thousand? (10) How many hundreds are in ten thousand? (100) How many tens are in ten thousand? (1000) Now we can count to ninety-nine thousand nine hundred ninety-nine. Then what do we do? We make another place.
1 0 0, 0 0 0 …	hundred thousand	This is called the hundred thousands place. How many ten thousands are in a hundred thousand? (10) How many thousands? (100)
9 9 9, 9 9 9		Read this number (nine hundred ninety-nine thousand, nine hundred ninety-nine). To add one more, we need another place.
1, 0 0 0, 0 0 0	million	This is called the millions place.

(Millions will be addressed more in the next lesson.)
Point out that we write a comma every three places in from the right.

 **p. 6**

Show your student a unit cube and a thousand-block from a **base-10 set**.

Ask: How many unit cubes are there in the block? (1000)

Ask: How many hundreds are there in a block? (10)

Show her a 10-rod and ask her to imagine each unit in it to be a thousand-block, as in the picture in the textbook. A rod of ten 1000-blocks has ten thousand unit cubes. Write 10,000.

Ask: How many hundreds are there in such a rod of 10,000? (100)

Ask: How many tens are there in 10,000? (1000)

Show your student a hundred-flat from the base-10 set. If each unit in the hundred-flat were actually a thousand-block, there would be a hundred thousand-blocks, or one hundred thousand unit-cubes. Write 100,000.

Ask: How many hundreds are there in such a flat? (1000)

Ask: How many tens are there in a flat with 100,000 cubes? (10,000)

Two such flats would be 200,000, as in the picture on this page.

Ask: How many thousand-blocks are in 200,000? (200)

Ask: How many hundreds are there in 200,000? (2,000)

Ask: How many tens are there in 200,000? (20,000)

Learning Tasks 1-3, p. 7

1. (a) **20,000** (b) **100,000**

2. (a) **four hundred thirty-five thousand, six hundred seventy-two**
   (b) **five hundred thousand, five hundred**
   (c) **four hundred four thousand, forty**
   (d) **three hundred forty-five thousand, seven hundred thirteen**
   (e) **seven hundred thousand, three hundred seventy**
   (f) **three hundred eleven thousand, twelve**
   (g) **eight hundred forty thousand, three hundred eighty-two**
   (h) **six hundred thousand, five**
   (i) **nine hundred ninety-nine thousand, nine hundred ninety-nine**

3. (a) **401,062** (b) **970,505** (c) **700,009**

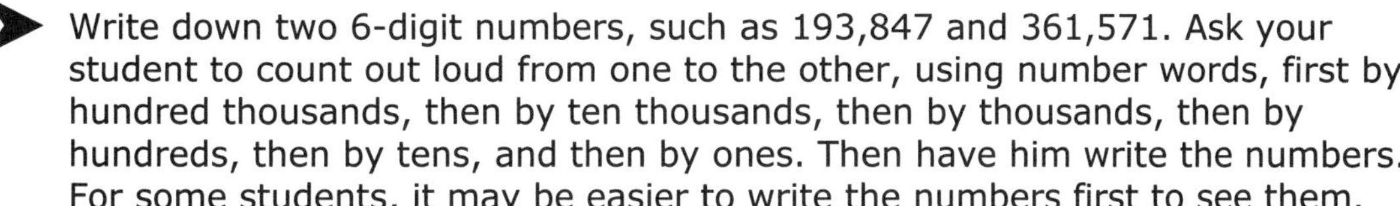

Write down two 6-digit numbers, such as 193,847 and 361,571. Ask your student to count out loud from one to the other, using number words, first by hundred thousands, then by ten thousands, then by thousands, then by hundreds, then by tens, and then by ones. Then have him write the numbers. For some students, it may be easier to write the numbers first to see them.

193,847; **2**93,847; **30**3,847; 3**1**3,847; 3**2**3,847; 3**3**3,847; 3**4**3,847, 3**5**3,847; 35**4**,847; 35**5**,847, 35**6**,847; 35**7**,847; 35**8**,847, 35**9**,847; 3**60**,847; 3**60**,**9**47; 36**1**,**0**47; 361,**1**47; 361,**2**47; 361,**3**47, 361,**4**47; 361,**5**47; 361,5**5**7; 361,5**6**7; 361,56**8**; 361,56**9**; 361,5**70**; 361,57**1**.

In the exercise in the workbook students will be putting numbers in order. This has been done in each level of *Primary Mathematics*. Review comparing and ordering numbers only if necessary.

Write down two numbers, such as 143,345 and 144,345 and ask your student which is larger. Show him that he must first compare the digits in the highest place value. Rewrite them, aligning the digits. If the first digits of both numbers are the same, he compares the digits in the next highest place value. If not, the one with the larger digit in that place is the larger number. The digits can be compared more easily by writing them one above the other, aligning the digits, and then comparing digits.

1 4 3, 3 4 5
1 4 4, 3 4 5

Write two more numbers, one with 5-digits and one with 6-digits, where the first digit of the 5-digit number is larger than the first digit of the 6-digit number, such as 56,743 and 256,473. Have him rewrite the numbers, aligning the digits. See if he writes them correctly. He should realize that 56,743 is smaller than 256,473, since it has nothing, or essentially 0, in the hundred thousands place, which is smaller than the 2 in the same place for 256,473

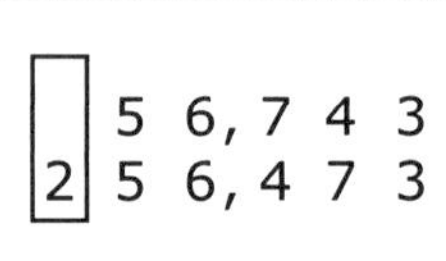

Workbook Exercise 1

Part 2 – Millions (pp. 8-9)

(1) Millions

- Understand how big a million is.
- Read and write 7-digit number and corresponding number words.
- Compare and order numbers within 10,000,000.
- Optional: Understand other large numbers.

Primary Mathematics 5A deals only with numbers up to 10 million. You may wish to discuss the names of larger numbers, though numbers beyond a trillion are not often used.

Ask your student if she remembers from the previous lesson what number follows 999,999. It is 1 million.

How big is a million? You may want to do or discuss some activities to give your student an idea about large numbers like a million. Help your student with calculations that involve division by 3 or 4 digit numbers (or use a calculator).

- How many liters are a million drops of water? Use an eye dropper and a medicine spoon and count the number of drops in a milliliter. There are about 20 drops in a milliliter. Multiply by 1000 to get the number of drops in a liter, and divide 1,000,000 by this number to get the number of liters. A million drops is about 50 liters.

- How long would it take to count to a million, if you counted at the rate of one number per second? There are 60 seconds in a minute, 3600 seconds in an hour, and 86,400 seconds in a day. Divide 1,000,000 by 86,400. It takes about 12 days.

- How big a square would a million unit-cubes from a base-10 set make? You would need 1,000 rows of 1,000 squares. 1,000 cm is 10 meters. So the square would be 10 meters on a side.

- If you lived a million days, how old would you be? Divide 1,000,000 by 365 days and the answer is about 2,740 years old.

- **US›** How high would a stack of a million pennies be? Measure a stack of pennies. There are 16 pennies in an inch, 192 pennies in a foot, 192 x 5280 = 1,013,760 pennies in a mile. So a stack of a million pennies would be about a mile high.

- **US›** If pennies were laid side by side, how long would a row of a million pennies be? Put pennies side by side until they are a foot long. There are 5,280 feet in a mile. There are 16 pennies side by side in a foot, and 84,480 in a mile. Divide 1,000,000 by 84,480. A million pennies side by side would be about 12 miles long.

➢ **US›** How much does a million pennies weigh? 1 penny weighs about one tenth of an ounce. So there are 160 pennies in a pound. Divide 1,000,000 by 160. A million pennies weigh about 6,250 pounds (about 3.12 tons). Or, there are about 353 pennies per kilogram. (160 pennies/lb ÷ 0.454 kg/lb). So a million pennies weigh about 2,833 kilograms, about the weight of a half-grown elephant.

Page 8
Learning Tasks 1-3, p. 9

1. (a) **2** (b) **millions**

2. (a) **five million**
   (b) **four million, one hundred twenty-six thousand**
   (c) **three million, six hundred ninety thousand**
   (d) **six million, eight hundred thousand**

3. (a) **6,000,000** (b) **7,003,000** (c) **8,000,000** (d) **9,023,000**

➤ Do this activity if your student needs extra practice in writing number words or comparing numbers.

Use 4 sets of number cards 0-9, shuffled. Have him turn over 8 of them and lay them out next to each other to form an 8-digit number. He then writes the number down on paper and next to it writes the number in words. After doing 3 to 5 numbers, he puts them in order.

Optional: Discuss the following with your student.
Numbers are arranged in groups of three places called periods. The places within periods repeat (hundreds, tens, ones). Commas are used in the U.S. to separate periods. The names for numbers larger than a million are based on the number of 000's after 1 thousand and prefixes. For example:

bi = 2 — a billion has two sets of ,000's after a thousand
tri = 3 — a trillion has three sets of ,000's after a thousand
quad = 4 — a quadrillion has four sets of ,000's after a thousand
quint = 5 — a quintillion has five sets of ,000's after a thousand
sext = 6 — a sextillion has six sets of ,000's after a thousand

3d› The European system is different after eight 0's, or after a hundred million, though the "American system" is being used more. The European system is given in brackets for some numbers on the next page.

million	1,000,000
ten million	10,000,000
hundred million	100,000,000
billion [thousand million or milliard]	1,000,000,000
trillion [billion]	1,000,000,000,000
quadrillion [billiard]	1,000,000,000,000,000
quintillion [trillion]	1,000,000,000,000,000,000
sextillion [trilliard]	1,000,000,000,000,000,000,000
septillion [quadrillion]	1,000,000,000,000,000,000,000,000
octillion [quadrilliard]	1,000,000,000,000,000,000,000,000,000
nonillion [quintillion]	1,000,000,000,000,000,000,000,000,000,000
decillion [quintilliard]	1,000,000,000,000,000,000,000,000,000,000,000
undecillion	1,000,000,000,000,000,000,000,000,000,000,000,000
duodecillion	1,000,000,000,000,000,000,000,000,000,000,000,000,000
centillion	1,000 followed by 100 groups of three zeros

One googol is a ONE followed by 100 zeros.
One googolplex is a 1 followed by googol number of zeros.
There are about 2 billion seconds in an average life time.
There are about 6 billion people on earth.
There are about 50 trillion cells in an average human being.
There are about one quadrillion grains of sand on a beach.
There are about one sextillion cups of water in the ocean.
US› The earth weighs about one septillion pounds.
US› The sun weighs about one nonillion pounds.

 **Workbook Exercise 2**

Practice 1A (p. 10)

Practice 1A, p. 10

1. (a) **11,012** (b) **115,600** (c) **700,013** (d) **880,005**
   (e) **5,000,000** (f) **4,200,000** (g) **10,000,000** (h) **8,008,000**

2. (a) **two hundred seven thousand, three hundred six**
   (b) **five hundred sixty thousand, three**
   (c) **seven hundred thousand**
   (d) **three million, four hundred fifty thousand**
   (e) **six million, twenty thousand**
   (f) **four million, three thousand**

3. (a) **800** (b) **80,000** (c) **80**
   (d) **800,000** (e) **8,000** (f) **8,000,000**
4. (a) **6,000** (b) **200,000** (c) **184,900**
   (d) **7,609,000** (e) **9,021,000** (f) **30,000**

5. (a) **44,668** **45,668** (b) **73,500** **74,500** (c) **103,002** **113,002**
   (d) **5,652,000** **5,662,000** (e) **7,742,000** **5,742,000**

6. (a) **53,607; 53,670; 53,760; 56,370**
   (b) **324,468; 324,648; 342,468; 342,486**
   (c) **425,700; 2,357,000; 2,537,000; 3,257,000**

Game

Material: Number cards 0-9, one more set than the number of players.

Procedure: Each player draws 7 lines on paper for the places for a 7-digit number. Players take turns drawing cards and writing the number drawn on one of the lines. Once the digit has been written it must stay in that place. After all players have drawn 8 cards, they compare their numbers. The one with the highest number wins. The players are allowed to see each other's number. They can apply some strategy to determine what numbers are likely to remain and what their chances are of drawing a high number to put in the highest place.

You can have your student write the number she has formed in words. Players can also compare all the numbers and put them in order.

Part 3 – Approximation and Estimation (pp. 11-13)

(1) Approximation

- Round whole numbers to the nearest 10, nearest 100, or nearest 1000.
- Understand the symbol ≈ to mean "is approximately" or "is about."

In *Primary Mathematics* 4A students learned to round numbers to the nearest ten and to the nearest 100. This concept is reviewed here and extended to rounding numbers to the nearest thousand.

Rounding numbers is an important skill for estimation, which will be discussed in the next section.

In these books if the next lower place has a 5, the number is always rounded up. For example, 65 is rounded up to 70.

p. 11

Ask your student to determine the divisions or sections on the first number line. Each division is 10. So the first division after 4850 is 4860, and the next one is 4870. 4865 is between 4860 and 4870 and so falls on the number line between these two divisions. Ask him to locate some other numbers between 4800 and 4900 on the number line, such as 4876, and determine whether they are nearer to 4800 or 4900.

Ask your student to determine the divisions on the second number line. Each one is now 100. Ask her to locate some other numbers as well, such as 4130. Tell her that in this book the convention is that 4500 is rounded to 5000 than 4000. (Some books might round 5 to the nearest even number, so 4500 would round to 4000 and 5500 would round to 6000.)

Point out the wavy equal sign and that it means "is approximately" or "is about."

Learning Tasks 1-7, pp. 12-13

1. **490**
2. (a) **600** (b) **800** (c) **1,000**
3. **5,700**
4. (a) **3,700** (b) **6,000** (c) **5,000**
5. **17,000**
6. (a) **23,000** (b) **55,000** (c) **40,000**

Read the top of p. 13.

In general, to round off whole numbers:

- Find the place value you want (the rounding digit) and look to the digit just to the right of it.
- If that digit is less than 5, just change digits to the right of the "rounding digit" to zero.
- If that digit is greater than or equal to 5, round up and change all digits to the right of the rounding digit to zero.

For example, to round 49,587 to the nearest 1000, locate the 9 in the thousands place. Then look at the 5 to the right of it. 49,|587 Since it 5, we round up (by adding 1 to 49, or going up to the next thousand), then change all the digits to the right of it to 0.

49,587 ≈ 50,000

7. (a) **49,000** (b) **74,000**
   (c) **804,000** (d) **130,000**

Ask your student to round 693 to the nearest thousand. (1000)
Now ask him to round 410 to the nearest thousand. (0)

If your student needs extra practice in locating numbers on a number line and rounding, draw some number lines, have him label it with consecutive tens, hundreds, or thousands, and ask him to locate a number on the number line and tell you which ten, hundred, or thousand it is closest to.

If your student needs extra practice in rounding, use 4 sets of number cards 0-9, shuffled. Turn over 5 of them and lay them out next to each other to form a 5-digit number. Ask him to round the number formed to the nearest 10, the nearest 100, and the nearest 1,000.

Workbook Exercise 3

(2) Estimation

- Review multiplication and division of tens, hundreds, or thousands by a 1-digit whole number.
- Estimate the answer in addition and subtraction of whole numbers.
- Estimate the answer in the multiplication and division of a whole number by a 1-digit number.

In *Primary Mathematics* 3A students learned to multiply tens, hundreds, and thousands by a 1-digit whole number. In *Primary Mathematics* 4A they learned to estimate the answer in addition, subtraction, multiplication, and division. This is reviewed here.

The purpose for estimation in these books is to determine if the answer to a problem is reasonable. Estimated answers can vary depending on the precision of the rounding. Your student should round to numbers with which it is easy to perform mental calculations. In addition and subtraction, he should generally round the smallest number to a number with one non-zero digit, and then the larger number to the same place. By now, a student should be able to add one digit to any number and subtract one digit from any number mentally.

6326 + 4608
↓ ↓
6000 + 5000 = 11,000

Both digits are rounded to the thousands place.

48,943 + 392
↓ ↓
48,900 + 400 = 49,300

Since 392 is rounded to 400 to get a number with one non zero digit, round 48,943 to the nearest hundred. Mentally add 489 + 4 and add two 0's to the sum.

When rounding to estimate the answer in multiplication by a 1-digit number, round the larger number to a number with one non-zero digit, unless it is easy to mentally multiply more than one non-zero digit with the single digit.

4592 x 9
↓
5000 x 9 = 4500

2319 x 3
↓
2300 x 3 = 6900

24,516 x 3
↓
25,000 x 3 = 75,000

In the second and third example, it may also be easy for the student to multiply 23 x 3 or 25 x 3 (3 quarters) mentally. The estimated answer will be closer to the actual answer. However, he can also round to 2000 x 3 or 20,000 x 3, and the answer will tell the student the correct number of places that the actual answer should have. This is useful when multiplying by larger numbers. For example, 25,000 x 30 will give a better estimate (750,000) than will 20,000 x 30 (600,000), of the actual answer (833,544). However, the latter estimate will still let the student know how many places the answer should have and help prevent errors in the multiplication process. (Estimating the answer for multiplication by a 2-digit number is covered in the next part.)

To roun numbers to estimate the answer for the division of 4-digit number by a 1-digit number, we round to the nearest multiple of the single digit, not necessarily to the nearest thousand.

3100 ÷ 4
↓
3200 ÷ 4 = 800

Rounding to 3000 would result in 3000 ÷ 4, which cannot be easily done mentally.

➤ If your student is shaky on multiplication and division facts, spend time reviewing them. There are many sites on the internet with interactive flash cards. You can play a version of the card game war.

Multiplication practice
Material: Number cards 1-10 (a card deck without face cards).
Procedure: Shuffle and deal out all cards. Each player turns over two cards and multiplies them together. The one with the highest product gets all the cards.

Division practice
Material: Number cards 1-10 (a card deck without face cards).
Procedure: Shuffle and deal out all cards. Each player turns over 3 cards. The first two cards form a 2-digit number, which is divided by the third card. There may be a remainder. The players add the quotient and the remainder. The one with the highest sum of quotient and remainder gets all the cards. For example, a player turns over 3, 5, and 6: 35 ÷ 6 = 5 R 5. The sum of the quotient and remainder is 10.

➤ Your student should be able to mentally add and subtract a 1-digit number from any number, or add or subtract a ten, hundred, or thousand from any number. Review, if necessary. (If your student does not know how to add and subtract these numbers mentally, and needs more practice than given below, consider using earlier levels of Primary Mathematics.)

345 + 6 = 351
Adding 5 and 6 increases the tens. Write down the hundreds then the tens plus 1 ten, then the ones resulting from 5 + 6.

34,500 + 600 = 35,100
Add in the same way, ignoring the two extra 0's during the addition. Notice that adding the hundreds increases the 4 in the thousands place.

345 – 6 = 339

Since 5 is less than 6, the tens must be decreased by 1. Write down the hundreds, then the tens less one ten, then the ones for either 15 – 6 or 3 + 6.

34,500 – 600 = 33,900

Subtract in the same way, except that it is the thousands place that is decrease by one.

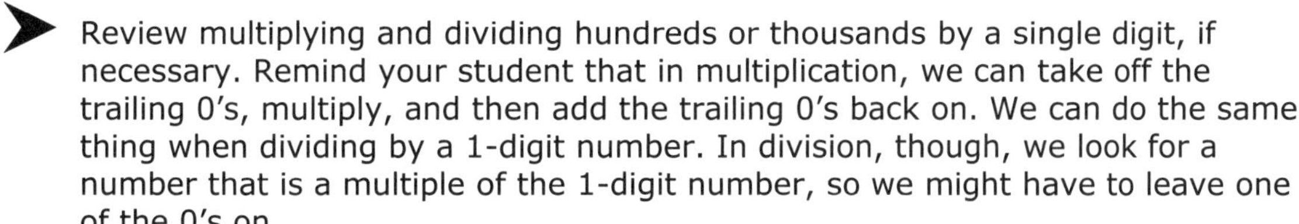

Review multiplying and dividing hundreds or thousands by a single digit, if necessary. Remind your student that in multiplication, we can take off the trailing 0's, multiply, and then add the trailing 0's back on. We can do the same thing when dividing by a 1-digit number. In division, though, we look for a number that is a multiple of the 1-digit number, so we might have to leave one of the 0's on.

900 x 4 = 9 hundreds x 4 = 36 hundreds = 3600
5,000 x 8 = 5 thousands x 8 = 40 thousands = 40,000
3600 ÷ 9 = 36 hundreds ÷ 9 = 4 hundreds = 400
30,000 ÷ 6 = 30 thousands ÷ 6 = 5 thousands = 5,000

Learning Tasks 8-12, p. 13

8. **600**

9. (a) **33,000** (b) **37,000**
   (c) **28,000** (d) **700**

10. **18,000**

11. **700**

12. (a) 6,390 + 5,992 ≈ 6,000 + 6,000 ≈ **12,000**
    (b) 78,123 + 8,969 ≈ 78,000 + 9,000 ≈ **87,000**
    (c) 8,307 - 4,265 ≈ 8,000 - 4,000 ≈ **4,000**
    (d) 45,627 - 7,324 ≈ 46,000 - 7,000 ≈ **39,000**
    (e) 3,806 x 9 ≈ 4,000 x 9 ≈ **36,000**
    (f) 9,794 x 5 ≈ 10,000 x 5 ≈ **50,000**
    (g) 4,785 ÷ 6 ≈ 4,800 ÷ 6 ≈ **800**
    (h) 3,782 ÷ 4 ≈ 3,600 ÷ 4 ≈ **900**

As a review, you can have your student find the actual answers to task 12:

(a) 12,382 (b) 87,092
(c) 4,042 (d) 38,303
(e) 34,254 (f) 48,970
(f) 797 r 3 (h) 945 r 2

Workbook Exercise 4

Practice 1B (p. 14)

Practice 1B, p. 14

1. (a) **70** (b) **660** (c) **1,290**
2. (a) **300** (b) **1,300** (c) **20,800**
3. (a) **7,000** (b) **11,000** (c) **125,000**
4. **$800**
5. **$70,000**
6. **1,000,000 km**
7. (a) Town A: **180,000**
   Town B: **176,000**
   Town C: **171,000**

   (b) 180,000 + 176,000 + 171,000
   = **527,000**
8. (a) 32,370 + 4,959
   ≈ 32,000 + 5,000
   = **37,000**

   (b) 24,890 + 5,016
   ≈ 25,000 + 5,000
   = **30,000**

   (c) 48,207 - 9,864
   ≈ 48,000 - 10,000
   = **38,000**

   (d) 54,500 - 6,892 ≈ 55,000 - 7,000
   = **48,000**
9. (a) 8,659 x 4 ≈ 9,000 x 4
   = **36,000**

   (b) 6,023 x 9 ≈ 6,000 x 9
   = **54,000**

   (c) 7,080 ÷ 8 ≈ 7,200 ÷ 8
   = **900**

   (d) 4,378 ÷ 7 ≈ 4,200 ÷ 7
   = **600**

The actual answers to 8 and 9 are:

8. (a) 37,329 (b) 29,906
   (c) 38,343 (d) 47,608
9. (a) 34,636 (b) 54,207
   (c) 885 (d) 625 r 3

Part 4 – Multiplying by Tens, Hundreds, or Thousands (pp. 15-16)

(1) Multiplying by Tens, Hundreds or Thousands

- Multiply a whole number by 10, 100, or 1000.
- Multiply a whole number by tens, hundreds, or thousands.
- Multiply tens, hundreds, or thousands by each other.
- Estimate the answer in the multiplication of a whole number by a 2-digit number.

In *Primary Mathematics* 4A students learned to multiply a 2-digit number by tens, and to multiply tens, hundreds, and thousands by each other (e.g. 400 x 60). They also learned to estimate the answer when multiplying a 3-digit number by a 2-digit number. These concepts are extended to 4-digit numbers here. The strategy simply involves adding on the correct number of 0's. Since estimation is used to help determine whether the actual answer to a problem is reasonable in terms of place value, it is important for the student to be able to estimate competently.

To multiply a number by 10, 100, or 1000, we can obtain the answer by simply adding the correct number of 0's.

To multiply a number by tens, we can do it in two steps:

45 x 30

$45 \xrightarrow{\times 3} 135 \xrightarrow{\times 10} 1350$

Your student can do 45 x 3 mentally, and then add a 0, or use the multiplication algorithm:

$$\begin{array}{r} 4\ 5 \\ \underline{\times\ \ \ 3\ \mathbf{0}} \\ 1\ 3\ 5\ \mathbf{0} \end{array} \quad \text{or} \quad \begin{array}{r} 4\ 5 \\ \underline{\times\ \ \ 3\ \mathbf{0}} \\ 1\ 3\ 5\ \mathbf{0} \end{array}$$

To multiply a number by hundreds, we can also do it in two steps:

86 x 200

$86 \xrightarrow{\times 2} 172 \xrightarrow{\times 100} 17{,}200$

Your student can do 86 x 2 mentally, and then add two 0's, or use the multiplication algorithm:

$$\begin{array}{r} 8\ 6 \\ \underline{\times\ \ \ 2\ \mathbf{0}\ \mathbf{0}} \\ 1\ 7\ 2\ \mathbf{0}\ \mathbf{0} \end{array} \quad \text{or} \quad \begin{array}{r} 8\ 6 \\ \underline{\times\ \ \ 2\ \mathbf{0}\ \mathbf{0}} \\ 1\ 7\ 2\ \mathbf{0}\ \mathbf{0} \end{array}$$

To multiply a number by thousands, we can also use two steps:

71 x 9000

$71 \xrightarrow{\times 9} 639 \xrightarrow{\times 1000} 639{,}000$

Your student can do 45 x 3 mentally, and then add three 0's, or use the multiplication algorithm:

$$\begin{array}{r} 7\ 1 \\ \underline{\times\quad 9\ \mathbf{0}\ \mathbf{0}\ \mathbf{0}} \\ 6\ 3\ 9\ \mathbf{0}\ \mathbf{0}\ \mathbf{0} \end{array} \quad \text{or} \quad \begin{array}{l} \quad\ \ 7\ 1 \\ \underline{\times\quad 9\ \mathbf{0}\ \mathbf{0}\ \mathbf{0}} \\ 6\ 3\ 9\ \mathbf{0}\ \mathbf{0}\ \mathbf{0} \end{array}$$

To multiply tens, hundreds, or thousands with each other, we take off trailing 0's, multiply the numbers together, and then add the trailing 0's from both numbers back on.

34**00** x 6**000** = 34 x 100 x 6 x 1000
= 34 x 6 x 100 x 1000
= 204 x 100 x 1000
= 20400 x 1000
= 20,4**00,000**

5**000** x 8**000** = 40,**000,000**

Page 15

Point out that to multiply a number by 10, 100, or 1000, we can multiply the digit in each place by 10, 100, or 1000. The result is the same as simply adding on the correct number of 0's (1, 2, or 3) to the number.

Learning Tasks 1-8, p. 16

Multiplication by a 2-digit number will be reviewed in a later section, so do not require your student to find the actual answers to tasks 7-9.

1. (a) **3,280** (b) **53,600** (c) **63,000**
3. (a) **1,440** (b) **14,400** (c) **144,000**
4. (a) **27,000** (b) **270,000** (c) **2,700,000**
5. (a) **100,000** (b) **540,000** (c) **4,800,000**
   (d) **1,000,000** (e) **2,400,000** (f) **10,000,000**
6. **14,000**
8. (a) 529 x 34 ≈ 500 x 30 = **15,000**
   (b) 75 x 386 ≈ 80 x 400 = **32,000**
   (c) 7,804 x 59 ≈ 8,000 x 60 = **480,000**

Workbook Exercise 5

Part 5 – Dividing by Tens, Hundreds, or Thousands (pp. 17-18)

(1) Dividing by Tens, Hundreds, or Thousands

- Divide a whole number by 10, 100, or 1000.
- Divide a whole number by tens, hundreds, or thousands (no remainder).
- Estimate the answer in the division of a whole number by a 2-digit number.

In *Primary Mathematics* 4A students learned to divide a 2-digit, 3-digit, or 4-digit number that had 0 in the ones place by 10 by simply removing the 0. This concept is reviewed here and extended to division by 100 or 1000.

To divide a whole number that has 0 in the ones place by tens, we can do it in two steps:

$$45{,}000 \div 30$$

$$45{,}000 \xrightarrow{\div 10} 4500 \xrightarrow{\div 3} 1500$$

Your student can do 45,000 ÷ 30 mentally by removing a 0 from 45,000 and then dividing 4500 by 3 mentally or use the division algorithm. Notice that when dividing by 3, we divide 45 by 3 and then add on the two 0's. We do not add back on any 0's that we took off of *both* numbers. So

$$\begin{aligned} 45 \text{ thousands} \div 3 \text{ tens} &= 45 \text{ thousands} \div \text{ten} \div 3 \\ &= 45 \text{ hundreds} \div 3 \\ &= 15 \text{ hundreds} \end{aligned}$$

Similarly, to divide a whole number that ends in at least two 0's by hundreds, remove two of the zeros and then divide by the digit in the hundreds place:

$$45{,}0\cancel{00} \div 3\cancel{00} = 150$$

To divide by thousands, remove three zeros.

$$45{,}\cancel{000} \div 3\cancel{000} = 15$$

So to divide by tens, hundreds, or thousands, we take off the same number of 0's from both, and then divide the numbers.

Page 17

Point out that when we divide each thousand or hundred by 10, we remove a zero. When we divide each thousand or hundred by 100, we remove two zeros. And when we divide by 1000, we remove three 0's. We remove the same number of zeros as the number of zeros in the number we are dividing by.

Learning Tasks 1-6, p. 18

Division by a 2-digit number will be taught in a later section, so do not require your student to find the actual answers to tasks 4-6.

1. (a) **52** (b) **74** (c) **40**

3. (a) $28\underline{0} \div 4\underline{0}$
   $= 28 \div 4$
   $= \mathbf{7}$

   (b) $64{,}\underline{000} \div 8\underline{00}$
   $= \mathbf{64}0 \div \mathbf{8}$
   $= \mathbf{80}$

   (c) $200{,}\underline{000} \div 5\underline{000}$
   $= \mathbf{200} \div \mathbf{5}$
   $= \mathbf{40}$

4. 70

6. (a) $6{,}398 \div 81$
   $\approx 6{,}400 \div 80$
   $= \mathbf{80}$

   (b) $2{,}205 \div 34$
   $\approx 2{,}100 \div 30$
   $= \mathbf{70}$

   (c) $638 \div 67$
   $\approx 630 \div 70$
   $= \mathbf{9}$

Workbook Exercise 6

Part 6 - Order of Operations (pp. 19-20)

(1) Mixed Operations without Parentheses

- Do mixed operations involving addition and subtraction without parentheses.
- Do mixed operations involving multiplication and division without parentheses.
- Do mixed operations involving all four operations without parentheses.

If an expression involves only addition, we can add in any order. (Addition is commutative — changing the order of addends does not change the sum — and associative — changing the grouping of addends does not change the sum.)

$\underline{42 + 25} + 75 = 67 + 75 = 142$ or $42 + \underline{25 + 75} = 42 + 100 = 142$

Note that the second way is easier because there were two numbers that were easy to add mentally. So the student can look for compatible pairs of numbers, that is, numbers that they can easily add mentally. These are usually numbers that make 100, or that end in 5 or 0.

100

$35 + 32 + 41 + 68 + 25 = 100 + 60 + 41 = 201$

60

If an expression involves only subtraction from the first number, we subtract from left to right.

$\underline{10 - 4} - 3 = 6 \quad 3 = 3$ (**not** $10 - \underline{4 - 3} = 10 - 1 = 9$)

Note: The numbers can be subtracted from the first number in any order, but the subtraction sign must stay with the number following it. So 10 - 4 - 3 = 10 - 3 - 4. This is not the same as doing 4 - 3 first; we are not supposed to subtract from the 4. With a problem like 115 - 20 - 15 we can do it as 115 - 15 - 20 = 100 - 20 = 80, but we can **not** do it as 115 - $\underline{20 - 15}$ = 115 - 5 = 110. If this is confusing to your student, do not teach it at this point. Have him simply subtract from left to right.

If an expression involves both addition and subtraction, we add and subtract from left to right.

$\underline{22 - 8} + 10 = 14 + 10 = 24$

(We can also rearrange the problem, but make sure the operation stays with the number following it, and that is the operation that is being done on that number.)

If the expression involves only multiplication, we can multiply in any order. So we can look for factors that are easy to multiply mentally.

$$\overbrace{25 \times 36 \times 4}^{100} = 100 \times 36 = 3600$$

If the expression involves only division we divide from left to right.

$\underline{32 \div 4} \div 2 = 8 \div 2 = 4$ (**not** $32 \div \underline{4 \div 2} = 32 \div 2 = 16$)

If an expression involves both multiplication and division, we multiply or divide from left to right (multiplication does not have precedence over division).

$\underline{32 \div 4} \times 2 = 8 \times 2 = 16$ (**not** $32 \div \underline{4 \times 2} = 32 \div 8 = 4$)

If an expression involves all four operations, we first do multiplication and division from left to right, and then addition and subtraction from left to right. Multiplication and division take precedence over addition and subtraction.

$$\begin{aligned} & 10 - \underline{4 \div 2} + 6 \times 5 \\ = \; & 10 - 2 + \underline{6 \times 5} \\ = \; & \underline{10 - 2} + 30 \\ = \; & \underline{8 + 30} \\ = \; & 38 \end{aligned}$$

Note that $4 \div 2$ could be done at the same time as 6×5 in this instance, since the result from one does not affect the result from the other. This is not the case in the following, where the division operation must be done before the multiplication operation, since it is the answer to the division that is multiplied:

$$\begin{aligned} & 10 - \underline{4 \div 2} \times 5 \\ = \; & 10 - \underline{2 \times 5} \\ = \; & \underline{10 - 10} \\ = \; & 0 \end{aligned}$$

Let your student take shortcuts only if she thoroughly understands the process and whether the shortcut will affect the outcome. Otherwise, require that the operations be done one step at a time, since that will lead to a correct answer.

Many courses teach acronyms such as PEDMAS (parentheses, exponents, division and multiplication, addition and subtraction) to help remember order of operations, but many people using these acronyms forget that the correct order is multiplication **and** division from left to right, not multiplication followed by division. Because of this, do not teach this acronym. It leads to confusion.

---

p. 19

Tell your student that the equation given on this page can be used to find the total number of stamps. From looking at the picture, we know that we must first multiply 4 x 3 and then add the product to 10 to get the total number of stamps. Ask what equation would he write for the total number of stamps if he had put 10 of one kind of stamp and 4 of another kind on each of 3 pages. He might write the same equation: 10 + 4 x 3 = 14 x 3 = 42. We need a way to indicate in which order the problem should be done, multiplication first or addition first.

By convention, when there is nothing else in the problem to tell us what order to do the operations, we do multiplication or division first, then addition or subtraction. If we want to show that instead the addition should be done first, we use parentheses to indicate what operation should be done first:

(10 + 4) x 3

The parentheses tell us that the addition should be done first. We could write parentheses around the multiplication part to show that the multiplication should be done first:

10 + (4 x 3)

But if there are no parentheses, we follow the convention of doing the multiplication first.

Order of operation simply means the order in which we compute the operations in a problem such as this.

3d› Rewrite the rule on the bottom of p. 19 to read, "Do multiplication or division from left to right, then addition or subtraction from left to right."

 Give your student the following problem:

25 + 21 + 15 + 9 + 75

Ask for suggestions on how to do the problem. Point out that when all the operations are addition, the numbers can be added in any order. Some problems can be made easier by adding numbers that are easy to add mentally first. In particular, have your student try to find pairs that make 100, or add pairs that end in 0 or 5 first:

100 (25 + 75)
25 + 21 + 15 + 9 + 75 = 145
30 (21 + 9)

Show that this answer is the same as the answer if the numbers were added in the order they are written.

Give your student some additional problems and have him find the sum in the easiest way.

45 + 62 + 73
153 + 341 + 59
29 + 62 + 41

Tell your student that if the problem has only subtraction, it should be done from left to right:

$$\begin{aligned} & \underline{20 - 5} - 4 - 1 \\ = & \underline{15 - 4} - 1 \\ = & \underline{11 - 1} \\ = & 10 \end{aligned}$$

Show her that doing them in a different order may give a different and incorrect answer. In the problem above, she cannot first do 5 – 4 – 1 = 0 and subtract that from 20.

Tell your student that a problem with both addition and subtraction is also done from left to right. Addition is not done before subtraction unless it comes before in the problem.

$$\begin{aligned} & \underline{90 - 40} + 10 \\ = & \underline{50 + 10} \\ = & 60 \end{aligned}$$

 **Learning Task 1, p. 20**

1. (a) $\underline{12 + 8} - 10 = \underline{20 - 10} = \mathbf{10}$
   (b) $\underline{60 - 12} - 24 = \underline{48 - 24} = \mathbf{24}$
   (c) $\underline{31 - 19} + 11 = \underline{12 + 11} = \mathbf{23}$
   (d) $\underline{43 + 16} - 27 = \underline{59 - 27} = \mathbf{32}$
   (e) $\underline{64 + 26} + 57 = \underline{90 + 57} = \mathbf{147}$
   (f) $\underline{90 - 12} + 21 = \underline{78 + 21} = \mathbf{99}$
   (g) $\underline{55 + 69} - 25 = \underline{124 - 25} = \mathbf{99}$
   (h) $\underline{111 - 89} - 11 = \underline{22 - 11} = \mathbf{11}$
   (i) $\underline{58 - 25} + 42 = \underline{33 + 42} = \mathbf{75}$

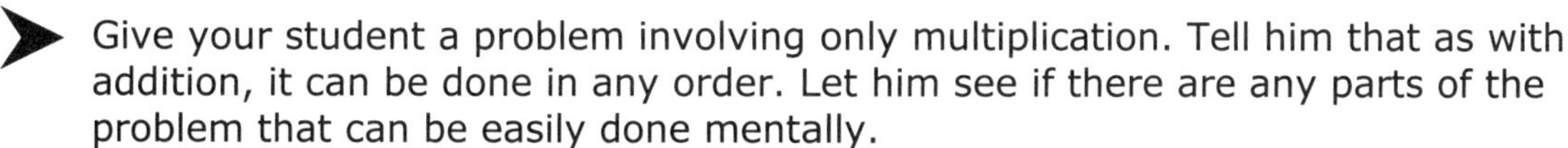

Give your student a problem involving only multiplication. Tell him that as with addition, it can be done in any order. Let him see if there are any parts of the problem that can be easily done mentally.

$$\overbrace{2 \times 16 \times 5}^{10} = 160 \qquad 91 \times \overbrace{4 \times 25}^{100} = 9100$$

Tell your student that division should be done from left to right, and so should a problem that involves both division and multiplication. Do the division or multiplication in order from left to right. Show her that doing the operations in a different order can give a different answer, which is incorrect.

$$\begin{aligned} &\underline{32 \div 4} \div 2 \\ =& \underline{\;8 \;\div 2} \\ =& \;4 \end{aligned} \qquad \begin{aligned} &\underline{32 \div 4} \times 2 \\ =& \underline{\;8 \;\times 2} \\ =& \;16 \end{aligned}$$

Learning Tasks 2, p. 20

2. (a) $\underline{2 \times 4} \times 8$
   $= \underline{8 \times 8}$
   $= \mathbf{64}$

   (b) $\underline{60 \div 4} \div 3$
   $= \underline{15 \div 3}$
   $= \mathbf{5}$

   (c) $\underline{54 \div 6} \times 3$
   $= \underline{9 \times 3}$
   $= \mathbf{27}$

   (d) $\underline{9 \times 8} \times 6$
   $= \underline{72 \times 6}$
   $= \mathbf{432}$

   (e) $\underline{72 \div 6} \div 4$
   $= \underline{12 \div 4}$
   $= \mathbf{3}$

   (f) $\underline{4 \times 24} \div 8$
   $= \underline{96 \div 8}$
   $= \mathbf{12}$

   (g) $\underline{4 \times 7} \times 25$
   $= \underline{28 \times 25}$
   $= \mathbf{700}$
   or $4 \times 25 = 100$
   $100 \times 7 = 700$

   (h) $\underline{64 \div 8} \div 8$
   $= \underline{8 \div 8}$
   $= \mathbf{1}$

   (i) $\underline{9 \times 81} \div 9$
   $= \underline{729 \div 9}$
   $= \mathbf{81}$

Tell your student that if the problem has all four operations, we first do multiplication or division from left to right, and then addition or subtraction. Give some examples:

$$\begin{aligned} &10 - \underline{4 \div 2} + 6 \times 5 \\ =& 10 - 2 + \underline{6 \times 5} \\ =& \underline{10 - 2} + 30 \\ =& \underline{8 + 30} \\ =& 38 \end{aligned} \qquad \begin{aligned} &100 - \underline{7 \times 42} \div 3 + 18 \\ =& 100 - \underline{294 \div 3} + 18 \\ =& \underline{100 - 98} + 18 \\ =& \underline{2 + 18} \\ =& 20 \end{aligned}$$

 **Learning Task 3, p. 20**

3\. (a) $9 + \underline{3 \times 6}$
$= \underline{9 + 18}$
$= \mathbf{27}$

(b) $27 - \underline{12 \div 3}$
$= \underline{27 - 4}$
$= \mathbf{23}$

(c) $4 + \underline{15 \times 12}$
$= \underline{4 + 180}$
$= \mathbf{184}$

(d) $80 - \underline{5 \times 10}$
$= \underline{80 - 50}$
$= \mathbf{30}$

(e) $54 - \underline{48 \div 6}$
$= \underline{54 - 8}$
$= \mathbf{46}$

(f) $9 + \underline{81 \div 9}$
$= \underline{9 + 9}$
$= \mathbf{18}$

(g) $56 - \underline{8 \times 5} + 4$
$= \underline{56 - 40} + 4$
$= \underline{16 + 4}$
$= \mathbf{20}$

(h) $70 + \underline{80 \div 5} \times 4$
$= 70 + \underline{16 \times 4}$
$= \underline{70 + 64}$
$= \mathbf{134}$

(i) $\underline{96 \div 8} - 6 \times 2$
$= 12 - \underline{6 \times 2}$
$= \underline{12 - 12}$
$= \mathbf{0}$

(j) $6 + \underline{54 \div 9} \times 2$
$= 6 + \underline{6 \times 2}$
$= \underline{6 + 12}$
$= \mathbf{18}$

(k) $49 - \underline{45 \div 5} \times 3$
$= 49 - \underline{9 \times 3}$
$= \underline{49 - 27}$
$= \mathbf{22}$

(l) $62 + \underline{42 \div 7} - 6$
$= \underline{62 + 6} - 6$
$= \underline{68 - 6}$
$= \mathbf{62}$

 **Workbook Exercise 7**

(2) Mixed Operations with Parentheses

- Do mixed operations involving all four operations with parentheses.

If an expression includes parentheses, we do the operations within the parentheses first. If there are several operations within the parentheses, we follow the same order of operation, doing multiplication and division from left to right first, then addition and subtraction from left to right. Once we get the value for the expression in the parentheses, then we do the rest of the operations.

Learning Task 4, p. 20

Point out that in this case we do the addition in the parentheses first. We can treat the problem in the parentheses as an expression that we need to solve first.

4. 27 – 2 x (3 + 5)
   = 27 – 2 x 8
   = 27 – 16
   = **11**

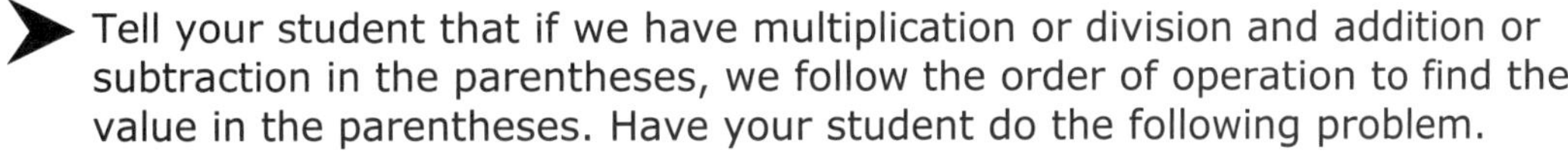

Tell your student that if we have multiplication or division and addition or subtraction in the parentheses, we follow the order of operation to find the value in the parentheses. Have your student do the following problem.

23 – (8 + 2 x 5) ÷ 6
= 23 – (8 + 10) ÷ 6
= 23 – 18 ÷ 6
= 23 – 3
= 20

Learning Tasks 5-6, p. 20

5. (a) 76 + (36 + 164)
   = 76 + 200
   = **276**

   (b) 200 – (87 – 13)
   = 200 – 74
   = **126**

   (c) 99 – (87 + 12)
   = 99 – 99
   = **0**

   (d) 18 x (5 x 2)
   = 18 x 10
   = **180**

   (e) 490 ÷ (7 x 7)
   = 490 ÷ 49
   = **10**

   (f) 153 x (27 ÷ 9)
   = 153 x 3
   = **459**

6. (a) 60 ÷ (4 + 8)
   = 60 ÷ 12
   = **5**

   (b) 20 – 2 x (18 ÷ 6)
   = 20 – 2 x 3
   = 20 – 6
   = **14**

(c) $25 + (\underline{5 + 7}) \div 3$
$= 25 + \underline{12 \div 3}$
$= \underline{25 + 4}$
$= \mathbf{29}$

(d) $(\underline{22 + 10}) \div 8 \times 5$
$= \underline{32 \div 8} \times 5$
$= \underline{4 \times 5}$
$= \mathbf{20}$

(e) $(\underline{50 - 42}) \div 2 \times 7$
$= \underline{8 \div 2} \times 7$
$= \underline{4 \times 7}$
$= \mathbf{28}$

(f) $100 \div 10 \times (\underline{4 + 6})$
$= \underline{100 \div 10} \times 10$
$= \underline{10 \times 10}$
$= \mathbf{100}$

➤ Ask your student to use the digit 4 four times in an expression with any of the four operations, with or without parentheses, to make up the numbers from 0 to 9. More than one solution is possible. Here are some possible solutions:

$(4 + 4) - (4 + 4) = 0$
$(4 + 4) \div (4 + 4) = 1$
$4 \div 4 + 4 \div 4 = 2$
$(4 + 4 + 4) \div 4 = 3$
$4 \times (4 - 4) + 4 = 4$
$(4 \times 4 + 4) \div 4 = 5$
$(4 + 4) \div 4 + 4 = 6$
$4 + 4 - 4 \div 4 = 7$
$4 + 4 + 4 - 4 = 8$
$4 \div 4 + 4 + 4 = 9$

Workbook Exercise 8

Practice 1C (p. 21)

Practice 1C (p. 21)

1. (a) **2,380** (b) **70,000** (c) **37,000**
   (d) **4,000** (e) **28,000** (f) **520,000**

2. (a) **3,920** (b) **39,200** (c) **392,000**

3. (a) **6,750** (b) **67,500** (c) **675,000**

4. (a) $720{,}00\cancel{0} \div 8\cancel{0} = \mathbf{9{,}000}$
   (b) $720{,}0\cancel{00} \div 8\cancel{00} = \mathbf{900}$
   (c) $720{,}\cancel{000} \div 8{,}\cancel{000} = \mathbf{90}$

5. (a) $90{,}00\cancel{0} \div 6\cancel{0} = \mathbf{1{,}500}$
   (b) $90{,}0\cancel{00} \div 6\cancel{00} = \mathbf{150}$
   (c) $90{,}\cancel{000} \div 6{,}\cancel{000} = \mathbf{15}$

6. (a) $36\cancel{0} \div 9\cancel{0} = \mathbf{4}$
   (b) $7{,}60\cancel{0} \div 4\cancel{0} = \mathbf{190}$
   (c) $90{,}6\cancel{00} \div 6\cancel{00} = \mathbf{151}$
   (d) $4{,}08\cancel{0} \div 8\cancel{0} = \mathbf{51}$
   (e) $350{,}0\cancel{00} \div 5\cancel{00} = \mathbf{700}$
   (f) $412{,}\cancel{000} \div 4{,}\cancel{000} = \mathbf{103}$

7. (a) 48 – 17 + 25
   = 31 + 25
   = **56**

   (b) 6 x 5 x 10
   = 30 x 10
   = **300**

   (c) 81 ÷ 9 ÷ 3
   = 9 ÷ 3
   = **3**

   (d) 50 ÷ 5 + 5
   = 10 + 5
   = **15**

   (e) 64 – 3 x 9
   = 64 – 27
   = **37**

   (f) 72 – 36 ÷ 9
   = 72 – 4
   = **68**

   (g) 27 + 15 ÷ 3 x 2
   = 27 + 5 x 2
   = 27 + 10
   = **37**

   (h) 40 ÷ 2 – 2 x 5
   = 20 – 10
   = **10**

   (i) 10 + 24 ÷ 8 + 8
   = 10 + 3 + 8
   = **21**

   (j) (38 - 17) ÷ 3 x 10
   = 21 ÷ 3 x 10
   = 7 x 10
   = **70**

   (k) 35 ÷ (10 – 3) x 10
   = 35 ÷ 7 x 10
   = 5 x 10
   = **50**

   (l) (13 + 7) ÷ (9 – 4)
   = 20 ÷ 5
   = **4**

8. (a) 372 – (45 – 29)
= 372 – 16
= **356**

(b) 372 – 45 + 29
= 327 + 29
= **356**

(c) 372 – 45 – 29
= 327 – 29
= **298**

(d) 372 – (45 + 29)
= 372 – 74
= **298**

(e) 128 ÷ 4 ÷ 2
= 32 ÷ 2
= **16**

(f) 128 ÷ (4 x 2)
= 128 ÷ 8
= **16**

(g) 128 ÷ 4 x 2
= 32 x 2
= **64**

(h) 128 ÷ (4 ÷ 2)
= 128 ÷ 2
= **64**

➤ Write some of the following problems and ask your student to insert parentheses if needed so that the problem's answer is the answer given.

	Solution:
2 + 4 ÷ 2 = 3	(2 + 4) ÷ 2
6 – 2 x 3 = 0	6 – 2 x 3
2 x 4 – 3 + 2 = 7	2 x 4 – 3 + 2
2 x 4 – 3 + 2 = 4	2 x (4 – 3) + 2
2 x 4 – 3 + 2 = 3	2 x 4 – (3 + 2)
12 – 3 x 2 + 9 = 15	12 – 3 x 2 + 9
12 – 3 x 2 + 9 = 99	(12 – 3) x (2 + 9)
24 ÷ 6 ÷ 2 + 3 = 5	24 ÷ 6 ÷ 2 + 3
24 ÷ 6 ÷ 2 + 3 = 11	24 ÷ (6 ÷ 2) + 3
2 x 6 – 1 + 8 = 3	2 x 6 – (1 + 8)
14 ÷ 1 + 6 x 8 – 1 = 15	14 ÷ (1 + 6) x 8 – 1
4 + 2 x 7 – 9 x 4 = 6	(4 + 2) x 7 – 9 x 4
2 + 3 x 6 – 3 x 7 + 1 = 8	(2 + 3) x 6 – (3 x 7 + 1)
6 + 2 x 9 – 13 – 7 x 7 = 30	(6 + 2) x 9 – (13 – 7) x 7
8 x 10 – 36 ÷ 9 + 2 – 2 x 5 x 5 = 0	8 x (10 – 36 ÷ 9) + 2 – 2 x 5 x 5

Game

Material: Number cards 0-9, as many sets as number of players. Operation cards "+", "–", "x", and "÷", and parentheses cards "**(**" and "**)**", two sets per player. (Use half an index card to make each of the operation cards.) Alternatively, players can place the number cards on a lap white board and write the operations and parentheses between them, or simply write their expression on paper.

Procedure: For each round shuffle the number cards and deal 6 cards to each player face up. Turn one more card face up and place in the center. Make the operation and parentheses cards available to all players. Each player must form an expression whose answer is the number in the middle using any of the four operations and parentheses. The player gets one point for each number card used. The first player who gets 25 points first wins.

Game

Material: Number cards 0-9, as many sets as number of players. Operation cards "+", "–", "x", "÷", and "=", and parentheses cards "**(**" and "**)**", two sets per player. You can use half an index card to make each of the operation cards.

Procedure: For each round, shuffle the number cards and deal 6 cards to each player face up. Make the operation and parentheses cards available to all players. Each player must form an equation with his cards. The player gets one point for each number card used. The first player who gets 25 points first wins. For example, a player with the cards 2, 4, 4, 6, 7 and 9 can make the equations

$$(4 + 2) \times 7 - 9 \times 4 = 6 \quad \text{or} \quad (4 + 4) \div 2 + (9 - 6) = 7$$

Part 7 – Word Problems (pp. 22-24)

In Primary Mathematics 3, students learned to draw part-whole and comparison models to illustrate concepts and to solve 1-step and 2-step word problems. In this section they will be solving word problems of 2-steps or more.

<u>Part-whole model for addition and subtraction</u>

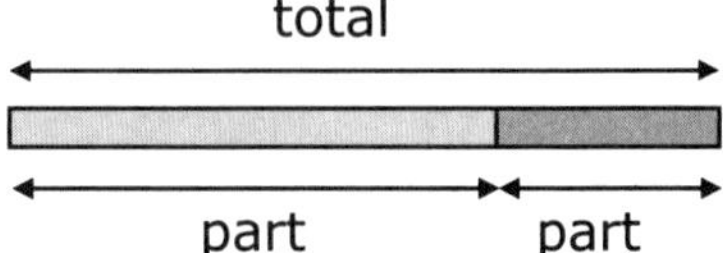

The total is made up of two or more parts.

If the problem gives the parts, we use the model to see that we add to find the whole. For example:

There are 20 marbles in a bag. Sam put in 10 more marbles. How many are in the bag now?

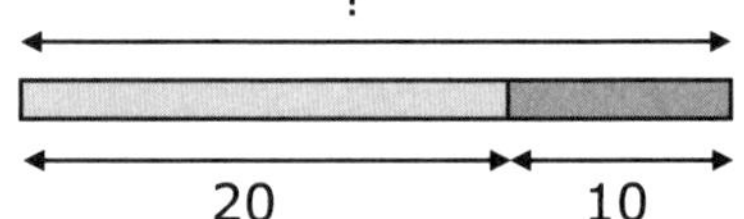

20 + 10 = 30

There are 30 marbles total.

If the problem gives a part and the total, we can see from the model that we subtract to find the missing part. For example:

There are 30 red and blue marbles in a bag. 20 were red marbles. How many blue marbles are there?

30

20 ?

30 – 20 = 10

There are 10 blue marbles.

<u>Comparison model for addition and subtraction</u>

Two (or more) quantities are compared. We draw two bars, one longer than the other, to represent the two quantities.

If the problem gives the value of one quantity and the difference between the two quantities, we can see from the model that we can find the value of the other quantity by addition. For example:

A bag has red and blue marbles. There are 80 blue marbles. There are 120 more red marbles than blue marbles. How many marbles are there?

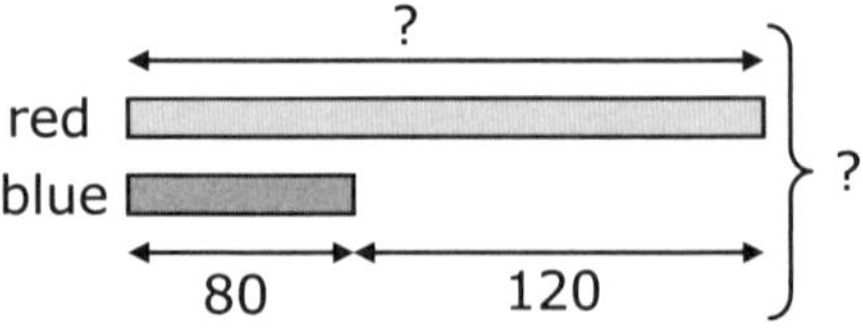

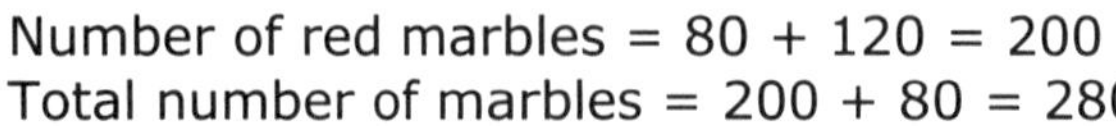
Number of red marbles = 80 + 120 = 200
Total number of marbles = 200 + 80 = 280

If the problem gives the value of both quantities, we can find the difference by subtraction. Or, if the problem gives the value of the larger number and the difference, we can see from the model that we can find the value of the second quantity by subtraction. For example:

There are red and blue marbles in a bag. There are 200 red marbles. There are 120 more red marbles than blue marbles. How many marbles are in the bag?

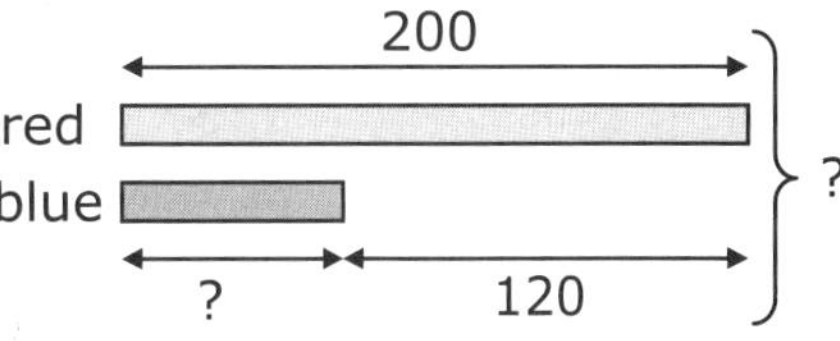

Number of blue marbles = 200 – 120 = 80
Total number of marbles = 200 + 80 = 280

If the problem gives the total and the difference between the quantities, we can find the value of the smaller quantity by subtracting the difference from the total and dividing the result by 2. For example:

There are 280 red and blue marbles in the bag. There are 120 more red marbles than blue marbles. How many blue marbles are there?

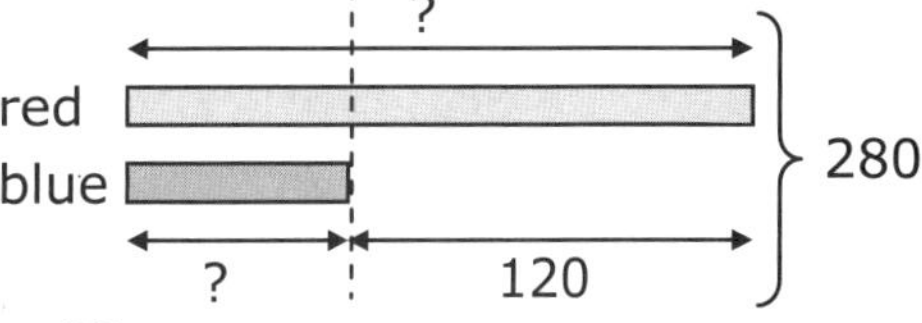

Number of blue marbles = (280 – 120) ÷ 2 = 80

Part-whole model for multiplication and division

The total is represented with a long bar which can be divided up into equal parts. Each equal part is called a **unit**.

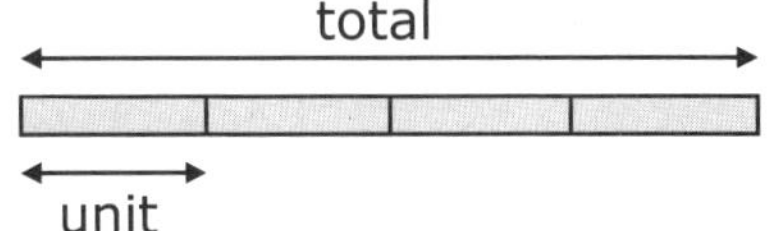

If the problem gives the number of equal parts and the number in each part, we divide the total bar into the number of equal parts (units) and label a part with the number in the part. We can see from the model that we must multiply to find the total. For example:

There are 4 jars. Each has 10 marbles. Find the total number of marbles.

1 unit is the number of marbles in one jar.

1 unit = 10 marbles.

The total number of marbles is 4 units.

4 units = 10 x 4 = 40 marbles

There are 40 marbles total.

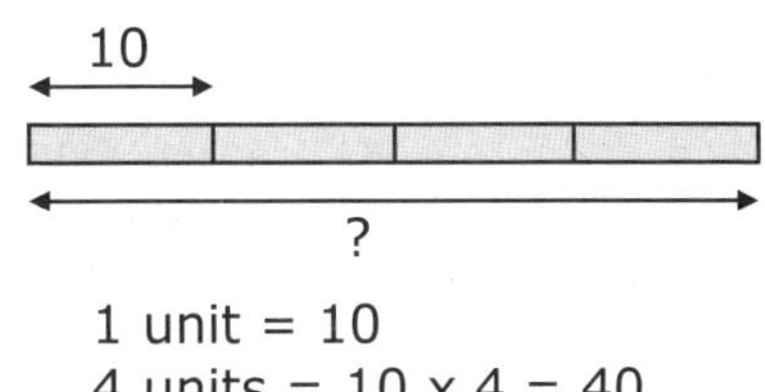

1 unit = 10
4 units = 10 x 4 = 40

If the problem gives a total and the number of equal groups, divide the total bar into the number of equal parts (units) and label the total. We can see from the model that we must divide to find the amount in each unit. For example:

40 marbles are divided equally into 4 jars. Find the number of marbles in each jar.

1 unit is the number of marbles in a jar.

There are 4 units total.

4 units = 40

We need to find the number of marbles in 1 unit.

1 unit = 40 ÷ 4 = 10

Each jar gets 10 marbles.

4 units = 40
1 unit = 40 ÷ 4 = 10

If the problem gives the amount in each group or part, we can divide to find the number of parts. For example:

There are 40 marbles total. 10 are put into each jar. How many jars do we need? In this problem we don't know the number of units, but we know the amount in each unit. We can find the number of units by division.

40 ÷ 10 = 4

There are 4 jars.

We can also solve this problem by making a unit the number of jars. There will be 10 units, because a marble is put into each jar 10 times. One unit represents putting the first marble in each jar, the next unit represents putting the second marble into each jar, etc. In all, a marble is put into each jar 10 times.

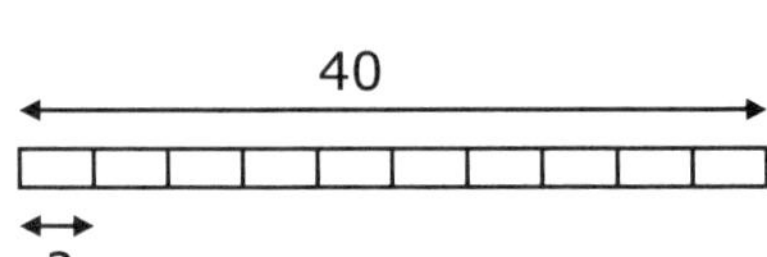

<u>Comparison model for multiplication and division</u>

In the **comparison model** for multiplication and division, two (or more) quantities are compared. We are told how many times as much one quantity is than the other. The smaller quantity is the unit. We can draw both quantities as a number of equal sized units. We generally want to find the value of one unit.

If the problem gives the smaller quantity, the amount in one unit, we can use that information to find the value of the larger quantity, the difference between the quantities, or the total amount by multiplication. For example:

There are 4 times as many blue marbles in a jar as red marbles. There are 10 red marbles. How many blue marbles are there? How many more blue marbles are there than red marbles? How many marbles are there altogether?

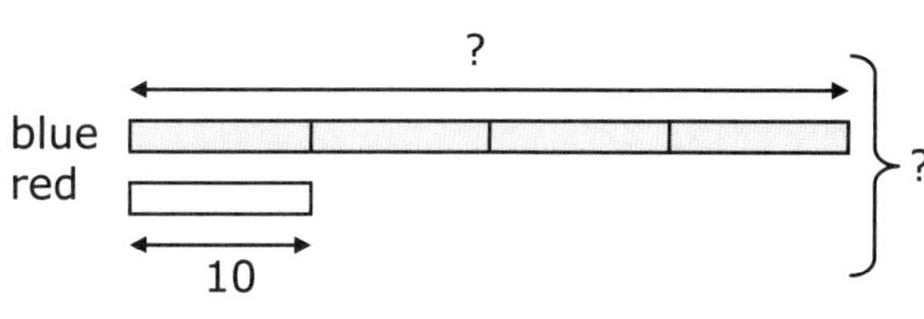

1 unit is the number of red marbles. There are 4 units of blue marbles, 3 units more blue marbles than red marbles, and 5 units of marbles altogether.

1 unit = 10
4 units = 10 x 4 = 40
3 units = 10 x 3 = 30
5 units = 10 x 5 = 50

There are 40 blue marbles.

There are 30 more blue marbles than red marbles. We can also find this by subtraction: 40 - 10 = 30.

There are 50 marbles altogether. We can also find this by addition: 10 + 40 = 50.

If the problem gives the larger quantity (more than one unit), we see from the model that we can find the smaller quantity, or one unit, by division. Once we find the value for 1 unit, we can answer other questions. For example:

There are 4 times as many blue marbles in a jar as red marbles. There are 40 blue marbles.

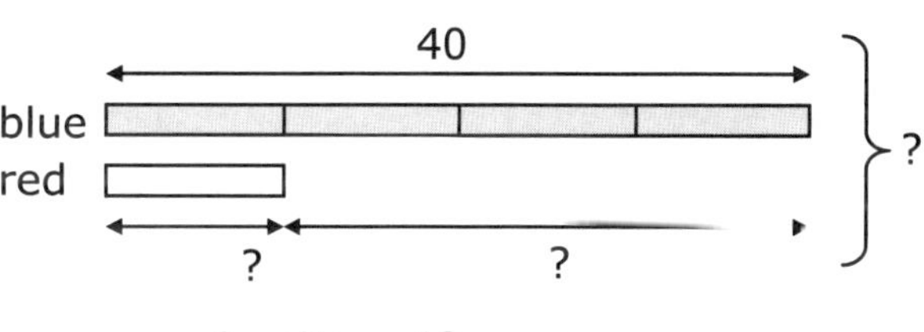

1 unit is the number of red marbles.

Once we find the value of 1 unit (the number of red marbles) we can find the difference between the blue and red marbles and the number of total marbles.

4 units = 40
1 unit = 40 ÷ 4 = 10
3 units = 10 x 3 = 30
5 units = 10 x 5 = 50

Combined models

Students have already encountered problems that can be modeled using a part-whole model where one part is a multiple of a unit. From the model, we can see which operation needs to be used to find the answer to each step of the problem.

If the problem gives one part as a multiple of a given unit, we can find the total by first finding that part by multiplication, then adding the other part. For example:

There are 4 small jars each with 10 marbles, and a large jar with 15 marbles. How many marbles are there in all?

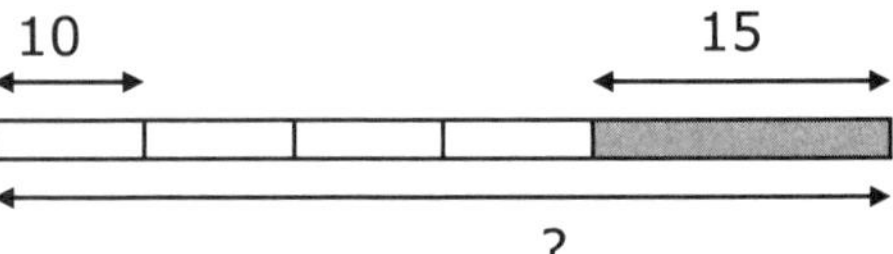

Here we have two parts, the small jars and the large jar. We can model the problem by making two parts, dividing one part into 4 units, labeling the amount in 1 unit and the amount in the other part. This helps to show that we have to first find the number of marbles in the small jars by multiplication.

1 unit = 10
4 units = 10 x 4 = 40
total = 4 units + 10 = 40 + 10 = 55

The student has also encountered problems where a total and the differences between two or more quantities are given. To solve these types of problems, we need to get a number of equal units. For example:

There are 56 marbles in all. There are three times as many red marbles as blue marbles. There are 6 fewer blue marbles than green marbles. How many green marbles are there?

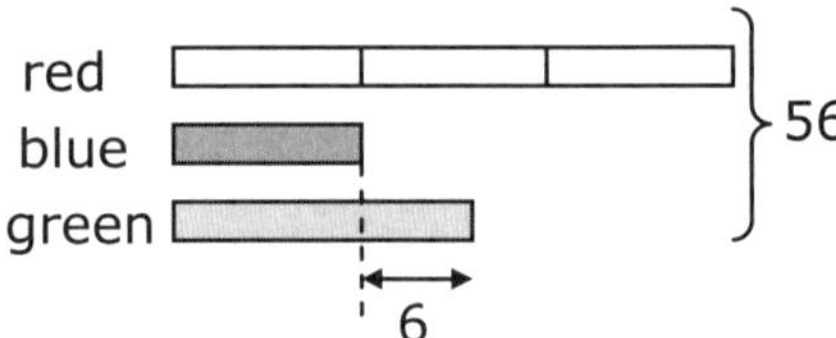

To solve this problem, we need to find the value of 1 unit. First, we need to find what a number of units are equal to so we can divide. We can see by the model that if we take away 6 green marbles, we get 5 equal units. So we can take away 6 from the total to get the value of 5 units. Then we can find the number of green marbles.

5 units = 56 – 6 = 50
1 unit = 50 ÷ 5 = 10
green marbles = 10 + 6 = 16

Modeling is a tool that can be used in solving word problems. It is not the only tool and not all problems lend themselves to modeling using bars. However, for those that do, modeling provides students with systematic means of organizing the information and determining the calculations needed to solve the problem. Some students can work out solutions to the problems in the workbook and practices by forming a mental picture of a model or without a pictorial model. Your student should be able to draw a pictorial representation when necessary, but do not insist that he or she always draw one if it is not necessary for him to solve the problem, or that drawing the models is the only way to solve the problem.

(1) Word Problems I

➢ Solve multi-step word problems.

Review some of the modeling techniques using examples from the notes, if necessary.

p. 22

Discuss this problem. What do we need to know to find how much money she made (her profit)? One thing we need to know how much she made selling the mangoes. How can we find that? We know how much a bag costs. To find out how much she made selling the mangoes, we need to find how many bags she sold. We can draw a bar showing the total. We have the number in each bag but we don't have the total number of bags. Since this is a problem involving equal parts, we can use a part-whole model and show a unit for a bag. To find the total number of bags, we divide. We now have the number of bags and can solve the problem.

Note that not every bit of information in the problem is modeled, just enough to be able to solve the problem. We could draw an additional comparison model showing the selling price and cost price, but by now most students don't need to draw a model for this part. Your student might not even have to draw a model to find the number of bags.

She made $**252.**

Learning Tasks 1-2, p. 23

1. The problem gives us information comparing two quantities, how much more Ryan received than Juan. (In the **3rd** edition Raju and Samy are Ryan and Juan respectively.) So we can draw a comparison model for the amount each boy received. Whose bar is longer? (Ryan's, since he got $100 more) So Ryan's bar is drawn longer than Juan's bar, and the difference is labeled. What other information do we have? (The total amount) We can label that on the diagram. What do we have to find? (How much Juan received, which is the value of the shorter bar) How is that labeled on the diagram? (With a question mark) How can we find that value? We can look at the picture and see that if we take $100 off of Ryan's bar, we get the same amount for both, or two equal units. If we know what 2 units is, we can find 1 unit, which is how much Ryan received.

   2 units = $410 - $100 = $310
   1 unit = $310 ÷ 2 = $**155**
   Juan received $**155**.

2. The statement that there are four times as many U.S. (**3d›** Singapore) stamps tells us that two quantities are being compared, and that one is a multiple of the other. So use the comparison model for multiplication and division, and show the number of U.S. stamps as 4 units and the number of foreign stamps as one unit. What information are we given? (The total number of stamps) That is labeled on the diagram. What do we need to find? (The number of U.S. stamps.) How many units is this? (4) If we can find one unit, we can then find 4 units. How do we find one unit? We see that 5 units equal 1170. So we can divide to find 1 unit.

    5 units = 1,170
    1 unit = 1,170 ÷ 5 = 234
    4 units = 234 x 4 = 936
    He collects **936** U.S. stamps.

 **Workbook Exercise 9**

(2) Word Problems II

- Solve multi-step word problems.

Learning Tasks 3-4, p. 24

3. A part-whole model can be used here, since we are given the cost of each item, plus the total. Since two of the items are the same, we show that by drawing two of the parts the same. We could also draw an added part to the diagram in the book which includes the change, and make the total \$50. From the diagram, we can see that since the two T-shirts cost the same, if we can find the cost of the two T-shirts, then we can find the cost of 1 T-shirt. So we first find the amount spent, then the amount of the 2 T-shirts. (We could also combine this step as
   \$50 - \$3 - \$29 = \$18)
   How much did the T-shirts cost? \$47 - \$29 = \$18
   How much did one T-shirt cost? \$18 ÷ 2 = \$9
   The cost of each T-shirt was \$**9**.

4. The words twice as much tell us that two amounts are being compared, with one a multiple of the other. Use the comparison model, showing the CD to be twice the cost of a tape. From the diagram, we see that we can find the cost of one tape.
   How much does the CD cost? \$16.
   How much does a tape cost? \$16 ÷ 2 = \$8
   How much do 3 tapes cost? \$8 x 3 = \$24
   How much did he spend altogether? \$24 + \$16 = \$**40**
   He spent \$**40** altogether.

Workbook Exercise 10

Practice 1D (p. 25)

Some of these problems in Practice 1D are challenging. If your student likes challenges, you can have him try them on his own first. But you can also discuss some of them first and then have him try the rest on his own. Good ones to discuss are #3, #5, and #10.

Solutions can vary. If your student does not get a correct answer, have her explain what she did. Don't just give her a solution. If she has trouble knowing where to start, give her suggestions on how to diagram the information given in the problem. Do not just diagram it yourself. Often, the solution involves finding units in the diagram, then finding the value of a certain number of units, and then finding the value of 1 unit. The value of that unit may be the answer to the problem, or it may lead to the answer to the problem.

At least one method of solution is given for each problem below.

Practice 1D, p. 25

1. John's weight is being compared to Peter's weight, so we can try a comparison model. Since we are trying to find John's weight, we can make his weight the unit.

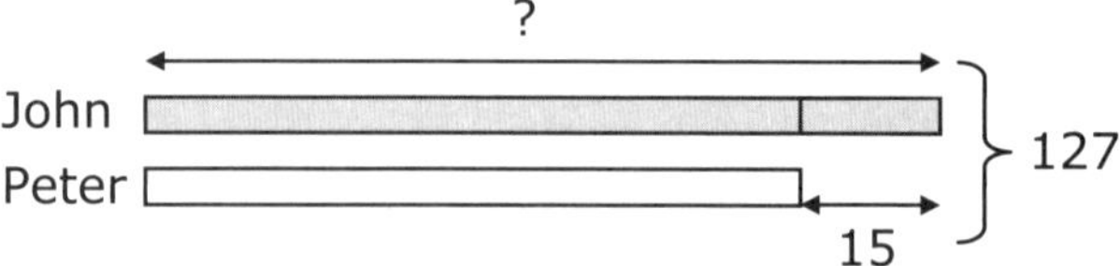

If 15 kg is added to Peter's weight, they would both weigh the same. Add 15 to the total weight to get the total weight if both weighed the same.

1 unit = John's weight.
2 units = 127 kg + 15 kg = 142 kg
1 unit = 142 ÷ 2 = 71 kg

Or, we can make Peter's weight the unit, and get 2 units by subtracting 15 from the total weight.

1 unit = Peter's weight
2 units = 127 kg - 15 kg = 112 kg
1 unit = 112 ÷ 2 = 56 kg
John's weight = 1 unit + 15 kg = 56 kg + 15 kg = 71 kg

John weighs **71 kg**

2. There are 2 more units of boys than girls.
2 units = 24
1 unit = 24 ÷ 2 = 12
4 units = 12 x 4 = 48
There are **48** children altogether.

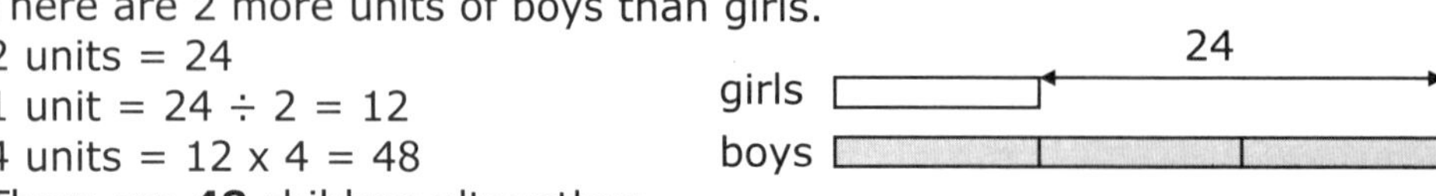

3. Three weights are being compared. Draw bars for each weight and label the diagram with any information that is given in the problem. Since Peter is heavier than David his bar will be longer than David's, and since David is lighter than Henry, Henry's bar is longer than David's. Since Henry is 3 kg heavier, whereas Peter is 15 kg heavier, Henry's bar will be shorter than Peter's.

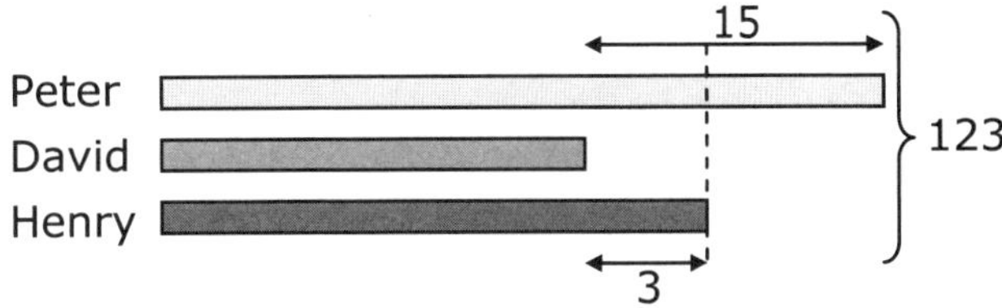

Now try to get equal units. Since we want to find Henry's weight, we can make that the unit. If 3 kg were added to David's weight, his weight would be 1 unit. If 15 kg – 3 kg = 12 kg is taken off Peter's weight, it would be 1 unit.

1 unit = Henry's weight.
3 units = 123 + 3 - 12 = 114 kg
1 unit = 114 ÷ 3 = 38 kg

Henry weighs **38 kg**.

The problem can also be solved by making Peter's or David's weight 1 unit.

4. Draw bars to show the comparison. (**3d›** Pablo ↔ Ahmad, Ryan ↔ Raju.)

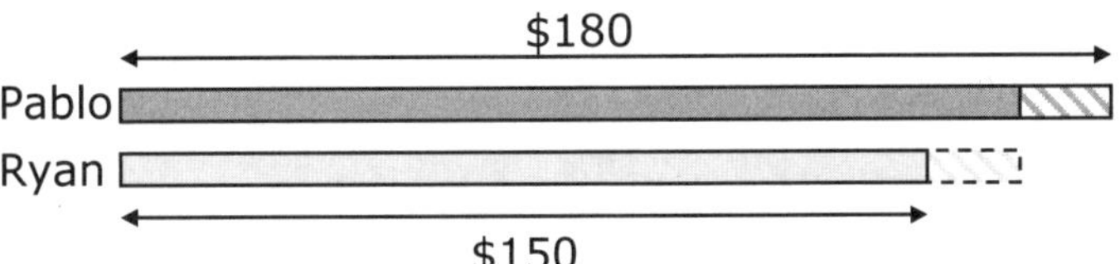

For them to both have an equal amount of money, Pablo would have to give Ryan half of the amount he has more than Ryan, or half the difference.
Amount Pablo has more than Ryan = $180 - $150 = $30
$\frac{1}{2}$ of $30 = $15.
He will have to give **$15** for them to have the same amount.

5. Draw a comparison model. (**3d›** Matthew ↔ Minghui.) Matthew has 2 units and David has 1 unit. The total does not change. In order for them to have the same amount, Matthew must give David half the difference, which is half of a unit. We can divide all the units into half so that Matthew has 4 units and David has 2. Then if Matthew gives David 1 unit, they will both have 3 units.

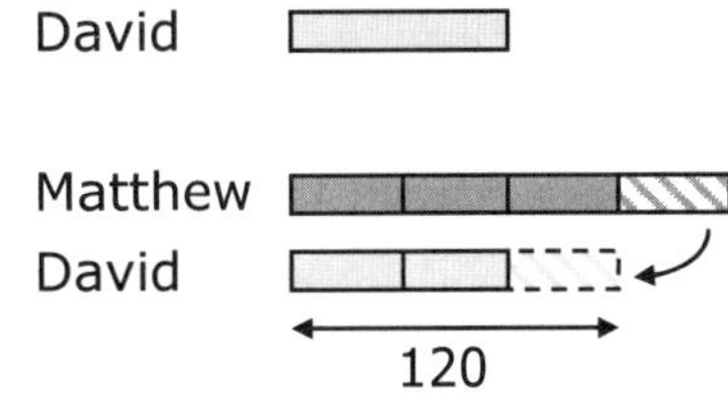

3 units = 120 stickers
1 unit = 120 ÷ 3 = 40
He must give David **40** stickers.

6. 4 units = 300 + 40 = 340
1 unit = 340 ÷ 4 = 85
2 units = 85 x 2 = 170
Peter has **170** stickers.
(**3d>** Joe ↔ Ali, Emily ↔ Lihua)

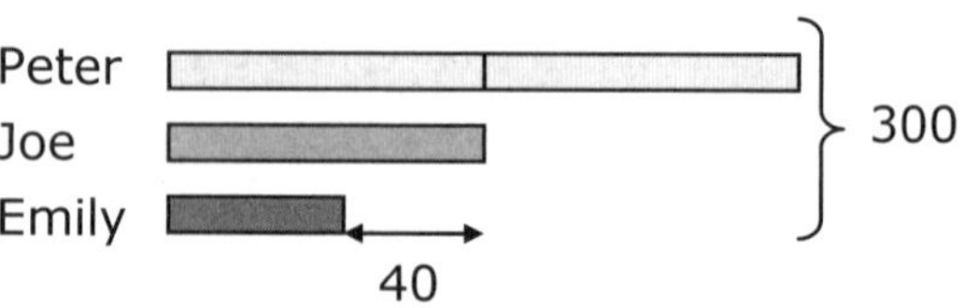

7. 3 books = 1 unit
24 books = 8 units
1 unit = $5
8 units = $5 x 8 = $40
Total money = $40 + $2 = $42
He had **$42** at first.

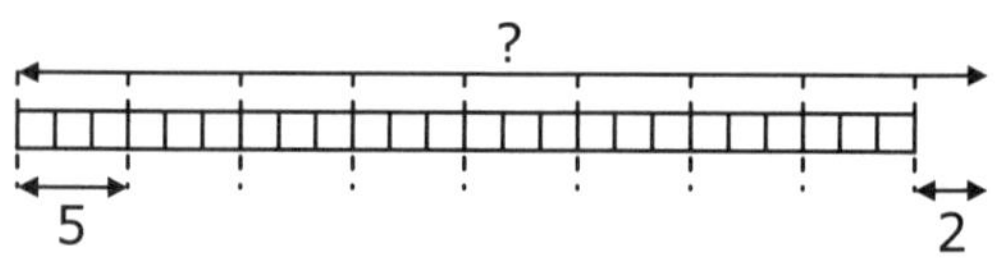

Or: 3 books cost $5

1 book cost $\$\frac{5}{3}$

24 books cost $\$\frac{5}{3}$ x 24 = $40

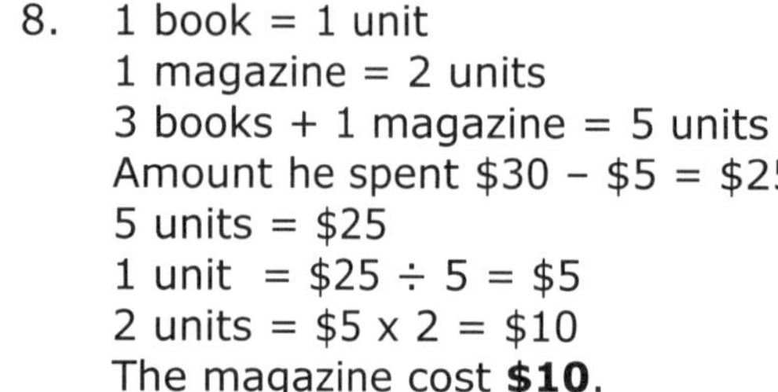

8. 1 book = 1 unit
1 magazine = 2 units
3 books + 1 magazine = 5 units
Amount he spent $30 – $5 = $25
5 units = $25
1 unit = $25 ÷ 5 = $5
2 units = $5 x 2 = $10
The magazine cost **$10**.

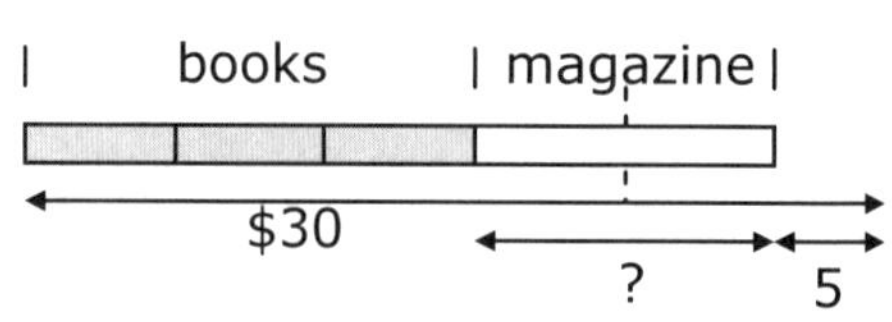

9. Remaining oranges = 155 - 15 = 140
140 ÷ 7 = 20 groups of 7 oranges
$2 x 20 = $40
His profit is $40 - $35 = **$5**

Or:
7 oranges for $2

1 orange for $\$\frac{2}{7}$

140 oranges for $\$\frac{2}{7}$ x 140 = $40

His profit is $40 – $35 = $5

10. Draw a bar to show the total for John and Paul, and another to show the total for John and Henry. For each, the bar for John is the same. Draw Henry's bar to show it as 3 times Paul's bar. If Paul's bar is 1 unit, we can see that John + Henry is 2 units longer than John + Paul. So we can find the value for 2 units, and then for 1 unit, which is how much Paul spent.

2 units = $65 - $45 = $20
1 unit = $20 ÷ 2 = $10
Amount John spent = $45 – $10
= $35
John spent **$35**.

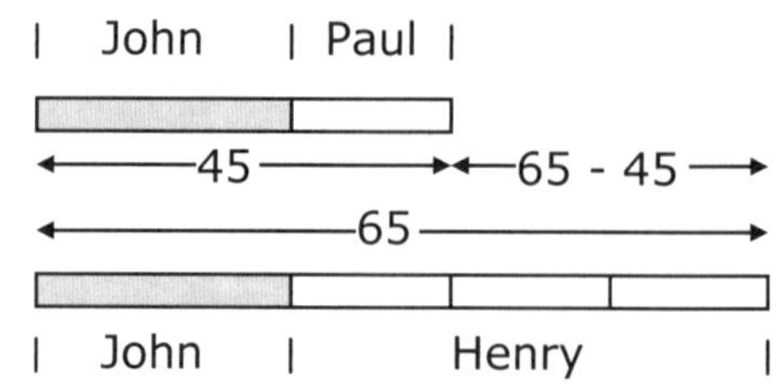

Unit 2 – Multiplication and Division by a 2-digit Whole Number

Part 1 – Multiplication (pp. 26-27)

Students learned to multiply a 2-digit or a 3-digit whole number by a 2-digit whole number in *Primary Mathematics* 4A. This is reviewed here and extended to multiplying a 4-digit whole number by a 2-digit whole number.

When we multiply a number by tens, we can write a 0 down in the ones column and then multiply the whole number by the digit in the tens place. For example, in 1234 x 50, we write a 0 down in the ones place, and then find 1234 x 5 = 6170.
(1234 x 50 = 1234 x 5 x 10)

```
   1234
x    50
  61700
```

When we multiply a whole number by a 2-digit number, we first multiply by the ones, then by the tens, and then add the two products. For example, in 1234 x 56 we first find 1234 x 6, then 1234 x 50, and then add the two products.

```
   1234
x    56
   7404 ←— 1234 x 6
  61700 ←— 1234 x 50
  69104
```

Students should determine whether their answer is reasonable using estimation. For example, 1234 x 56 ≈ 1**000** x 6**0** = 6**0,000**, so 69,104 is a reasonable answer. If the student forgot to write the 0 down when multiplying by the ten, for example, he will get the answer 13,547, which is not reasonable according to the estimate. If he does get an incorrect answer, it may help to have him estimate each step of the process to find the error. For example, multiplying by the tens can be estimated as 1000 x 50 and should have 4 0's.

Multiplication by 2-digits can be a tedious task for students first learning it. The sessions in this guide divide the material into smaller sections than the text does.

(1) Multiplication I

- Multiply a whole number by tens.
- Multiply a 2-digit or 3-digit whole number by a 2-digit whole number.

p. 26

(a)

Method 1 reminds the student that multiplying by a ten is the same as multiplying by the digit in the tens place and then adding a 0. Method 2 shows this in the vertical format. Have your student actually do the problem and compare the steps to 78 x 3 with attention to the place value of the digits. In 78 x 3, he might write a little 2 over the 7 to remind himself to add the tens in when multiplying the tens. In 78 x 30, he can do the same thing, but should realize that the 2 is 200, not a 20, even though it is written above the tens column. So is the 21 that he must add it to. Writing it above the 7 reminds him to add it after multiplying the 7 and 3.

```
  2
  78          78
x  3        x  3
 234          24 ← 8 x 3
             210 ← 70 x 3
             234

  2
  78          78
x 30        x 30
2340         240 ← 8 x 30
            2100 ← 70 x 30
            2340
```

(b)

In this problem we can write down two 0's, and then find 65 x 4. 650 x 40 = 65 x 10 x 4 x 10 = 65 x 4 x 100. The 2 resulting from 5 x 4 is actually 2 thousands (50 x 40 = 2000). We write it above the 6, knowing it actually belongs one place over, in order to remember to add it when multiplying 4 and 6 (for 40 x 600).

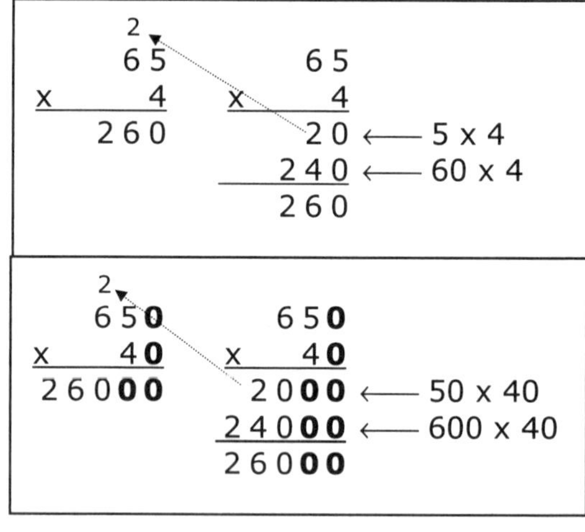

See if the answer to (b) is reasonable using estimation. 650 x 40 ≈ 600 x 40 = 24,000

Learning Tasks 1-2, p. 27

Have your student estimate to check the reasonableness of her answer. The problems in task 2 should be rewritten vertically.

1. (a) **3,180** (b) **19,760**

2. (a) **4,640** (b) **2,300** (c) **2,430**
   (d) **12,420** (e) **29,560** (f) **44,870**

Learning Tasks 3-4, p. 27

To multiply by a 2-digit number, we first multiply by the ones, and then by the tens of the 2-digit number, writing both products below the line. Then we add them.

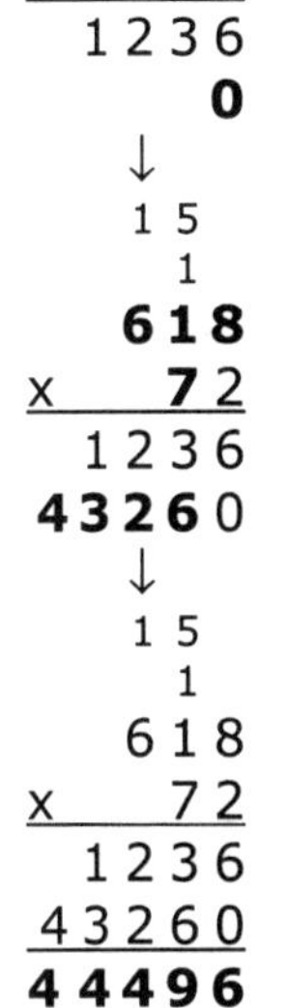

Step through the problems in task 3 with your student. The information in the text in (a) and (c) just shows the result of one step. Emphasize the place values. For example, in the last multiplication step for (d), say, "7 tens times 6 hundreds is 42 thousands. Add the thousands from regrouping...."

Have your student do task 4. He should estimate to check if his answer is reasonable. The problems in task 4 should be rewritten vertically.

3. (b) **2,444** (c) **17,550** (d) **44,496**

4. (a) **2,948** (b) **2,544** (c) **2,784**
(d) **19,352** (e) **15,995** (f) **28,482**

Give your student additional problems for practice. You can make up random problems by using number cards 0-9. Your student shuffles the cards, turns over 3 to make a 3 digit number, turns over another 2 to make a 2-digit number, writes them down and multiplies them. You can let him arrange the cards he turns over to get the largest or the smallest product. You can make it into a game where you deal out all cards and each player turns over 3 cards to make a 3-digit number and 2 more cards to make a 2-digit number, and multiplies the two numbers together. The player with the largest product (or smallest product) gets a point, or gets all the cards. Play to a specified number of points, or until only one player has cards.

Workbook Exercise 11, #1

(2) Multiplication II

➢ Multiply a 4-digit whole number by a 2-digit whole number.

Learning Tasks 5-6, p. 27

Step through the problems in task 5 with your student, emphasizing the place values of the digits in each step, if necessary. Let your student work through the problems in task 6, and estimate to check her answers.

5. (a) **120,510** (b) **313,386**

6. (a) **162,127** (b) **440,510** (c) **121,776**
   (d) **266,340** (e) **364,458** (f) **405,668**

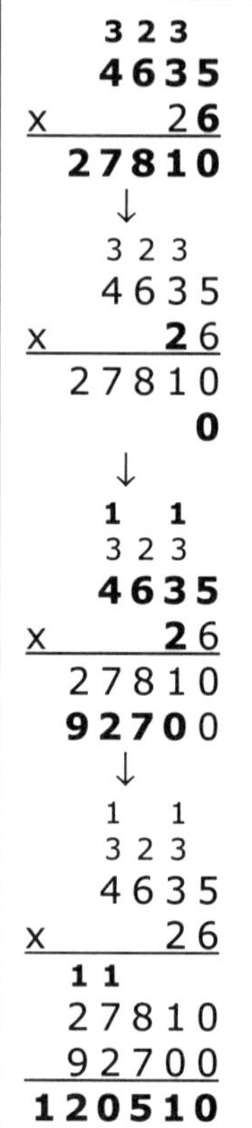

Give your student additional problems for practice. You can make up random problems by using number cards 0-9. Your student shuffles the cards, turns over 4 to make a 4 digit number, turns over another 2 to make a 2-digit number, writes them down and multiplies them. You can let him arrange the cards he turns over to get the largest or the smallest product. You can make it into a game where you deal out all cards and each player turns over 4 cards to make a 4-digit number and 2 more cards to make a 2-digit number, and multiplies the two numbers together. The player with the largest product (or smallest product) gets a point, or gets all the cards. Play to a specified number of points.

Workbook Exercise 11, #2

Part 2 – Division (pp. 28-31)

Students learned to divide a whole number by a 1-digit number. Here they will learn to divide by a 2-digit number.

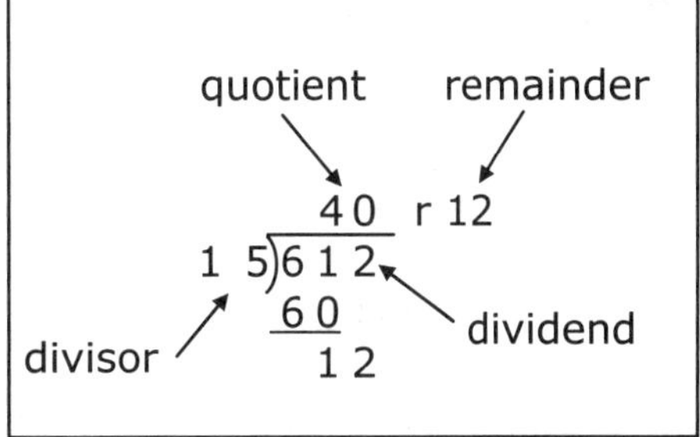

Students have learned the terms *quotient* and *remainder*. The terms *dividend* and *divisor* have not been formally taught in the *Primary Mathematics* curriculum. They are used in this guide to facilitate the explanations. If you use the words *dividend* and *divisor* when discussing the problems, tell your student what they mean. Do not require that he memorize them; you can point to the number as you use the word. Otherwise use the words "total" for dividend and "the number we are dividing by" for divisor.

In this section we will deal only with whole number quotients. When the division is not exact, the remainder is written as a whole number, not as a fraction or a decimal.

A number is divided by a 2-digit number through a process involving the estimated quotient. To find the quotient, first round the divisor to the nearest ten. Then, find the number that, when multiplied by the rounded divisor, gives the value closes to the dividend. Then, multiply that number by the actual divisor to find the actual product. Use that to find the remainder. When dividing a 4-digit number by a 2-digit number, we do it in steps, first finding the quotient for the hundreds, then the tens (including the remainder from dividing the hundreds), and then the ones (including the remainder from dividing the tens).

```
      1 4 8  r 42
 6 4)9 5 1 4
     6 4
     3 1 1
     2 5 6
       5 5 4
       5 1 2
         4 2
```

For example, in 9514 ÷ 64, first divide the hundreds; 95 hundreds ÷ 64. Round 64 to the ten to *estimate* 95 hundreds ÷ 60: 60 x 1 = 60, but 60 x 2 = 120. Try the quotient 1 hundred. 1 hundred x 64 hundreds = 64 hundreds. Subtract this product from 95 hundreds to get the remainder 31 hundreds. Now divide the tens. 31 hundreds and 1 ten is 311 tens. *Estimate* 311 ÷ 60: 60 x 5 = 300. Try 5 tens as the quotient. 5 tens x 64 = 320 tens, which is more than the remainder tens. So 5 tens is too high. Try one less ten: 4 tens x 64 = 256 tens. Subtract this product from the tens to get a remainder of 55 tens. Now divide the ones. 55 tens + 4 = 554 ones. *Estimate* 554 ÷ 60. 60 x 9 = 540. 9 will be too high, so try 8. 8 x 64 = 512. Subtract that from the ones to get a remainder of 42.

(1) Division I

- Divide a whole number by tens.
- Divide a 2-digit or 3-digit whole number by a 2-digit whole number where the quotient is a 1-digit number.

p. 28

Remind your student that we can divide by tens by first dividing by 10 and then by the digit in the tens place.

$$140 \div 20 = 140 \div 10 \div 2 = 14 \div 2 = 7$$

This works only if there is no remainder. In 150 ÷ 20, 15 ÷ 2 gives a remainder, so we must find the number which, when multiplied by 20, gives a number closest to but less than 150. The remainder of 15 ÷ 2 is 1, but the remainder of 150 ÷ 20 is 10. So to get the correct remainder, we can't just cross off 0's and divide. We have to do the division without removing 0's. But we can find the quotient by finding the multiple of 7 closest to 15 as if we could just cross off the 0's. To estimate the answer to 150 ÷ 20, we can find the answer to 140 ÷ 20 (since 14 is the multiple of 2 closest to 15), solve 140 ÷ 20 as 14 ÷ 2 = 7, and use 7 as the quotient in the *original* problem. We use the original problem to find the correct remainder.

```
        7  r 10
2 0)1 5 0
    1 4       = 7 x 20
      1 0
```

Learning Tasks 1-2, p. 29

Discuss task 1

(a): Find the multiple of 30 closest to 70 using the digit in the tens place: 3 x 2 = 6, 30 x 2 = 60. Use 2.

```
      2  r 10
3 0)7 0
    6 0
    1 0
```

(b): Estimate the quotient by looking at the tens. If we could cross out 0's, we would have 43 ÷ 6. Think: 6 x 7 = 42, 6 x 8 = 56, which is too big. So try 7 as the quotient, multiply it by 60 to get 420 and subtract that from the total to get the remainder.

```
        7  r 10
6 0)4 3 0
    4 2 0
      1 0
```

(c): Estimate the quotient by looking at tens: 2 x 4 = 8. 2 x 5 = 10, which is too large. (20 x 5 = 100, which is more than 89) So we try the quotient 4.

```
      4  r 9
2 0)8 9
    8 0
      9
```

(d): Look at tens only to estimate the quotient: 7 x 8 = 56, so 70 x 8 = 560. 9 would be too high. (70 x 9 = 630). Try 8 as the quotient. Note that the remainder needs to always be less than the divisor (the number we are dividing by).

```
        8  r 65
7 0)6 2 5
    5 6 0
      6 5
```

Have your student do task 2. The problems should be rewritten in the vertical format.

1. (a) **2 r10** (b) **7 r10**
   (c) **4 r9** (d) **8 r65**

2. (a) **1 r40** (b) **1 r39** (c) **2 r25**
   (d) **7 r50** (e) **6 r73** (f) **7 r18**

Learning Tasks 3-5, p. 29

Discuss task 3 and 4.

Task 3: Estimate the answer by rounding the divisor to 20, and then mentally finding what number times 2 gives an answer closest to 7. 2 x 3 = 6, so 20 x **3** = 60, which is less that 74. 4 would give too high a number (20 x 4 = 80). Put 3 down as the quotient and multiply it by 21 to find the remainder by subtracting the product (63) from the dividend (the total).

Task 4: Estimate again by looking at the tens. First round 47 to 50, then find the multiple of 50 closest to 256: 256 ÷ 47 ≈ 256 ÷ 50. 50 x **5** = 250. So use 5 as the quotient.

Have your student do task 5, rewriting the problems in the vertical format. Note that we are not finding the closest estimate. We need to find the quotient which when multiplied by the divisor gives a number smaller than the dividend (the total). So for (f), as an example, though 60 ÷ 30 gives the closest estimate of 2 (the answer is 1 r28), we use 1, since 30 x 1 = 30, but 30 x 2 = 60 which is greater than 57.

5. (a) **3 r12** (b) **2 r2** (c) **2 r9**
   (d) **2 r8** (e) **2 r8** (f) **1 r28**
   (g) **2 r15** (h) **6 r5** (i) **7 r91**
   (j) **9 r20** (k) **4 r55** (l) **4 r7**

Workbook Exercise 12, #1

(2) Division II

➤ Divide a 2-digit or 3-digit whole number by a 2-digit whole number where the quotient is a 1-digit number.

Learning Tasks 6-8, pp. 29-30

Discuss tasks 6 and 7.

Task 6: Round 24 to 20. 20 x 4 = 80, whereas 20 x 5 = 100, which is too big. So we try 4 as the quotient first. 4 turns out to be too big, since 24 x 4 = 96, which is greater than 89. So try the number that is 1 less.

Task 7: Round 26 to 30. 30 x 2 = 60, but 30 x 3 = 90, which is greater than the dividend (the total). Try 2 as a quotient. Multiply 26 by 2 and subtract the product from the dividend. The remainder is larger than the divisor 26, so the estimated quotient is too small. So try a number that is one more (3).

(Note that if the estimated quotient is too small, as 2 was, when we try 3, we can do a shortcut to find the new remainder. We don't really have to find the product of 26 x 3. We could simply subtract another 26 from the remainder we found when trying out 2. If this is confusing, don't worry about teaching it to your student at this point.)

Have your student do task 8, rewriting the problems in the vertical format.

8. (a) **4** (b) **3 r2** (c) **2 r28**
   (d) **3 r20** (e) **1 r41** (f) **5**

Learning Tasks 9-11, p. 29

Discuss tasks 9 and 10.

Task 9: Round 33 to 30. 30 x 9 = 270, so try 9 as the quotient first. It turns out to be too big, so try 8.

Task 10: Round 78 to 80. 80 x 5 = 400, but 80 x 6 = 480, which is larger than 473. So try 5 as the quotient first. This turns out to be too small, so we try 6.

Have your student do task 11, rewriting the problem in the vertical format.

11. (a) **9** (b) **6 r2** (c) **6**
    (d) **8 r60** (e) **8** (f) **6 r82**

Workbook Exercise 12, #2

(3) Division III

- Divide a 3-digit whole number by a 2-digit whole number where the quotient may be a 2-digit number.

Learning Tasks 12-14, p. 31

Have your student look at the division problems in tasks 10 and 11 on p. 30. Compare the first 2 digits of the dividend (total) with the divisor (number we are dividing by). In each case the number formed by the first 2 digits is smaller than the divisor. The dividend is always less than 10 times the divisor, so the quotient is a 1-digit number.

Now look at the problem in task 12 on p. 31. The first two digits form a number greater than the divisor (57 is greater than 16). So the dividend 570 is greater than 10 x 16. The quotient will therefore be a 2-digit number.

Do this problem in two steps. Step 1: divide 57 tens by 16 and get a remainder. Round 16 to 20, estimate the quotient for 570 ÷ 20. 20 x 2 tens = 40 tens so try 2 tens first. We would write 2 in the tens place for the quotient. (We are actually trying 20 first, 20 x 20 = 400). 16 x 2 tens = 32 tens. The remainder for the tens is 57 tens – 32 tens = 25 tens, which is too big (25 is greater than 16). So we try 3 tens. 16 x 3 tens = 48 tens, subtract this from 57 tens to find a remainder of 9 tens. 9 tens 0 ones is 90. Step 2: divide 90 by 16. Again, round 16 to 20. 20 x 4 = 80. So we try 4 first, but it is too small. Then we try 5. We did the problem in 2 steps, first dividing the tens by 16, then the remainder plus the ones by 16.

Work through the problems in task 13 with your student, discussing each step.

```
       14   r 45
 47 ) 703
      47
      233
      188
       45
```

```
       40  r 12
 15 ) 612
      60
       12
```

(c): 70 is bigger than 47, so we first find the quotient for the tens. Since 50 x 1 = 50, try 1 first as the quotient for the tens. It works, and the remainder is 23 tens. 23 tens and 3 ones is 233 ones. Now divide 233 by 47. Since 50 x 4 = 200, try 4. 47 x 4 = 188, and 233 – 188 gives a remainder of 45. 4 worked, just barely.

(d): Round 15 up to 20 and try 3 tens first. This will be too small, so we then try 4.

Have your student do task 14, rewriting the problems vertically.

14. (a) **23** (b) **22 r22** (c) **20 r5**
 (d) **12 r27** (e) **10 r38** (f) **20 r14**

Workbook Exercise 13, #1

(4) Division IV

➢ Divide a 4-digit whole number by a 2-digit whole number.

Learning Tasks 15-16, p. 31

Work through task 15 with your student.

(a): The first two digits of the dividend form the number 65, which is larger than the divisor 28, so the quotient will be a 3-digit number. We do the problem in 3 steps. First we divide 65 hundreds by 28. The remainder is 9 hundreds. 9 hundreds and 5 tens is 95 tens. Divide 95 tens by 28. The remainder is 11 tens. 11 tens and 2 ones is 112. Divide 112 by 28.

(b): The first two digits of the dividend form the number 43, which is smaller than the divisor 52. So the quotient will have 2 digits, and we start by dividing 432 tens by 52.

(c): 68 is larger than 64. Start by dividing the hundreds. The remainder from dividing the hundreds is 4 hundreds. 4 hundreds and 2 tens is 42 tens. Since 42 tens is smaller than 64, the quotient will not have any tens. So we now have to rename the tens as ones and divide 420 ones by 64.

```
       106  r 36
 64)6820
    64
      420
      384
       36
```

(d): 31 is less than 45, so we start by dividing the tens by 45: 318 tens ÷ 45. The remainder from dividing the tens plus the ones is less than 45, so there are no ones in the quotient.

```
        70  r 35
 45)3185
    315
      35
```

Have your student do task 16, rewriting the problems vertically.

16. (a) **239** (b) **133 r15** (c) **33 r10**
(d) **107 r16** (e) **28 r18** (f) **340 r4**

Provide your student with plenty of practice in dividing a whole number by a 2-digit whole number. You can give him several problems each day for a while. You can make up random problems by using number cards 0-9. Your student shuffles the cards, turns over 3 or 4 to make a 3-digit or 4-digt digit number, turns over another 2 to make a 2-digit number, and divides the first number by the second.

Workbook Exercise 13, #2

Practice 2A (p. 32)

Practice 2A, p. 32
The student can do this practice independently.

1. (a) **34,188** (b) **33,810** (c) **68,693**
2. (a) **275,145** (b) **629,340** (c) **194,796**
3. (a) **3 r17** (b) **2 r26** (c) **3 r2**
4. (a) **53** (b) **6 r1** (c) **9 r28**
5. (a) **19** (b) **38 r21** (c) **23 r33**
6. (a) **98 r40** (b) **58 r6** (c) **179 r4**

7. 1 cake → 12 eggs
   36 cakes → 12 eggs x 36 = 432 eggs
   He needs **432** eggs.

8. 240 ÷ 15 = 16 ℓ
   He needs **16 ℓ**.

9. 1,064 ÷ 38 = 28
   Each student receives **28** balloons.

10. Number of boxes = 96 ÷ 12 = 8
    Total money = 8 x $7 = $56
    She received **$56**.

11. Amount paid for 72 installments = $827 x 72 = 59,544
    Total amount paid = $59,544 + $280 = $59,824
    The car cost **$59,824**.

12. Money for tickets = 2,034 x $16 = $32,544
    Money for programs = 840 x $3 = $2,520
    Total money = $32,544 + $2,520 = **$35,064**

13. 1 team → 2 girls
    14 teams → 14 x 2 girls = 28 girls
    Number of boys = total students - girls = 70 - 28 = 42 boys
    There were **42** boys.

14. Number of packets = 840 ÷ 24 = 35
    Total money = 35 x $3 = $105
    She received **$105**.

Workbook Review 1

Unit 3 - Fractions

Part 1 - Fractions and Division (pp. 33-35)

(1) Fractions and Division

- Review improper fractions and mixed numbers.
- Associate division with fractions.
- Change an improper fraction to a mixed number or whole number by division.
- Express the quotient as a whole number or a mixed number.

In *Primary Mathematics* 4A students learned to convert from improper fractions to mixed numbers and vice versa by finding the number of fractional parts that made wholes. For example: $\frac{21}{4} = \frac{20}{4} + \frac{1}{4} = 5\frac{1}{4}$.

In this section, the student will relate the steps for converting to a mixed number to the steps in division, where we need to think of the multiple of 4 that is closest to 21 when dividing 21 by 4. The whole number remainder is 1. If the remainder is further divided, each group would get $\frac{1}{4}$. $\frac{21}{4} = 21 \div 4 = 5\frac{1}{4}$.

$$\begin{array}{r} 5 \\ 4\overline{)21} \\ \underline{20} \\ 1 \end{array}$$

In a proper fraction, the value is less than 1, and the numerator is smaller than the denominator. In an improper fraction, the value is equal to or greater than 1, and the numerator is equal to or greater than the denominator. Note that there is nothing wrong with an improper fraction, despite its name, and it is OK to write a fraction this way. A mixed number has both a whole number part and a fraction part.

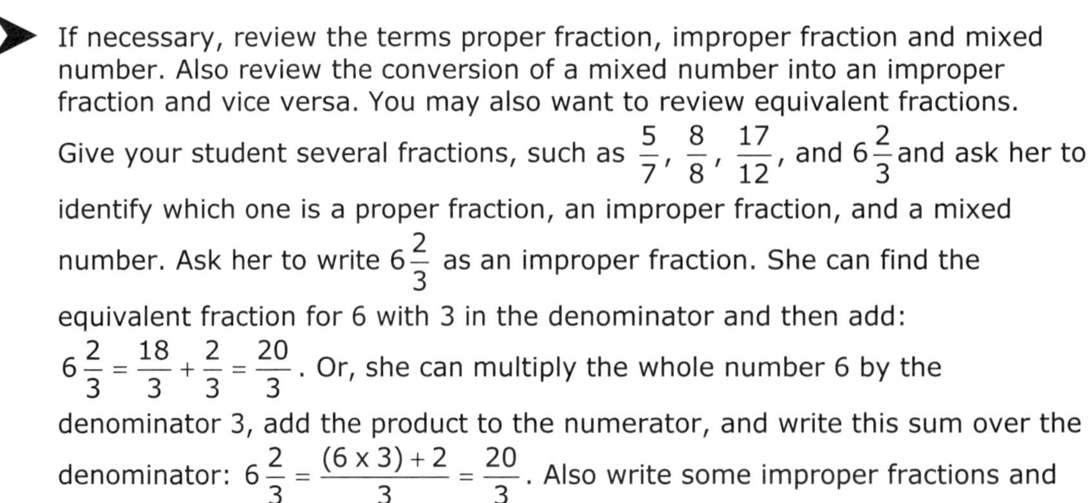

If necessary, review the terms proper fraction, improper fraction and mixed number. Also review the conversion of a mixed number into an improper fraction and vice versa. You may also want to review equivalent fractions. Give your student several fractions, such as $\frac{5}{7}$, $\frac{8}{8}$, $\frac{17}{12}$, and $6\frac{2}{3}$ and ask her to identify which one is a proper fraction, an improper fraction, and a mixed number. Ask her to write $6\frac{2}{3}$ as an improper fraction. She can find the equivalent fraction for 6 with 3 in the denominator and then add: $6\frac{2}{3} = \frac{18}{3} + \frac{2}{3} = \frac{20}{3}$. Or, she can multiply the whole number 6 by the denominator 3, add the product to the numerator, and write this sum over the denominator: $6\frac{2}{3} = \frac{(6 \times 3) + 2}{3} = \frac{20}{3}$. Also write some improper fractions and ask her to write them as mixed numbers. Do some other examples if more review is necessary.

You may want to use Review A, #15-18, #20-23, pp. 62-63 for review.

➤ Write 1 ÷ 4. Give your student a paper circle or square and ask him to divide it so that 4 groups get the same amount. Tell him that each group can get a part of a square, but all 4 groups have to get the same size part. Let him solve it on his own before discussing the solution. He can divide the square into fourths, and put one fourth in each group. Write $1 \div 4 = \frac{1}{4}$.

$$1 \div 4 = \frac{1}{4}$$

Write 9 ÷ 4. Give your student 9 paper circles or squares and ask him to divide them into 4 equal groups. Each group can get a part of a square. Allow him to do this on his own before discussing the result.

He could put 2 squares in each group, using 8 of them with a remainder of 1. Then he can divide the one square into fourths and put a fourth in each group. Write $9 \div 4 = 2\frac{1}{4}$. Show this as a vertical division problem. The remainder is 1. If we do not want only whole number answers, we can put the remainder over the divisor (the number we are dividing by) to show the fraction each group gets.
Ask him to convert the mixed number answer to an improper fraction. Point out that $9 \div 4 = \frac{9}{4}$.
We can write any division problem as a fraction, and then convert into a mixed number, or we can perform the division and then divide the remainder as well; the quotient from dividing the remainder is the fraction with the remainder in the numerator and the divisor in the denominator.

$$9 \div 4 = 2\frac{1}{4}$$

```
  2
4 9
  8
  1
```

$$9 \div 4 = 2\frac{1}{4} = \frac{9}{4}$$

pp. 33-34
Learning Tasks 1-4, pp. 34-35

1. $\mathbf{2\frac{3}{4}}$
2. $\mathbf{2\frac{2}{3}}$
3. **3; 11;** $\mathbf{2\frac{3}{4}}$
4. (a) $\mathbf{2\frac{1}{3}}$ (b) $\mathbf{2\frac{4}{5}}$ (c) $\mathbf{3\frac{1}{2}}$ (d) $\mathbf{8\frac{5}{9}}$

Workbook Exercise 14

Practice 3A (p. 36)

Practice 3A, p. 36

1. (a) $\frac{13}{5} = \frac{10}{5} + \frac{3}{5} = \mathbf{2\frac{3}{5}}$ (b) $\frac{21}{3} = \mathbf{7}$

   (c) $\frac{24}{9} = \frac{18}{9} + \frac{6}{9} = 2\frac{6}{9} = \mathbf{2\frac{2}{3}}$ (d) $\frac{50}{6} = \frac{25}{3} = \frac{24}{3} + \frac{1}{3} = \mathbf{8\frac{1}{3}}$

2. (a) $\frac{30}{8} = \frac{15}{4} = \frac{12}{4} + \frac{3}{4} = \mathbf{3\frac{3}{4}}$ (b) $\frac{21}{4} = \frac{20}{4} + \frac{1}{4} = \mathbf{5\frac{1}{4}}$

   (c) $\frac{35}{10} = \frac{7}{2} = \frac{6}{2} + \frac{1}{2} = \mathbf{3\frac{1}{2}}$ (d) $\frac{78}{7} = \frac{77}{7} + \frac{1}{7} = \mathbf{11\frac{1}{7}}$

3. Length of each piece = 26 m ÷ 8 = $\frac{26}{8} = \frac{13}{4} = \frac{12}{4} + \frac{1}{4} = \mathbf{3\frac{1}{4}}$ **m**

4. Cloth for each pillow case = 3 m ÷ 9 = $\frac{3}{9} = \mathbf{\frac{1}{3}}$ **m**

5. Cakes in each share = $\frac{10}{4} = \frac{5}{2} = \frac{4}{2} + \frac{1}{2} = \mathbf{2\frac{1}{2}}$

6. Milk in each jug = $\mathbf{\frac{2}{5}}$ **ℓ**

7. Length of blue ribbon = $\frac{11}{5} = \frac{10}{5} + \frac{1}{5} = \mathbf{2\frac{1}{5}}$ **m**

8. Weight of each share = $\frac{4}{6} = \mathbf{\frac{2}{3}}$ **kg**

Part 2 – Addition and Subtraction of Unlike Fractions (pp. 37-39)

In *Primary Mathematics* 4A students learned to add and subtract related fractions. Related fractions are fractions where the denominator of one fraction is a simple multiple of the denominator of the other fraction. Adding or subtracting the fractions therefore involves finding an equivalent fraction of only one of them. For example:

$$\frac{3}{4}+\frac{1}{8}=\frac{6}{8}+\frac{1}{8}=\frac{7}{8}$$

In this part students will learn to add and subtract unlike fractions, where the denominator of one is not a simple multiple of the denominator of the other. So addition and subtraction involves finding equivalent fractions of both. For example:

$$\frac{3}{8}+\frac{5}{6}=\frac{9}{24}+\frac{20}{24}=\frac{29}{24}=1\frac{5}{24}$$

In this example, the equivalent fractions have a denominator that is the lowest common multiple of both 8 and 6. Any equivalent fractions where the denominators are the same can be used. One possible denominator is the product of the denominators of each fraction. In this case equivalent fractions can be obtained by multiplying the numerator and denominator by the denominator of the other fraction:

$$\frac{3}{8}+\frac{5}{6}=\frac{3\times 6}{8\times 6}+\frac{5\times 8}{6\times 8}=\frac{18}{48}+\frac{40}{48}=\frac{58}{48}=\frac{29}{24}=1\frac{5}{24}$$

However, using the lowest common multiple of both denominators reduces the need for simplification at the end, and involves smaller numbers, making calculations easier.

Your student should reduce answers to their simplest form, and convert an answer that is an improper fraction to a mixed number. Some texts call the lowest common multiple of denominators the lowest common denominator.

(1) Addition of Unlike Fractions

- Review factors and multiples.
- Add unlike fractions.

Remind your student that any whole number can be expressed as the product of two or more whole numbers, or factors. Since 4 x 3 = 12, then 4 and 3 are factors of 12.

Guide him in systematically listing the factors of 24 (problem 8.a in Review 1). 1 is a factor of all whole numbers, and so is the number itself. 2, 3 and 4 divide 24 evenly, while 5 does not. 6 has already been found as the factor to go with 4. So the factors of 24 are 1, 2, 3, 4, 6, 8, 12, and 24. Those are all the numbers that divide 24 exactly.

1 x 24 = 24
2 x 12 = 24
3 x 8 = 24
4 x 6 = 24
6 x 4 = 24
8 x 3 = 24
12 x 2 = 24
24 x 1 = 24

You may want to review divisibility rules, which can help in finding factors.

- A number is divisible by 2 if the last digit is 0, 2, 4, 6, or 8.
- A number is divisible by 5 if the last digit is 5 or 0.
- A number is divisible by 3 if the sum of the digits is divisible by 3.
- A number is divisible by 9 if the sum of the digits is divisible by 9.
- A number is divisible by 4 if the last two digits are divisible by 4.

Remind your student that a common factor of two numbers is any factor that both numbers have. Ask your student for the factors of 48. Then ask her to list the factors of 60 and find the factors that are common to both 48 and 60.

48: 1, 2, 3, 4, 6, 8, 12, 16, 24, 48

60: 1, 2, 3, 4, 5, 6, 10, 12, 15, 20, 30, 60

1, 2, 3, 4, 6 and 12 are common factors of 48 and 60.

Remind your student that a multiple of a number is any number that is the product of the given number and a whole number. Ask her to list some multiples of 6 and of 8 and to find some multiplies common to both 6 and 8.

6: 6, 12, 18, 24, 30, 36, 42, 48, ...
8: 8, 16, 24, 32, 40, 48, ...

24 and 48 are common multiples of 6 and 8. 24 is the lowest common multiple. Note that the product of the two numbers is always a common multiple.

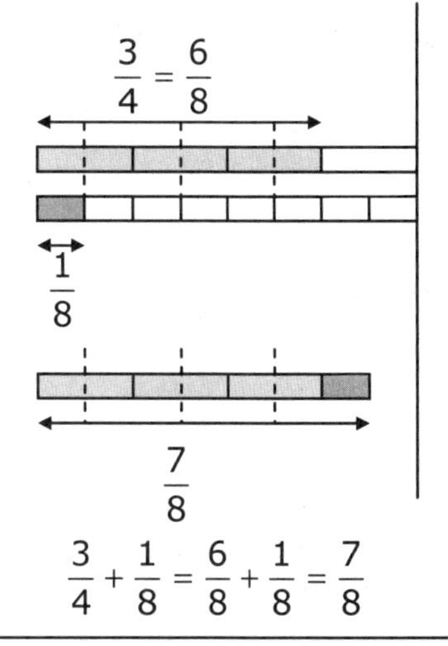

➤ Ask your student what she must do to add two fractions, such as $\frac{3}{4}$ and $\frac{1}{8}$. If necessary, draw two fraction bars illustrating these fractions and remind her that we need to make the parts the same size to add them. To do this, we need to cut up the larger pieces into smaller pieces. If we cut each fourth into half, we have $\frac{6}{8}$. $\frac{6}{8}$ is an equivalent fraction of $\frac{3}{4}$. We can add six eighth pieces to one eighth piece to get 7 eighth pieces.

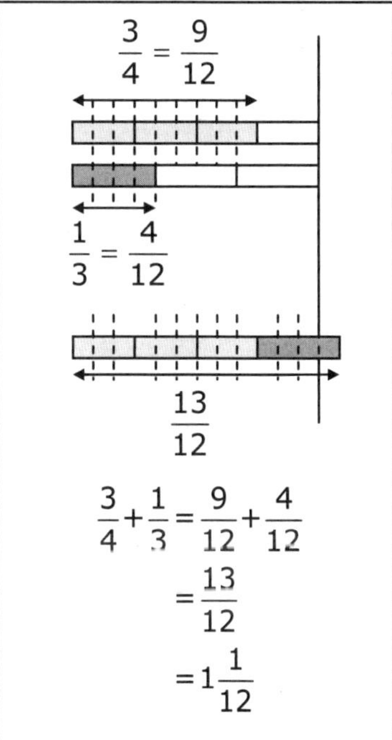

Now ask her to add $\frac{3}{4}$ and $\frac{1}{3}$. If necessary, you can draw fraction bars for these. We have to make the parts into equal size to add them, but we can't do this by simply dividing up the larger pieces. We have to divide each size piece so that we have equal sizes for both. We can figure out how we should divide each piece by finding a common multiple of the denominators, 4 and 3. 12 is a common multiple. If we divide up the whole into twelfths, each larger piece (third) needs to be divided into 4 smaller pieces, so there will be 4 times as many, and each smaller piece (fourths) needs to be divided into 3 smaller pieces. Then we can add the pieces together.

Tell your student that the final answer should be in the simplest form, and if it is an improper fraction it should be converted to a proper fraction.

p. 37

In order to add the two fractions together, we find equivalent fractions of each until we find ones with the same denominator. This denominator, 6, is a common multiple of 3 and 2. To find the sum of $\frac{1}{3}$ and $\frac{1}{2}$, we find equivalent fractions of $\frac{1}{3}$ and $\frac{1}{2}$ with the same denominator, and add them together. The sum is $\mathbf{\frac{5}{6}}$.

Learning Tasks 1-4, p. 38

For sums that will be greater than 1, the standard method for adding fractions shown in the learning tasks is to find the total number of parts and then convert into a mixed number. For example we can add $\frac{7}{8}$ and $\frac{3}{4}$ by finding the total number of eighths and then converting into a mixed number:

$$\frac{7}{8}+\frac{3}{4}=\frac{7}{8}+\frac{6}{8}=\frac{13}{8}=1\frac{5}{8}$$

You may want to point out another way to mentally add these fractions once the equivalent fractions are found. We can "make ones" by taking off one fraction what is needed to bring the other fraction to a one. For example, we can make a one out of the $\frac{7}{8}$ by taking an eighth from $\frac{6}{8}$:

$$\frac{7}{8}+\frac{3}{4}=\frac{7}{8}+\frac{6}{8}=\frac{8}{8}+\frac{5}{8}=1\frac{5}{8}$$

You can also choose several of the problems and show how another common multiple for the denominator, such as the product of the denominators, would result in the same answer, in simplest form.

1. $\frac{3}{8}+\frac{1}{6}=\mathbf{\frac{9}{24}}+\mathbf{\frac{4}{24}}$
   $=\mathbf{\frac{13}{24}}$

2. $\frac{2}{3}+\frac{2}{5}=\mathbf{\frac{10}{15}}+\mathbf{\frac{6}{15}}$
   $=\mathbf{\frac{16}{15}}$
   $=\mathbf{1\frac{1}{15}}$
   or: $\frac{10}{15}+\frac{6}{15}=\frac{15}{15}+\frac{1}{15}$

3. $\frac{7}{10}+\frac{5}{6}=\mathbf{\frac{21}{30}}+\mathbf{\frac{25}{30}}$
   $=\mathbf{\frac{46}{30}}$
   $=\mathbf{\frac{23}{15}}$
   $=\mathbf{1\frac{8}{15}}$
   or:
   $\frac{21}{30}+\frac{25}{30}=\frac{16}{30}+\frac{30}{30}$

4. (a) $\frac{7}{9}+\frac{5}{6}=\frac{14}{18}+\frac{15}{18}$
   $=\frac{18}{18}+\frac{11}{18}$
   $=\mathbf{1\frac{11}{18}}$

   (b) $\frac{3}{4}+\frac{5}{12}=\frac{9}{12}+\frac{5}{12}$
   $=\frac{12}{12}+\frac{2}{12}$
   $=\mathbf{1\frac{1}{6}}$

   (c) $\frac{3}{10}+\frac{5}{6}=\frac{9}{30}+\frac{25}{30}$
   $=\frac{4}{30}+\frac{30}{30}$
   $=1\frac{4}{30}$
   $=\mathbf{1\frac{2}{15}}$

Workbook Exercise 15

(2) Subtraction of Unlike Fractions

 ➢ Subtract unlike fractions.

 Remind your student that to subtract one fraction from another, the denominators have to be the same. Sometimes only one fraction needs to be changed, as with $\frac{3}{4} - \frac{1}{2} = \frac{3}{4} - \frac{2}{4} = \frac{1}{4}$, and sometimes both need to be changed, as with $\frac{5}{8} - \frac{1}{6} = \frac{15}{24} - \frac{4}{24} = \frac{11}{24}$. We find a common multiple (24) of the denominators (8 and 6) and then find equivalent fractions with that denominator. Note that we can find any common multiple. If we can't think of one easily, we can use the product of the two denominators. We could have used 48 (the product of 8 and 6) in the above example. Then all we do to find the equivalent fractions is to multiply the numerator of one with the denominator of the other: $\frac{5}{8} - \frac{1}{6} = \frac{5 \times 6}{48} - \frac{1 \times 8}{48} = \frac{30}{48} - \frac{8}{48} = \frac{22}{48} = \frac{11}{24}$. It is, however, easier to use the lowest common multiple since the resulting numbers are smaller and easier to compute mentally. Remind your student that the answer has to be in simplest form.

 **Learning Tasks 5-8, p. 39**

5. $\frac{7}{8} - \frac{1}{6} = \frac{\mathbf{21}}{24} - \frac{\mathbf{4}}{24}$
   $= \frac{\mathbf{17}}{24}$

6. $\frac{5}{6} - \frac{1}{10} = \frac{\mathbf{25}}{30} - \frac{\mathbf{3}}{30}$
   $= \frac{\mathbf{22}}{30}$
   $= \frac{\mathbf{11}}{15}$

7. $1\frac{7}{10} - \frac{5}{6} = \frac{\mathbf{30} + \mathbf{21}}{30} - \frac{\mathbf{25}}{30}$
   $= \frac{\mathbf{51}}{30} - \frac{\mathbf{25}}{30}$
   $= \frac{\mathbf{13}}{15}$

$\frac{5}{6}$ can first be subtracted from the whole, and the result added to $\frac{7}{10}$:

$1\frac{7}{10} - \frac{5}{6} = 1 - \frac{5}{6} + \frac{7}{10}$
$= \frac{1}{6} + \frac{7}{10}$
$= \frac{5}{30} + \frac{21}{30} = \frac{26}{30} = \frac{13}{15}$

8. (a) $\frac{5}{6} - \frac{3}{10} = \frac{25}{30} - \frac{9}{30}$

$= \frac{16}{30}$

$= \mathbf{\frac{8}{15}}$

(b) $1\frac{2}{3} - \frac{11}{12} = 1\frac{8}{12} - \frac{11}{12}$

$= \frac{20}{12} - \frac{11}{12}$

$= \frac{9}{12}$

$= \mathbf{\frac{3}{4}}$

Or: $1\frac{2}{3} - \frac{11}{12} = 1\frac{8}{12} - \frac{11}{12}$

$= 1 - \frac{11}{12} + \frac{8}{12}$

$= \frac{1}{12} + \frac{8}{12}$

$= \frac{3}{4}$

(c) $1\frac{1}{10} - \frac{5}{6} = 1\frac{3}{30} - \frac{25}{30}$

$= \frac{33}{30} - \frac{25}{30}$

$= \frac{8}{30}$

$= \mathbf{\frac{4}{15}}$

Or: $1\frac{1}{10} - \frac{5}{6} = 1\frac{3}{30} - \frac{25}{30}$

$= 1 - \frac{25}{30} + \frac{3}{30}$

$= \frac{5}{30} + \frac{3}{30}$

$= \frac{4}{15}$

 **Workbook Exercise 16**

Practice 3B (p. 40)

 **Practice 3B, p. 40**

1. (a) $\frac{7}{12}+\frac{5}{6}=\frac{7}{12}+\frac{10}{12}$ $=\mathbf{1\frac{5}{12}}$

   (b) $\frac{9}{10}+\frac{1}{6}=\frac{27}{30}+\frac{5}{30}$ $=\mathbf{1\frac{1}{15}}$

   (c) $\frac{5}{6}+\frac{7}{8}=\frac{20}{24}+\frac{21}{24}$ $=\mathbf{1\frac{17}{24}}$

2. (a) $\frac{2}{3}-\frac{5}{12}=\frac{8}{12}-\frac{5}{12}$ $=\frac{3}{12}$ $=\mathbf{\frac{1}{4}}$

   (b) $\frac{5}{6}-\frac{7}{10}=\frac{25}{30}-\frac{21}{30}$ $=\frac{4}{30}$ $=\mathbf{\frac{2}{15}}$

   (c) $\frac{3}{4}-\frac{1}{6}=\frac{9}{12}-\frac{2}{12}$ $=\mathbf{\frac{7}{12}}$

3. (a) $\frac{1}{6}+\frac{3}{10}=\frac{5}{30}+\frac{9}{30}$ $=\frac{14}{30}$ $=\mathbf{\frac{7}{15}}$

   (b) $\frac{2}{3}+\frac{1}{12}=\frac{8}{12}+\frac{1}{12}$ $=\frac{9}{12}$ $=\mathbf{\frac{3}{4}}$

   (c) $\frac{5}{12}+\frac{1}{8}=\frac{10}{24}+\frac{3}{24}$ $=\mathbf{\frac{13}{24}}$

4. (a) $1\frac{3}{8}-\frac{7}{12}=1\frac{9}{24}-\frac{14}{24}$ $=\mathbf{\frac{19}{24}}$

   (b) $1\frac{1}{3}-\frac{7}{10}=1\frac{10}{30}-\frac{21}{30}$ $=\mathbf{\frac{19}{30}}$

   (c) $1\frac{3}{10}-\frac{5}{6}=1\frac{9}{30}-\frac{25}{30}$ $=\frac{14}{30}$ $=\mathbf{\frac{7}{15}}$

5. $\frac{2}{5}+\frac{1}{4}=\frac{8}{20}+\frac{5}{20}=\frac{13}{20}$

   $\mathbf{\frac{13}{20}}$ of the lawn was mowed.

6. $1\frac{1}{4} - \frac{3}{4} = \frac{5}{4} - \frac{3}{4} = \frac{2}{4} = \frac{1}{2}$

It took $\mathbf{\frac{1}{2}}$ hour longer to return.

7. (a) $\frac{1}{8} + \frac{1}{4} = \frac{1}{8} + \frac{2}{8} = \frac{3}{8}$

They ate $\mathbf{\frac{3}{8}}$ of the cake together.

(b) $\frac{1}{4} - \frac{1}{8} = \frac{2}{8} - \frac{1}{8} = \frac{1}{8}$

Peter ate $\mathbf{\frac{1}{8}}$ of the cake more than Mary.

8. (a) $\frac{3}{5} + \frac{1}{4} = \frac{12}{20} + \frac{5}{20} = \frac{17}{20}$

He spent $\mathbf{\frac{17}{20}}$ of his money.

(b) $1 - \frac{17}{20} = \frac{20}{20} - \frac{17}{20} = \frac{3}{20}$

He had $\mathbf{\frac{3}{20}}$ of his money left.

Part 3 – Addition and Subtraction of Mixed Numbers (pp. 41-42)

(1) Addition of Mixed Numbers

➢ Add mixed numbers.

The process for adding two (or more) mixed numbers involves the following steps:

Add the whole number parts.

$$3\frac{1}{2} + 6\frac{3}{4} = 3 + \frac{1}{2} + 6 + \frac{3}{4}$$
$$= 3 + 6 + \frac{1}{2} + \frac{3}{4}$$
$$= 9 + \frac{1}{2} + \frac{3}{4}$$

Change the fractional parts to like fractions.

$$= 9 + \frac{2}{4} + \frac{3}{4}$$

Add the fractional parts.

$$= 9 + \frac{5}{4}$$

Write the answer in simplest form.

$$= 9 + 1\frac{1}{4}$$
$$= 10\frac{1}{4}$$

p. 41

Go through these problems, outlining the steps for adding mixed numbers. You may want to draw pictures of fraction bars or circles to illustrate the steps. You can also use concrete manipulatives, but illustrate a simpler problem, like the one in the notes, since manipulatives don't usually have twenty-fourths.

(a) $3\frac{5}{8} + 1\frac{7}{12}$

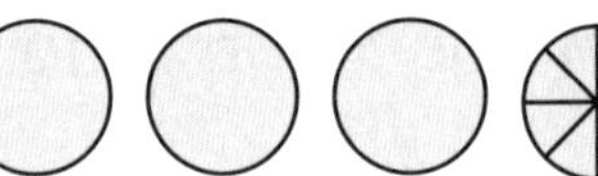
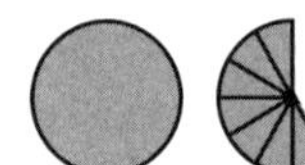

$= 4\frac{5}{8} + \frac{7}{12}$ Add the whole numbers together

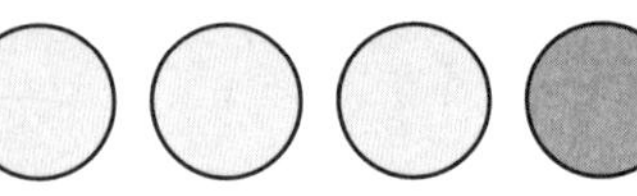
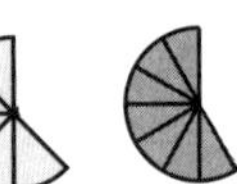

$= 4\frac{15}{24} + \frac{14}{24}$ Change eighths and twelfths to twenty-fourths.

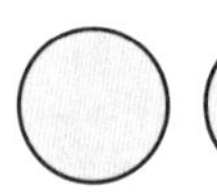
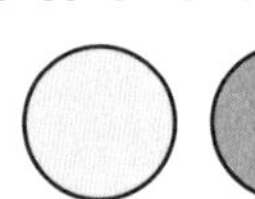
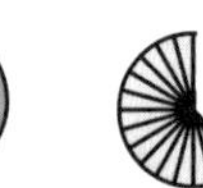

$= 4\mathbf{\frac{29}{24}}$ or $4\frac{24}{24} + \frac{5}{24}$ Add the twenty-fourths.

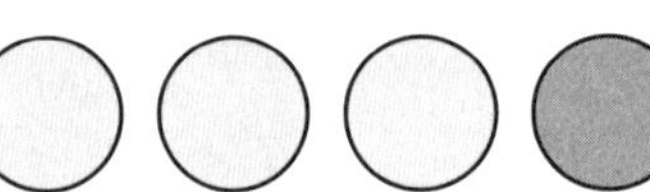

$= \mathbf{5\frac{5}{24}}$ Write the answer in simplest form.

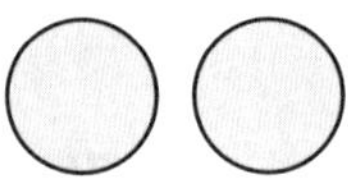
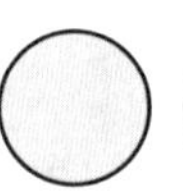

(b) $4\frac{7}{12} + 1\frac{3}{4} = 5\frac{7}{12} + \frac{3}{4}$ Add the whole numbers together.

$= 5\frac{7}{12} + \frac{9}{12}$ Change fourths to twelfths.

$= 5\mathbf{\frac{16}{12}}$ or $5\frac{4}{12} + \frac{12}{12}$ Add twelfths.

$= 5\frac{\mathbf{4}}{3}$ or $6\frac{4}{12}$ Simplify.

$= \mathbf{6\frac{1}{3}}$

 **Learning Task 1, p. 42**

1. $3\frac{1}{6} + 1\frac{9}{10} = 4\frac{1}{6} + \frac{9}{10}$

$= 4\mathbf{\frac{5}{30}} + \mathbf{\frac{27}{30}}$

$= 4\mathbf{\frac{32}{30}}$

$= \mathbf{5\frac{1}{15}}$

Workbook Exercise 17

(2) Subtraction of Mixed Numbers

 ➢ Subtract mixed numbers.

 The process for subtracting two mixed numbers involves the following steps:

$4\frac{1}{2} - 1\frac{3}{4}$

$= 3\frac{1}{2} - \frac{3}{4}$ Subtract the whole number parts.

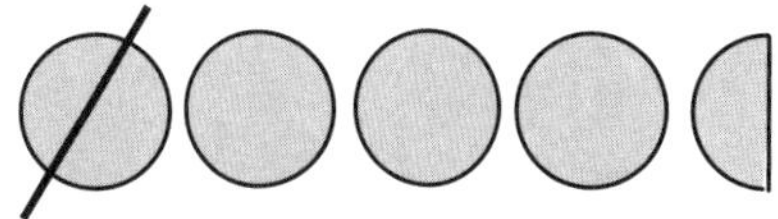

$= 3\frac{2}{4} - \frac{3}{4}$ Change the fractional parts to like fractions.

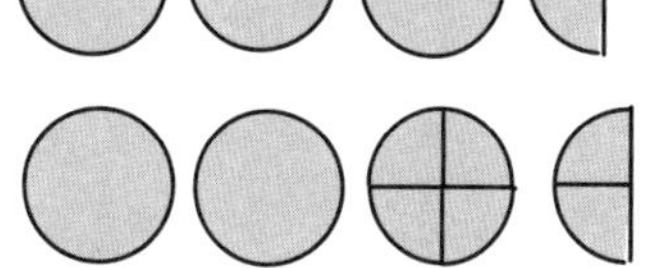

$= 2\frac{6}{4} - \frac{3}{4}$ Rename part of the mixed number if its fractional part is not enough to subtract.

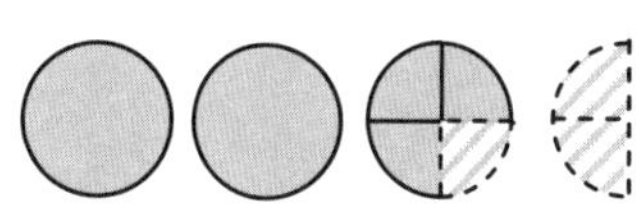

$= 2\frac{3}{4}$ Subtract fractional parts.

Simplify if necessary.

OR:

$4\frac{1}{2} - 1\frac{3}{4} = 3\frac{2}{4} - \frac{3}{4}$

$= 3 - \frac{3}{4} + \frac{2}{4}$ Subtract from a whole.

$= 2\frac{1}{4} + \frac{2}{4} = 2\frac{3}{4}$

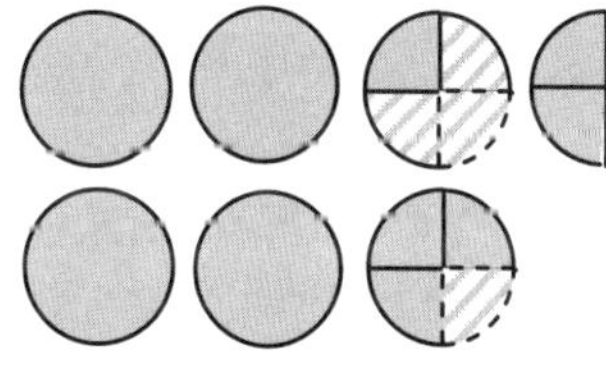

Learning Tasks 2-3, p. 42

Discuss the steps used in solving these problems. Illustrate with fraction discs or bar diagrams.

2. $4\frac{3}{4} - 3\frac{7}{12} = 1\frac{3}{4} - \frac{7}{12}$

$= 1\frac{9}{12} - \frac{7}{12}$

$= 1\frac{\mathbf{2}}{12}$

$= \mathbf{1\frac{1}{6}}$

3. (a) $3\frac{1}{6} - 1\frac{5}{9} = 2\frac{1}{6} - \frac{5}{9}$

$= 2\frac{3}{18} - \frac{10}{18}$

$= 1\frac{\mathbf{21}}{18} - \frac{10}{18}$

$= \mathbf{1\frac{11}{18}}$

(b) $4\frac{1}{6} - 1\frac{3}{10} = 3\frac{1}{6} - \frac{3}{10}$

$= 3\frac{\mathbf{5}}{30} - \frac{9}{30}$

$= 2\frac{\mathbf{35}}{30} - \frac{9}{30}$

$= 2\frac{\mathbf{26}}{30}$

$= \mathbf{2\frac{13}{15}}$

Workbook Exercise 18

Practice 3C (p. 43)

Practice 3C, p. 43

1. (a) $2\frac{2}{3}+1\frac{5}{9}$
$= 3\frac{6}{9}+\frac{5}{9}$
$= \mathbf{4\frac{2}{9}}$

(b) $2\frac{1}{8}+1\frac{5}{6}$
$= 3\frac{3}{24}+\frac{20}{24}$
$= \mathbf{3\frac{23}{24}}$

(c) $1\frac{1}{4}+2\frac{5}{6}$
$= 3\frac{3}{12}+\frac{10}{12}$
$= \mathbf{4\frac{1}{12}}$

2. (a) $3\frac{5}{6}-1\frac{1}{3}$
$= 2\frac{5}{6}-\frac{2}{6}$
$= 2\frac{3}{6}$
$= \mathbf{2\frac{1}{2}}$

(b) $3\frac{4}{5}-1\frac{3}{10}$
$= 2\frac{8}{10}-\frac{3}{10}$
$= 2\frac{5}{10}$
$= \mathbf{2\frac{1}{2}}$

(c) $4\frac{5}{6}-1\frac{1}{4}$
$= 3\frac{10}{12}-\frac{3}{12}$
$= \mathbf{3\frac{7}{12}}$

3. (a) $3\frac{2}{9}+1\frac{1}{6}$
$=4\frac{4}{18}+\frac{3}{18}$
$= \mathbf{4\frac{7}{18}}$

(b) $2\frac{5}{6}+5\frac{1}{2}$
$= 7\frac{5}{6}+\frac{3}{6}$
$= 8\frac{2}{6}$
$= \mathbf{8\frac{1}{3}}$

(c) $2\frac{5}{6}+1\frac{3}{8}$
$= 3\frac{20}{24}+\frac{9}{24}$
$= \mathbf{4\frac{5}{24}}$

4. (a) $4\frac{1}{6}-1\frac{2}{3}$
$= 3\frac{1}{6}-\frac{4}{6}$
$= 2\frac{7}{6}-\frac{4}{6}$
$= \mathbf{2\frac{1}{2}}$

(b) $3\frac{1}{6}-2\frac{1}{10}$
$= 1\frac{5}{30}-\frac{3}{30}$
$= 1\frac{2}{30}$
$= \mathbf{1\frac{1}{15}}$

(c) $3\frac{3}{10}-1\frac{1}{6}$
$=2\frac{9}{30}-\frac{5}{30}$
$= 2\frac{4}{30}$
$= \mathbf{2\frac{2}{15}}$

5. $2\frac{1}{2}-1\frac{2}{5}=1\frac{5}{10}-\frac{4}{10}=1\frac{1}{10}$

The brother jogged $\mathbf{1\frac{1}{10}}$ km farther.

6. $3\frac{1}{6} - 1\frac{2}{3} = 2\frac{1}{6} - \frac{4}{6} = 1\frac{7}{6} - \frac{4}{6} = 1\frac{3}{6} = 1\frac{1}{2}$

$1\frac{1}{2}$ cakes were eaten.

7. $3 - 1\frac{3}{4} = 2 - \frac{3}{4} = 1\frac{1}{4}$

$1\frac{1}{4}$ ℓ are needed to fill the container.

8. $1\frac{1}{2} - 1\frac{1}{12} = \frac{6}{12} - \frac{1}{12} = \frac{5}{12}$

She finished cooking **$\frac{5}{12}$ hours** earlier.

9. $2\frac{3}{4} - 1\frac{1}{3} = 1\frac{9}{12} - \frac{4}{12} = 1\frac{5}{12}$

The other ribbon is **$1\frac{5}{12}$ m**.

Part 4 – Product of a Fraction and a Whole Number (pp. 44-47)

(1) Product of a Fraction and a Whole Number

- Find the product of a fraction and a whole number.

Students learned to multiply a proper fraction by a whole number *in Primary Mathematics* 4A. This is reviewed here. In the next section the concept will be extended to multiplying an improper fraction or a mixed number by a whole number in the context of conversion of measurement. Make sure your student is comfortable with finding the product of a fraction and a whole number, and with using cancellation to simplify the calculations.

- Use or draw fraction discs to illustrate $10 \times \frac{1}{4}$.

$10 \times \frac{1}{4}$ means ten $\frac{1}{4}$'s, or ten fourths.

$10 \times \frac{1}{4} = \frac{10}{4} = 2\frac{1}{2}$.

We can first simplify $\frac{10}{4}$: $\frac{1}{4} \times 10 = \frac{\cancel{10}^{5}}{\cancel{4}_{2}} = 2\frac{1}{2}$

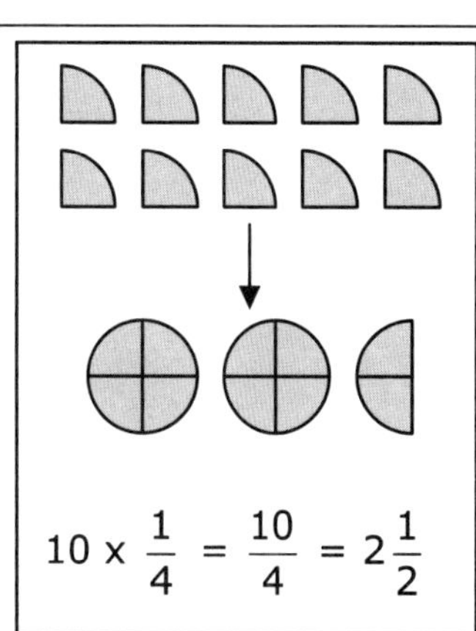

$10 \times \frac{1}{4} = \frac{10}{4} = 2\frac{1}{2}$

- Use the fraction discs to illustrate $\frac{1}{4}$ of 10.

We put 10 into four groups. To do so, we need to divide the last 2 wholes into half and put a half in each group. This gives us the same result as before. Your student should see that

$\frac{1}{4}$ of $10 = 10 \times \frac{1}{4} = \frac{1}{4} \times 10 = \frac{\cancel{10}^{5}}{\cancel{4}_{2}} = 2\frac{1}{2}$

We can interpret $\frac{1}{4}$ **of** 10 as meaning $\frac{1}{4} \times 10$.

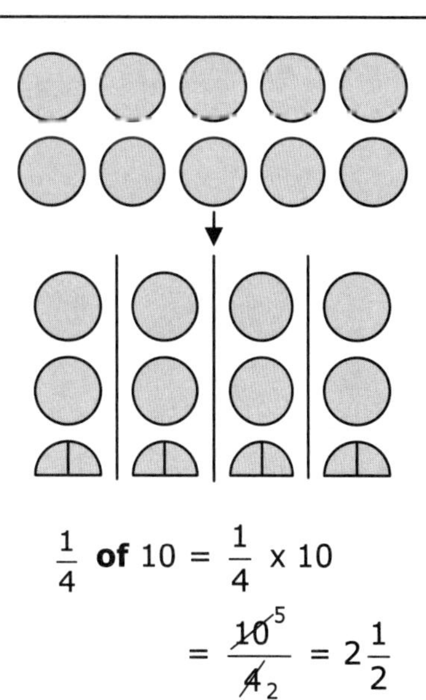

$\frac{1}{4}$ **of** $10 = \frac{1}{4} \times 10$

$= \frac{\cancel{10}^{5}}{\cancel{4}_{2}} = 2\frac{1}{2}$

Use your previous illustration to help your student interpret $\frac{3}{4}$ of 10. By looking at the illustration, we can see that $\frac{3}{4}$ of 10 = $7\frac{1}{2}$. We can find $\frac{1}{4}$ of 10 and then multiply the answer by 3. $\frac{3}{4}$ of 10 = 3 x $\frac{1}{4}$ x 10 = 3 x $2\frac{1}{2}$. We can find 3 x $2\frac{1}{2}$ by multiplying each of the parts by 3 and adding:

$$3 \times 2\frac{1}{2} = (3 \times 2) + (3 \times \frac{1}{2}) = 6 + 1\frac{1}{2} = 7\frac{1}{2}$$

Or we can convert the mixed number to an improper fraction and multiply:

$$3 \times 2\frac{1}{2} = 3 \times \frac{5}{2} = \frac{5}{2} \times 3 = \frac{5 \times 3}{2} = \frac{15}{2} = 7\frac{1}{2}$$

Note that $\frac{5}{2} = \frac{10}{4}$. We have shown that $\frac{3}{4}$ of 10 = 3 x $\frac{5}{2}$. We can solve as:

$$\frac{3}{4} \text{ of } 10 = \frac{3}{4} \times 10 = \frac{3 \times 10}{4} = 3 \times \frac{\cancel{10}^{5}}{\cancel{4}_{2}} = 7\frac{1}{2}$$

We can simplify these steps as:

$$\frac{3}{4} \text{ of } 10 = \frac{3}{4} \times 10 = \frac{3 \times \cancel{10}^{5}}{\cancel{4}_{2}} = \frac{15}{2} = 7\frac{1}{2}$$

And simplify the steps even farther as:

$$\frac{3}{4} \text{ of } 10 = \frac{3}{\cancel{4}_{2}} \times \cancel{10}^{5} = \frac{15}{2} = 7\frac{1}{2}$$

Crossing out a number in the numerator and denominator is called canceling. Each cancellation step is dividing the numerator and denominator by a common factor. We are simplifying the fractions before finding the product. We can cancel in steps.

$$\frac{3}{14} \text{ of } 28 = \frac{3 \times 28}{14} = \frac{3 \times \cancel{28}^{14}}{\cancel{14}_{7}} = \frac{3 \times \cancel{28}^{\cancel{14}^{2}}}{\cancel{14}_{\cancel{7}_{1}}} = 6$$

p. 44
Learning Tasks 1-2, p. 45

She used **8** eggs.

1. (a) $\mathbf{3\frac{1}{3}}$ (b) $\mathbf{3\frac{1}{3}}$ 2. $\mathbf{7\frac{1}{2}}$

(2) Conversion of Measurement I

- Convert a measurement expressed as a fraction (proper fraction or mixed number) to a smaller unit or a compound unit.

Students will learn to convert measurements involving fractions in this unit. They need to be familiar with conversion units, or how many smaller units equal a larger unit. (e.g. 1 kg = 1000 g, 1 yd = 3 ft, 1 minute = 60 seconds) To convert from a larger unit to a smaller unit, we multiply by the conversion unit. For example, $\frac{1}{2}$ year = $\frac{1}{2}$ x 12 months = 6 months. Your student can think of this as cutting something up into smaller parts, so there will be more of them. The size of the unit is smaller, but there are more of them. So we multiply.

Ask your student for the number of months in a year. Ask him how many months are in half of a year. Write:

$\frac{1}{2}$ year = $\frac{1}{2}$ of 12 months = $\frac{1}{2}$ x 12 months = 6 months.

By finding the number of months in half a year, we are essentially cutting up the year into 12 months, and then finding half of those 12 months. We can do this by multiplying the fraction of the year by the number of months in a year.

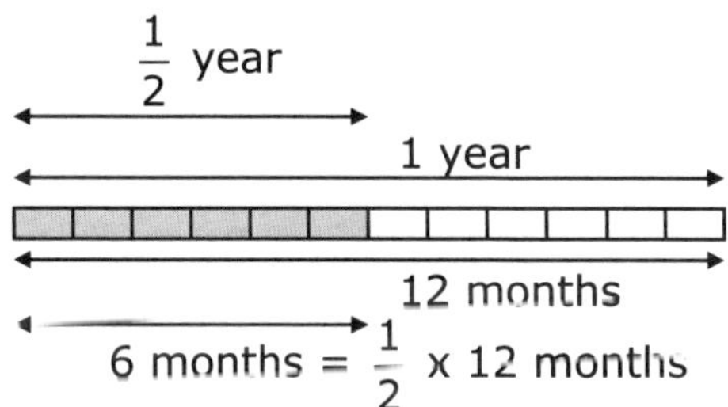

Ask him how many months are in one fourth of a year.

$\frac{1}{4}$ year = $\frac{1}{4}$ of 12 months = $\frac{1}{4}$ x 12 months = 3 months.

Ask him many months are in one sixth of a year.

$\frac{1}{6}$ year = $\frac{1}{6}$ of 12 months = $\frac{1}{6}$ x 12 months = 2 months.

If there are 2 months in one sixth of a year, how many are there in five sixths of a year?

2 months x 5 = 10 months

Learning Task 3, p. 46

We can solve this problem either by mentally finding a sixth of 12, then multiplying by 5, or as follows:

$$\frac{5}{\not{6}_1} \times \not{12}^2 = 5 \times 2 = \mathbf{10}$$

➤ Your student should know all the conversion units in the table on p. 46. For a brief review, have the student convert some whole numbers of a larger unit of measure to a smaller unit of measure.

2 m = _____ cm	2 m = 2 x 100 cm = 200 cm
7 kg = _____ g	7 kg = 7 x 1000 g = 7000 g
3 gal = ____ qt	3 gal = 3 x 4 qt = 12 qt
2 days = ____ hours	2 days = 2 x 24 hours = 48 hours
4 ft = ____ in.	4 ft = 4 x 12 in. = 48 in.
8 min = ____ s	8 min = 8 x 60 s = 480 s

Learning Task 4 p. 46

4. (a) 1 min = 60 s
$\frac{1}{2}$ min = $\frac{1}{2}$ x 60 s
= **30** s

(b) 1 kg = 1,000 g
$\frac{7}{10}$ kg = $\frac{7}{10}$ x 1,000 g
= 7 x 100 g
= **700** g

(c) 1 km = 1,000 m
$\frac{2}{5}$ km = $\frac{2}{5}$ x 1,000 m
= 2 x 200 m
= **400** m

(d) 1 ℓ = 1,000 ml
$\frac{3}{10}$ ℓ = $\frac{3}{10}$ x 1,000 ml
= 3 x 100 ml
= **300** ml

(e) 1 year = 12 mths
$\frac{3}{4}$ year = $\frac{3}{4}$ x 12 mths
= 3 x 3 mths
= **9** mths

(f) 1 h = 60 min
$\frac{1}{6}$ h = $\frac{1}{6}$ x 60 min
= **10** min

US› (g) 1 yd = 3 ft
$\frac{2}{3}$ yd = $\frac{2}{3}$ x 3 ft
= **2** ft

(h) 1 lb = 16 oz
$\frac{1}{4}$ lb = $\frac{1}{4}$ x 16 oz
= **4** oz

(i) 1 gal = 4 qt
$\frac{3}{4}$ gal = $\frac{3}{4}$ x 4 qt
= **3** qt

Learning Tasks 5-6, p. 46

To convert a measurement expressed as a mixed number into compound units, we only need to convert the fractional part to the smaller unit.

5. $\frac{3}{4}$h = $\frac{3}{4}$ x 60 min = **45** min

   $2\frac{3}{4}$ h = **2** h **45** min

6. (a) $\frac{1}{3}$ h = $\frac{1}{3}$ x 60 min
   = 20 min
   $2\frac{1}{3}$ h = **2** h **20** min

US› (b) $\frac{2}{3}$ yd = $\frac{2}{3}$ x 3 ft
   = 2 ft
   $4\frac{2}{3}$ yd = **4** yd **2** ft

3d› (b) $\frac{2}{3}$ min = $\frac{2}{3}$ x 60 s
   = 40 s
   $4\frac{2}{3}$ min = **4** min **40** s

3d› (c) $\frac{1}{4}$ m = $\frac{1}{4}$ x 100 cm
   = 25 cm
   $5\frac{1}{4}$ m = **5** m **25** cm

US› (c) $\frac{1}{4}$ gal = $\frac{1}{4}$ x 4 qt
   = 1 qt
   $5\frac{1}{4}$ gal = **5 gal 1 qt**

(d) $\frac{1}{2}$ km = $\frac{1}{2}$ x 1,000 m
   = 500 m
   $3\frac{1}{2}$ km = **3** km **500** m

(e) $\frac{9}{10}$ ℓ = $\frac{9}{10}$ x 1,000 ml
   = 900 ml
   $14\frac{9}{10}$ ℓ = **14** ℓ **900** ml

(f) $\frac{1}{4}$ years = $\frac{1}{4}$ x 12 months
   = 3 months
   $6\frac{1}{4}$ years = **6** years **3** months

Workbook Exercise 19

(3) Conversion of Measurement II

➢ Convert a measurement expressed as a mixed number to a smaller unit.

In this section your student will learn here to convert a measurement expressed as a mixed number by separating the mixed number into the whole number part and the fractional part, converting each part separately, then adding them back together.

Ask your student to convert $2\frac{3}{4}$ feet into inches.

Allow her to determine a method on her own. She may convert it into an improper fraction and then multiply:

$$2\frac{3}{4} \text{ feet} = \frac{11}{4} \text{ feet} = \frac{11}{\cancel{4}_1} \times \cancel{12}^3 \text{ inches} = 33 \text{ inches}$$

Guide her to see that she can also convert each part of the mixed number separately.

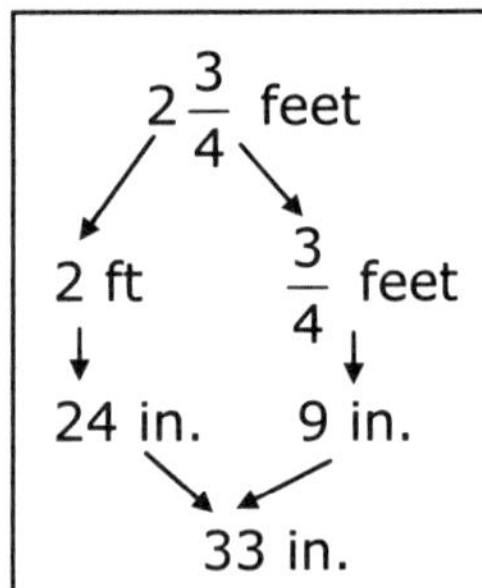

Learning Tasks p. 47

7. **400** m **3,400** m
8. **48** h **6** h **54** h
9. (a) 2 m = 200 cm; $\frac{1}{2}$ m = 50 cm; $2\frac{1}{2}$ m = **250** cm

   (b) **US›** 1 lb = 16 oz; $\frac{1}{2}$ lb = 8 oz; $1\frac{1}{2}$ lb = **24** oz

   (c) **US›** 3 gal = 12 qt; $\frac{1}{2}$ gal = 2 qt; $3\frac{1}{2}$ gal = **14** qt

   (b) **3d›** 1 kg = 1,000 g; $\frac{9}{10}$ kg = 900 g; $1\frac{9}{10}$ kg = **1,900** g

   (c) **3d›** 3 days = 72 h; $\frac{1}{2}$ days = 12 h; $3\frac{1}{2}$ days = **84** h

   (d) 2 years = 24 mths; $\frac{3}{4}$ years = 9 mths; $2\frac{3}{4}$ years = **33** mths

   (e) 1 ℓ = 1,000 ml; $\frac{3}{10}$ ℓ = 300 ml; $1\frac{3}{10}$ ℓ = **1,300** ml

   (f) 4 min = 240 s; $\frac{1}{3}$ min = 20 s; $4\frac{1}{3}$ min = **260** s

(g) 2 km = 2,000 m

$\frac{1}{10}$ km = 100 m

$2\frac{1}{10}$ km= **2,100** m

(h) 3 h = 180 min

$\frac{1}{3}$ h = 20 min

$3\frac{1}{3}$ h = **200** min

(i) **US›** 5 ft = 60 in.

$\frac{3}{4}$ ft = 9 in.

$5\frac{3}{4}$ ft = **69** in.

(i) **3d›** 5 m = 500 cm

$\frac{3}{4}$ m = 75 cm

$5\frac{3}{4}$ m = **575** cm

 **Workbook Exercise 20**

(4) Fraction of a Measurement

➢ Express a part of a measurement as a fraction of the whole.

Students learned in *Primary Mathematics* 4A to express a smaller part as a fraction of a total amount where the smaller part was expressed in a smaller unit of measurement and the larger part was 1 unit of a larger measurement. For example, they learned to express 10 minutes as a fraction of 1 hour. This is reviewed here and extended to multiples of a whole unit, such as expressing 10 minutes as a fraction of 3 hours.

When comparing two measurements, both must be in the same unit. Convert the larger unit of measure to the smaller unit of measure. For example, to express 10 minutes as a fraction of 2 hours, change 2 hours to 120 minutes. 10 minutes is $\frac{10}{120}$, or $\frac{1}{12}$ of 2 hours.

Use two different objects, such as two colors of counters, red and yellow. Set out 6 yellow counters and 9 red counters. Ask your student to tell you what fraction of the counters are yellow. 6 out of 15 counters are yellow. We put the part over the total number of counters:

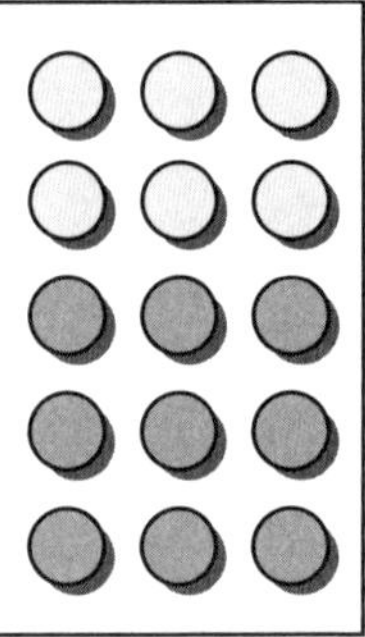

$\frac{6}{15} = \frac{2}{5}$ $\frac{2}{5}$ of the counters are yellow.

Use two rulers and set them side by side. Ask how many feet there are (you may have to overlap if 0 isn't at the beginning of the ruler). There are 2 feet. Point to 6 inches and ask your student what fraction 6 inches is of 2 feet. He should be able to see that 6 inches is a fourth of 2 feet. Ask him how he would find the answer if he could not "see" it either with the rulers or in his head. He should realize that he needs to change 2 feet to 24 inches:

$\frac{6}{24} = \frac{1}{4}$ 6 inches is $\frac{1}{4}$ of two feet.

Ask her to find 12 ounces as a fraction of 3 quarts.

3 qt = 3 x 16 oz = 48 oz $\frac{12}{48} = \frac{1}{4}$ 12 oz is $\frac{1}{4}$ of 3 qt.

Learning Task 10, p. 47

10. (a) $\frac{80}{200} = \mathbf{\frac{2}{5}}$

(b) 1 ℓ = 1,000 ml
$\frac{600}{1,000} = \frac{6}{10} = \mathbf{\frac{3}{5}}$

(c) 3 m = 300 cm
$\frac{90}{300} = \frac{9}{30} = \mathbf{\frac{3}{10}}$

(d) 1 min = 60 s
$\frac{45}{60} = \mathbf{\frac{3}{4}}$

(e) 2 h = 120 min
$\frac{50}{120} = \mathbf{\frac{5}{12}}$

Workbook Exercise 21

Practice 3D (p. 48)

Practice 3D, p. 48

1. (a) $\frac{1}{\cancel{2}_1} \times \cancel{14}^7 = \mathbf{7}$ (b) $\frac{1}{4_2} \times \cancel{26}^{13} = \frac{13}{2} = \mathbf{6\frac{1}{2}}$ (c) $\frac{2}{\cancel{5}_1} \times \cancel{40}^8 = \mathbf{16}$

2. (a) $\cancel{30}^6 \times \frac{4}{\cancel{5}_1} = \mathbf{24}$ (b) $40 \times \frac{2}{3} = \frac{80}{3} = \mathbf{26\frac{2}{3}}$ (c) $\cancel{15}^5 \times \frac{5}{\cancel{9}_3} = \frac{25}{3} = \mathbf{8\frac{1}{3}}$

3. (a) $\frac{7}{\cancel{3}_1} \times \cancel{21}^7 = \mathbf{49}$ (b) $\frac{13}{\cancel{5}_1} \times \cancel{20}^4 = \mathbf{52}$ (c) $\cancel{40}^5 \times \frac{9}{\cancel{8}_1} = \mathbf{45}$

4. (a) $\frac{2}{3}$ h $= \frac{2}{3} \times 60$ min
$= 2 \times 20$ min
$=$ **40** min

(b) $\frac{3}{5}$ kg $= \frac{3}{5} \times 1{,}000$ g
$= 3 \times 200$ g
$=$ **600** g

5. (a) $\frac{4}{5}$ m $= \frac{4}{5} \times 100$ cm
$= 4 \times 20$ cm
$=$ **80** cm

(b) $\frac{9}{10}$ km $= \frac{9}{10} \times 1{,}000$ m
$= 9 \times 100$ m
$=$ **900** m

6. (a) $\frac{3}{4}$ years $= \frac{3}{4} \times 12$ months
$= 3 \times 3$ months
$= 9$ months

$8\frac{3}{4}$ years $=$ **8** years **9** months

(b) $\frac{3}{5}$ ℓ $= \frac{3}{5} \times 1{,}000$ ml
$= 3 \times 200$ ml
$= 600$ ml

$3\frac{3}{5}$ ℓ $=$ **3** ℓ **600** ml

US› 7. (a) $\frac{1}{4}$ lb $= \frac{1}{4} \times 16$ oz $= 4$ oz

$9\frac{1}{4}$ lb $=$ **9** lb **4** oz

(b) $\frac{1}{3}$ h $= \frac{1}{3} \times 60$ min $= 20$ min

$5\frac{1}{3}$ h $=$ **5** h **20** min

3d› 7. (a) $\frac{1}{4}$ kg $= \frac{1}{4} \times 1{,}000$ g
$= 250$ g

$9\frac{1}{4}$ kg $=$ **9** kg **250** g

(b) $\frac{1}{3}$ h $= \frac{1}{3} \times 60$ min $= 20$ min

$5\frac{1}{3}$ h $=$ **5** h **20** min

US› 8. (a) 3 ft = 36 in.

$\frac{1}{2}$ ft = $\frac{1}{2}$ x 12 in.
= 6 in.

$3\frac{1}{2}$ ft = **42** in.

(b) 4 gal = 16 qt

$\frac{1}{4}$ gal = $\frac{1}{4}$ x 4 qt
= 1 qt

$4\frac{1}{4}$ gal = **17** qt

3d› 8. (a) 3 m = 300 cm

$\frac{1}{2}$ m = $\frac{1}{2}$ x 100 cm
= 50 cm

$3\frac{1}{2}$ m = **350** cm

(b) 4 h = 4 x 60 min
= 240 min

$\frac{1}{4}$ h = $\frac{1}{4}$ x 60 min
= 15 min

$4\frac{1}{4}$ h = 240 min + 15 min
= **255** min

9. (a) 2 km = 2,000 m

$\frac{7}{10}$ km = $\frac{7}{10}$ x 1,000 m
= 7 x 100 m
= 700 m

$2\frac{7}{10}$ km = **2,700** m

(b) 4 days = 4 x 24 h
= 96 h

$\frac{2}{3}$ days = $\frac{2}{3}$ x 24 h
= 2 x 8 h
= 16 h

$4\frac{2}{3}$ days = 96 h + 16 h
= **112** h

10. (a) \$1 = 100 ¢

$\frac{90}{100} = \mathbf{\frac{9}{10}}$

(b) 2 ℓ = 2,000 ml

$\frac{750}{2,000} = \frac{75}{200} = \mathbf{\frac{3}{8}}$

(c) 3 lb = 48 oz

US› $\frac{12}{48} = \mathbf{\frac{1}{4}}$

11. (a) 1 year = 12 mths

$\frac{9}{12} = \mathbf{\frac{3}{4}}$

(b) 2 h = 2 x 60 min
= 120 min

$\frac{50}{120} = \mathbf{\frac{5}{12}}$

(c) 2 ft = 24 in.

US› $\frac{8}{24} = \mathbf{\frac{1}{3}}$

12. Fraction of students that passed $= \frac{40}{44} = \mathbf{\frac{10}{11}}$

13. Fraction that she saved $= \frac{70}{350} = \frac{7}{35} = \mathbf{\frac{1}{5}}$

Part 5 – Product of Fractions (pp. 49-51)

(1) Meaning of Product of Fractions

- Understand product of fractions.

In this section, students will learn to multiply a fraction by a fraction. Grids are used to give the students a concrete understanding of the procedure.

p. 49

You can use 3″ x 5″ index cards to do this activity. Some students find a drawing sufficient.

- Draw a rectangle and divide it in fifths with vertical lines. Shade $\frac{3}{5}$. Then draw three lines horizontally to show fourths. Ask your student to shade $\frac{3}{4}$ of $\frac{3}{5}$ with a darker color. Ask him how to calculate the total number of small rectangles. Since there are 4 rows and 5 columns the total number is 4 x 5 = 20. Each small rectangle is $\frac{1}{20}$ of the total. Ask him how to calculate the number of darker rectangles. There 3 rows and 3 columns, so there are 3 x 3 = 9 dark rectangles.

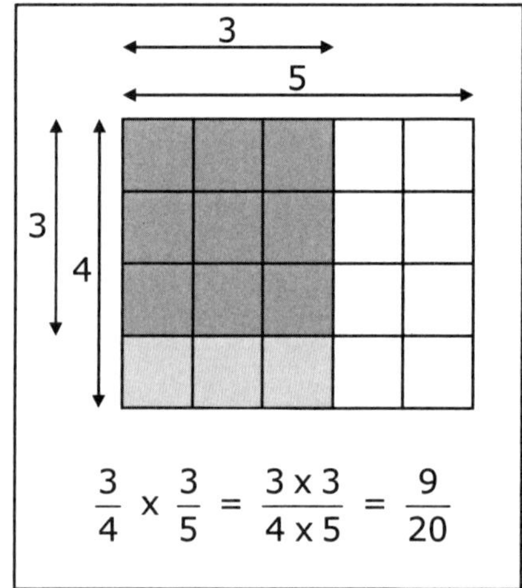

The dark rectangles are $\frac{9}{20}$ of the whole. So $\frac{3}{4} \times \frac{3}{5} = \frac{9}{20}$. Note that the total number of rectangles is the same as the product of the denominators and that the number of dark rectangles is the product of the numerators.

So we can find $\frac{3}{4} \times \frac{3}{5}$ by multiplying the numerators together to find the number of parts and multiplying the denominators together to find the total parts.

Use another drawing to show that $\frac{3}{5} \times \frac{3}{4} = \frac{3}{4} \times \frac{3}{5}$.

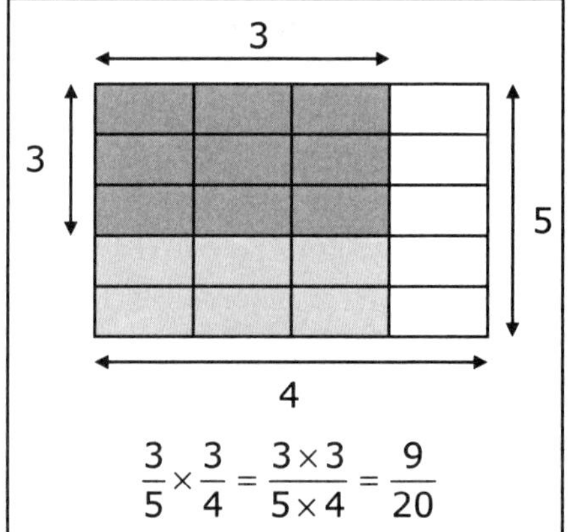

➤ Ask your student to find 2 x 2. When multiplying two whole numbers together, the product is greater than each of the numbers by itself. Ask her to find $2 \times \frac{1}{2}$. In the answer, the $\frac{1}{2}$ doubled. The product is larger than $\frac{1}{2}$, but smaller than 2. Ask her to find $\frac{1}{2}$ of 2: $\frac{1}{2} \times 2$. In the answer, the 2 is halved, so the product is smaller than the 2. Ask her to find $\frac{1}{2} \times \frac{1}{2}$. The product is smaller than both the factors.

$2 \times 2 = 4$

$2 \times \frac{1}{2} = 1$

$\frac{1}{2} \times 2 = 1$

$\frac{1}{2} \times \frac{1}{2} = \frac{1}{4}$

This idea that multiplication leads to a smaller number is sometimes hard for students to grasp, particularly in finding area when fractions are used. The area of a rectangle measuring $\frac{1}{2}$ m by $\frac{1}{2}$ m is $\frac{1}{4}$ m^2. If a student just looks at the numbers, it may seem odd that the area seems to be less than each side.

Draw a square, label the side of the square as 1 m, and mark $\frac{1}{2}$ on two sides with a solid line. Make a square with these sides. Show that the area of the little square is $\frac{1}{4}$ of the area of the larger square. It is $\frac{1}{2}$ of a meter on each side, but it is $\frac{1}{4}$ of a square meter.

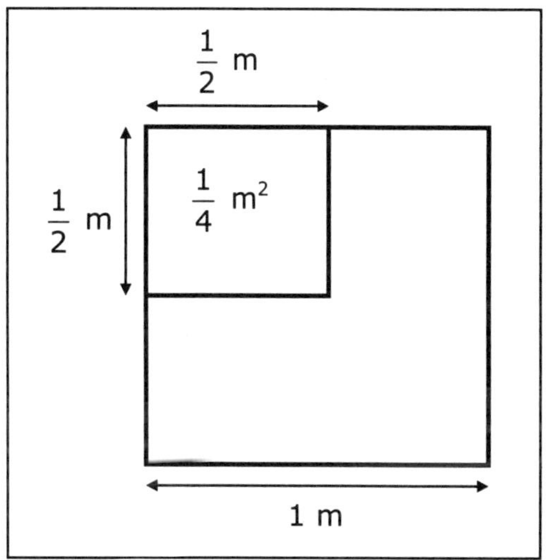

➤ Have your student draw rectangles to find the product of some other simple fractions, such as:

$\frac{1}{2} \times \frac{2}{3}$ $\frac{1}{4} \times \frac{3}{4}$ $\frac{3}{4} \times \frac{4}{5}$

(2) Product of Fractions

➢ Multiply a fraction by a fraction.

Learning Tasks 1-5, pp. 50-51

1. $\mathbf{\frac{3}{10}}$
2. $\mathbf{\frac{9}{20}}$
3. $\mathbf{\frac{5}{18}}$
4. $\mathbf{\frac{1}{12}}$

   The drawing accompanying this problem in the first printing (2003) of the US edition is incorrect. It should be:

   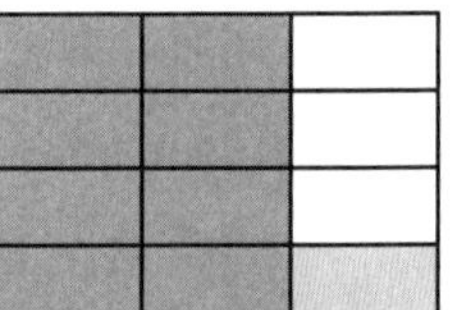

5. $\mathbf{\frac{8}{15}}$

Learning Task 6, p. 51

Show your student that all of the following are equivalent:

$$\frac{9}{10} \times \frac{5}{12} = \frac{9 \times 5}{10 \times 12} = \frac{9 \times 5}{12 \times 10} = \frac{9}{12} \times \frac{5}{10} = \frac{3}{4} \times \frac{1}{2} = \mathbf{\frac{3}{8}}$$

So we can simplify the fraction before multiplying the factors by dividing the 9 and 12 by 3, and the 5 and 10 by 2, even though they were not originally in the same fraction. We show this by crossing out the number and writing the quotient next to it. Method 2 shows that we can skip the step of showing the product of the numerators over the product of the denominators. We can also skip the step of showing 3 x 1 over 2 x 4 and simply show:

$$\frac{\cancel{9}^{3}}{\cancel{10}_{2}} \times \frac{\cancel{5}^{1}}{\cancel{12}_{4}} = \frac{3}{8}$$

Dividing the numerator and denominator by the same number is essentially factoring out 1's. You might also want to show him the following:

$$\frac{9 \times 5}{10 \times 12} = \frac{3 \times 3 \times 5}{2 \times 5 \times 3 \times 4} = \frac{3 \times 5 \ \times \ 3}{3 \times 5 \times 2 \times 4} = \frac{3}{3} \times \frac{5}{5} \times \frac{3}{2 \times 4} = \frac{3}{8}$$

Learning Task 7, p. 51

7\. (a) $\frac{1}{2}$ of $\frac{1}{2} = \frac{1}{2} \times \frac{1}{2} = \frac{1 \times 1}{2 \times 2} = \mathbf{\frac{1}{4}}$

(b) $\frac{1}{3}$ of $\frac{3}{4} = \frac{1}{\cancel{3}_1} \times \frac{\cancel{3}^1}{4} = \frac{1 \times 1}{1 \times 4} = \mathbf{\frac{1}{4}}$

(c) $\frac{1}{4}$ of $\frac{8}{9} = \frac{1}{\cancel{4}_1} \times \frac{\cancel{8}^2}{9} = \frac{1 \times 2}{1 \times 9} = \mathbf{\frac{2}{9}}$

(d) $\frac{\cancel{5}^1}{6} \times \frac{1}{\cancel{5}_1} = \frac{1 \times 1}{6 \times 1} = \mathbf{\frac{1}{6}}$

(e) $\frac{\cancel{3}^1}{4} \times \frac{5}{\cancel{6}_2} = \frac{1 \times 5}{4 \times 2} = \mathbf{\frac{5}{8}}$

(f) $\frac{\cancel{4}^1}{5} \times \frac{3}{\cancel{8}_2} = \frac{1 \times 3}{5 \times 2} = \mathbf{\frac{3}{10}}$

(g) $\frac{5}{\cancel{8}_2} \times \frac{\cancel{4}^1}{9} = \frac{5 \times 1}{2 \times 9} = \mathbf{\frac{5}{18}}$

(h) $\frac{1}{\cancel{3}_1} \times \frac{\cancel{6}^2}{7} = \frac{1 \times 2}{1 \times 7} = \mathbf{\frac{2}{7}}$

(i) $\frac{\cancel{5}^1}{6} \times \frac{7}{\cancel{10}_2} = \frac{1 \times 7}{6 \times 2} = \mathbf{\frac{7}{12}}$

(j) $\frac{\cancel{15}^5}{\cancel{4}_1} \times \frac{\cancel{8}^2}{\cancel{3}_1} = \frac{5 \times 2}{1 \times 1} = \mathbf{10}$

(k) $\frac{\cancel{9}^3}{\cancel{4}_1} \times \frac{16^4}{\cancel{3}_1} = \frac{3 \times 4}{1 \times 1} = \mathbf{12}$

(l) $\frac{\cancel{12}^4}{\cancel{5}_1} \times \frac{\cancel{20}^4}{\cancel{9}_3} = \frac{4 \times 4}{1 \times 3} = \frac{16}{3} = \mathbf{5\frac{1}{3}}$

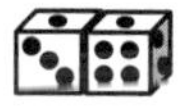

Game

Material: 4 sets of number cards 1-9 (playing cards with face cards removed).
Procedure: Shuffle cards and deal them all out. Each player turns over four cards to form two fractions and multiplies the fractions together. The player with the highest product gets all the cards. The player with the most cards at the end wins.

Workbook Exercises 22-23

Practice 3E (p. 52)

 **Practice 3E, p. 52**

1. (a) $\frac{\cancel{3}^{1}}{8} \times \frac{1}{\cancel{3}_{1}} = \mathbf{\frac{1}{8}}$ (b) $\frac{\cancel{4}^{1}}{9} \times \frac{5}{\cancel{8}_{2}} = \mathbf{\frac{5}{18}}$ (c) $\frac{\cancel{7}^{1}}{8} \times \frac{3}{\cancel{7}_{1}} = \mathbf{\frac{3}{8}}$

2. (a) $\frac{\cancel{2}^{1}}{\cancel{7}_{1}} \times \frac{\cancel{7}^{1}}{\cancel{10}_{5}} = \mathbf{\frac{1}{5}}$ (b) $\frac{\cancel{8}^{2}}{\cancel{9}_{3}} \times \frac{\cancel{3}^{1}}{\cancel{4}_{1}} = \mathbf{\frac{2}{3}}$ (c) $\frac{\cancel{9}^{3}}{\cancel{10}_{2}} \times \frac{\cancel{5}^{1}}{\cancel{6}_{2}} = \mathbf{\frac{3}{4}}$

3. (a) $\frac{\cancel{5}^{1}}{\cancel{6}_{3}} \times \frac{\cancel{2}^{1}}{\cancel{5}_{1}} = \mathbf{\frac{1}{3}}$ (b) $\frac{\cancel{3}^{1}}{\cancel{4}_{2}} \times \frac{\cancel{2}^{1}}{\cancel{3}_{1}} = \mathbf{\frac{1}{2}}$ (c) $\frac{\cancel{3}^{1}}{\cancel{10}_{2}} \times \frac{\cancel{5}^{1}}{\cancel{6}_{2}} = \mathbf{\frac{1}{4}}$

4. (a) $\frac{\cancel{16}^{4}}{\cancel{3}_{1}} \times \frac{\cancel{9}^{3}}{\cancel{4}_{1}} = \mathbf{12}$ (b) $\frac{\cancel{14}^{2}}{\cancel{9}_{3}} \times \frac{\cancel{12}^{4}}{\cancel{7}_{1}} = \frac{8}{3} = \mathbf{2\frac{2}{3}}$ (c) $\frac{\cancel{10}^{2}}{\cancel{7}_{1}} \times \frac{\cancel{14}^{2}}{\cancel{5}_{1}} = \mathbf{4}$

5. (a) $\frac{\cancel{20}^{5}}{\cancel{7}_{1}} \times \frac{\cancel{7}^{1}}{\cancel{4}_{1}} = \mathbf{5}$ (b) $\frac{\cancel{11}^{1}}{\cancel{5}_{1}} \times \frac{\cancel{20}^{4}}{\cancel{11}_{1}} = \mathbf{4}$ (c) $\frac{\cancel{15}^{5}}{\cancel{8}_{1}} \times \frac{\cancel{8}^{1}}{\cancel{3}_{1}} = \mathbf{5}$

6. Length of string used = $\frac{1}{3}$ of $\frac{1}{2}$ m = $\frac{1}{3} \times \frac{1}{2}$ m = $\mathbf{\frac{1}{6}}$ **m**

US› 7. Amount of oil she used = $\frac{2}{5}$ of $\frac{3}{4}$ qt = $\frac{\cancel{2}^{1}}{5} \times \frac{3}{\cancel{4}_{2}}$ qt = $\mathbf{\frac{3}{10}}$ **qt**

3d› 7. Amount of oil she used = $\frac{2}{5}$ of $\frac{3}{4}$ ℓ = $\frac{\cancel{2}^{1}}{5} \times \frac{3}{\cancel{4}_{2}}$ ℓ = $\mathbf{\frac{3}{10}}$ $\boldsymbol{\ell}$

8. Amount she cooked = $\frac{3}{4}$ of $\frac{4}{5}$ kg = $\frac{3}{\cancel{4}_{1}} \times \frac{\cancel{4}^{1}}{5}$ kg = $\mathbf{\frac{3}{5}}$ **kg**

9. The remainder is $1 - \frac{1}{6} = \frac{5}{6}$ of the cake

   Fraction of the cake she gave away = $\frac{1}{5}$ of $\frac{5}{6} = \frac{1}{\cancel{5}_{1}} \times \frac{\cancel{5}^{1}}{6} = \mathbf{\frac{1}{6}}$

10. Area = $\frac{\cancel{5}^{1}}{8} \times \frac{3}{\cancel{5}_{1}} = \mathbf{\frac{3}{8}}$ $\mathbf{m^2}$

Part 6 – Dividing a Fraction by a Whole Number (pp. 53-54)

(1) Dividing a Fraction by a Whole Number

- Divide a proper fraction by a whole number.

In this section students are introduced to division of a fraction by a whole number. They will learn that dividing by 4, for example, is the same as multiplying by $\frac{1}{4}$. Your student should understand the concepts learned here thoroughly before learning the skill of "invert and multiply," which will be covered in *Primary Mathematics* 6B (US edition only, not 3rd edition).

p. 53

Discuss this example. You can use actual fraction discs if you have some. Your student should see that $\frac{2}{3} \div 4$ is the same as $\frac{1}{4}$ of $\frac{2}{3}$. He should also see that we can find the value of $\frac{2}{3} \div 4$ by simply changing $\mathbf{\div 4}$ to $\mathbf{\times \frac{1}{4}}$.

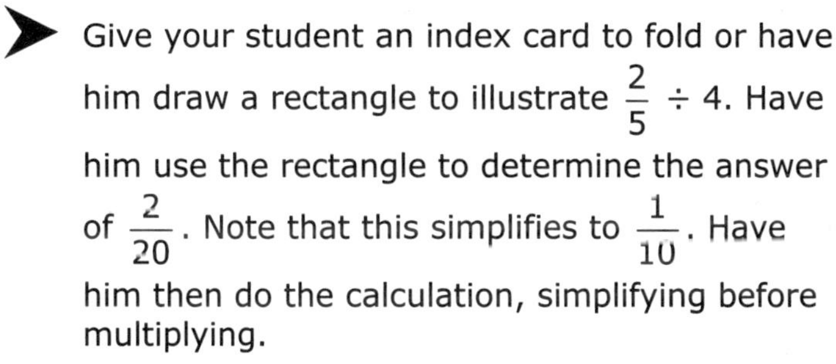

Give your student an index card to fold or have him draw a rectangle to illustrate $\frac{2}{5} \div 4$. Have him use the rectangle to determine the answer of $\frac{2}{20}$. Note that this simplifies to $\frac{1}{10}$. Have him then do the calculation, simplifying before multiplying.

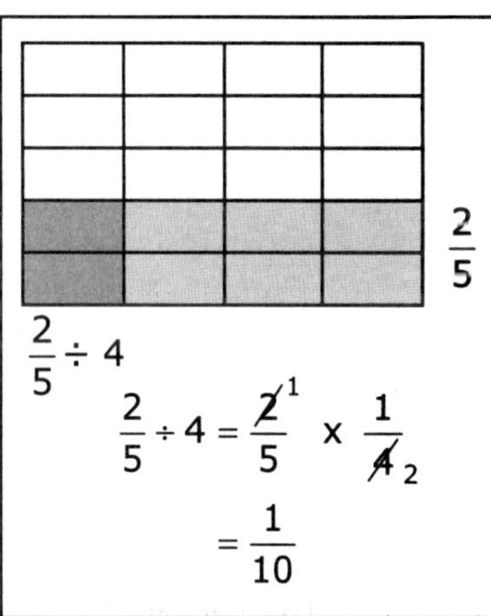

Learning Tasks 1-3, p. 54

1. $\mathbf{\frac{2}{9}}$

2. (a) $\mathbf{\frac{1}{8}}$ (b) $\mathbf{\frac{1}{15}}$

   (c) $\mathbf{\frac{1}{5}; \frac{1}{6}}$ (d) $\mathbf{\frac{1}{3}; \frac{3}{10}}$

3. (a) $\frac{1}{3} \div 2 = \frac{1}{3} \times \frac{1}{2} = \mathbf{\frac{1}{6}}$

   (b) $\frac{4}{5} \div 3 = \frac{4}{5} \times \frac{1}{3} = \mathbf{\frac{4}{15}}$

   (c) $\frac{5}{7} \div 4 = \frac{5}{7} \times \frac{1}{4} = \mathbf{\frac{5}{28}}$

   (d) $\frac{4}{5} \div 4 = \frac{\cancel{4}^{1}}{5} \times \frac{1}{\cancel{4}_{1}} = \mathbf{\frac{1}{5}}$

   (e) $\frac{6}{7} \div 2 = \frac{\cancel{6}^{3}}{7} \times \frac{1}{\cancel{2}_{1}} = \mathbf{\frac{3}{7}}$

   (f) $\frac{2}{3} \div 8 = \frac{\cancel{2}^{1}}{3} \times \frac{1}{\cancel{8}_{4}} = \mathbf{\frac{1}{12}}$

   (g) $\frac{9}{16} \div 3 = \frac{\cancel{9}^{3}}{16} \times \frac{1}{\cancel{3}_{1}} = \mathbf{\frac{3}{16}}$

   (h) $\frac{3}{8} \div 6 = \frac{\cancel{3}^{1}}{8} \times \frac{1}{\cancel{6}_{2}} = \mathbf{\frac{1}{16}}$

   (i) $\frac{9}{10} \div 6 = \frac{\cancel{9}^{3}}{10} \times \frac{1}{\cancel{6}_{2}} = \mathbf{\frac{3}{20}}$

Game

Material: 4 sets of number cards 1-9 (playing cards with face cards removed).

Procedure: Shuffle cards and deal them all out. Each player turns over three cards to form one fraction and a whole number. The fraction must be a proper fraction. The players divide the fraction by the whole number. The player with the highest answer gets all the cards. The player with the most cards at the end wins.

You could also use the cards to form random fractions for practice.

Workbook Exercises 24-25

Practice 3F (p. 55)

 **Practice 3F, p. 55**

1. (a) $\frac{1}{3} \div 3 = \frac{1}{3} \times \frac{1}{3} = \mathbf{\frac{1}{9}}$
   (b) $\frac{5}{6} \div 3 = \frac{5}{6} \times \frac{1}{3} = \mathbf{\frac{5}{18}}$
   (c) $\frac{9}{10} \div 3 = \frac{\cancel{9}^{3}}{10} \times \frac{1}{\cancel{3}_{1}} = \mathbf{\frac{3}{10}}$

2. (a) $\frac{3}{4} \div 5 = \frac{3}{4} \times \frac{1}{5} = \mathbf{\frac{3}{20}}$
   (b) $\frac{1}{5} \div 4 = \frac{1}{5} \times \frac{1}{4} = \mathbf{\frac{1}{20}}$
   (c) $\frac{8}{9} \div 6 = \frac{\cancel{8}^{4}}{9} \times \frac{1}{\cancel{6}_{3}} = \mathbf{\frac{4}{27}}$

3. (a) $\frac{2}{5} \div 3 = \frac{2}{5} \times \frac{1}{3} = \mathbf{\frac{2}{15}}$
   (b) $\frac{5}{9} \div 5 = \frac{\cancel{5}^{1}}{9} \times \frac{1}{\cancel{5}_{1}} = \mathbf{\frac{1}{9}}$
   (c) $\frac{5}{6} \div 10 = \frac{\cancel{5}^{1}}{6} \times \frac{1}{\cancel{10}_{2}} = \mathbf{\frac{1}{12}}$

4. Length of each piece = $\frac{4}{5} \div 2 = \frac{\cancel{4}^{2}}{5} \times \frac{1}{\cancel{2}_{1}} = \mathbf{\frac{2}{5}}$ **m**

5. Fraction each club received = $\frac{4}{5} \div 4 = \frac{\cancel{4}^{1}}{5} \times \frac{1}{\cancel{4}_{1}} = \mathbf{\frac{1}{5}}$

6. Weight of one packet = $\frac{3}{10} \div 6 = \frac{\cancel{3}^{1}}{10} \times \frac{1}{\cancel{6}_{2}} = \mathbf{\frac{1}{20}}$ **kg**

7. Amount of fruit juice in each cup = $\frac{2}{5} \div 4 = \frac{\cancel{2}^{1}}{5} \times \frac{1}{\cancel{4}_{2}} = \mathbf{\frac{1}{10}}$ (**US›** pt; **3d›** ℓ)

8. Length of each side = $\frac{3}{4} \div 4 = \frac{3}{4} \times \frac{1}{4} = \mathbf{\frac{3}{16}}$ **m**

9. Amount each child received = $\frac{3}{4} \div 6 = \frac{\cancel{3}^{1}}{4} \times \frac{1}{\cancel{6}_{2}} = \mathbf{\frac{1}{8}}$ **kg**

Part 7 - Word Problems (pp. 56-59)

In *Primary Mathematics* 4A students learned to solve two-step word problems involving fractions. In this section they will learn to solve multi-step word problems involving fractions.

Illustrating the problem with a part-whole model can help with finding a solution. Each fractional part of the bar is a unit, similar to the unit in the part-whole model for multiplication and division. Encourage your student to draw models when needed.

For example, to find $\frac{2}{3}$ x 18, we can draw a bar and divide it into thirds, or 3 units. Knowing the value of 3 units (18) we can find the value of 1 unit and of 2 units.

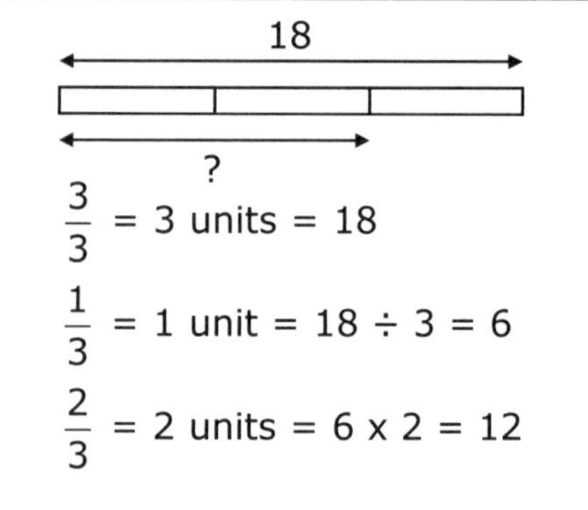

The part-whole model is also used to find the whole when given a fractional part. For example, if we know that $\frac{3}{5}$ of some number is 15, we can use the model to find the number. We can draw a bar, divide it into fifths, and label 3 units as 15. Then we see that we can find $\frac{1}{5}$, or 1 unit, by dividing by 3, and then find the total (5 units) by multiplying the value for 1 unit by 5.

?

15

$\frac{3}{5}$ = 3 units = 15

$\frac{1}{5}$ = 1 unit = 15 ÷ 3 = 5

$\frac{5}{5}$ = 5 units = 5 x 5 = 25

This kind of problem is essentially a fractional division problem; we need to find $\frac{3}{5}$ of what is 15, or 15 ÷ $\frac{3}{5}$. Students have not yet learned to divide by a fraction. Instead, they will solve these kinds of problems with a unitary approach; that is, by finding the value for 1 unit or for the unit fraction. Modeling the problem makes this easy to visualize.

(1) Word Problems I

- Solve multi-step word problems involving a fractional part of a given whole.
- Solve multi-step word problems involving a given value of a fractional part.

p. 56

Discuss the example on this page with your student. Three methods are shown. The first involves finding the fraction that she saved first and using that to find the fraction of the total. The second involves finding the amount spent first, and then subtracting that from the total to find the amount saved.

The third involves a part-whole model. Your student should know why the bar was divided into 5 units, and what the shaded and unshaded parts represent. Point out that a unit is the same as $\frac{1}{5}$. Once the value of $\frac{1}{5}$ is found, then the value of any number of fifths can be easily found. When using this approach, we often try to find the value of one unit first.

She saved $**75**.

1 unit = $**25**. 3 units = $**75**

Learning Tasks 1-3, p. 57

Have your student identify each part of the diagram for these problems. Discuss other ways to solve the problems. Point out that in each of these problems, we can find the total value of a certain number of units. In 1 and 2 we know the value for the total number of units; in task 3 we know the value for 5 of the units. From that, we can find the value of one unit, and then the answer to the problem. Discuss alternate solutions.

1. 8 units = 96
   1 unit = 96 ÷ 8 = 12
   3 units = 12 x 3 = 36

   Or: Fraction of boys = $1 - \frac{5}{8} = \frac{3}{8}$

   Number of boys = $\frac{3}{8} \times 96 = 3 \times 12 = 36$

   Or: Number of girls = $\frac{5}{8} \times 96 = 60$

   Number of boys = 96 – 60 = 36

   There are **36** boys.

2. We can first draw a bar with 5 units. Each unit is $\frac{1}{5}$. Then we can divide each unit in half to show tenths. Or, we can realize ahead of time that we will need like fractions. David spent $\frac{1}{5} = \frac{2}{10}$ of his money on a storybook.

   10 units = \$40
   1 unit = \$40 ÷ 10 = \$4
   5 units = \$4 x 5 = **\$20**

   Or: 5 is half of 10 units, or the total. Half of \$40 is \$20.

   Or: Amount he spent = $\frac{5}{10}$ x \$40 = \$20

   He spent **\$20**.

3. The shaded 5 units represent 300 eggs. From this, find how many eggs one unit represents, and then how many are represented by 8 units, or the whole.
   5 units = 300
   1 unit = 300 ÷ 5 = 60
   8 units = 60 x 8 = 480

   Or: $\frac{5}{8}$ of total = 300; $\frac{1}{8}$ of total = $\frac{300}{5}$ = 60; $\frac{8}{8}$ of total = 60 x 8 = 480

   He had **480** eggs at first.

 **Workbook Exercises 26-27**

(2) Word Problems II

➢ Solve multi-step word problems involving remainders.

Learning Tasks 4-6, pp. 58-59

4. In method 2 the bar is divided up into 3 parts to represent thirds and one third is shaded to represent the number of stamps sold on Monday. Because we know the value of 3 parts, we can find the value of 2 parts, which is the remainder. Then the remainder is divided into four units to represent fourths. Because we know the value of 4 units from the first step, we can find the value of 1 unit, which is the number of stamps he sold on Tuesday. He sold **60** stamps on Tuesday.

   Method 3:
   Find the number of stamps sold on Monday:

   $\frac{1}{3} \times 360 = 120$

   Find the remainder:

   $360 - 120 = 240$

   Find the number sold on Tuesday:

   $\frac{1}{4} \times 240 = 60$

   Method 4:
   Draw a bar showing thirds. See that dividing the remainder into fourths involves dividing the part in half. Divide all the parts in half. There are now 6 units. 1 unit represents the number of stamps he sold on Tuesday:

   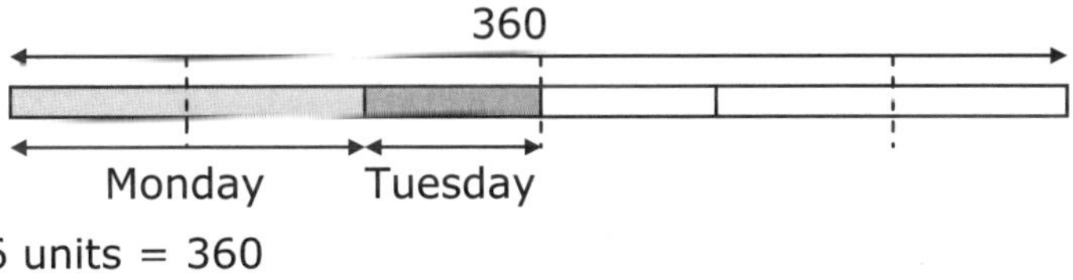

   6 units = 360
   1 unit = 360 ÷ 6 = 60

5.

Method 1:	Method 2:
Use diagram. 4 parts = 300 1 part = 300 ÷ 4 = 75 She had 75 unsold. 3 units = 75 1 unit $= \frac{75}{3} = 25$ 2 units = 25 x 2 = 50 She had **50** tarts left.	Use diagram. Subdivide entire bar into 12 units. 2 units are what she had left. 12 units = 300 1 unit $= \frac{300}{12}$ 2 units $= \frac{300}{12} \times 2 = 50$

Method 3:	Method 4:
Remainder: $1 - \frac{3}{4} = \frac{1}{4}$ Amount remaining: $\frac{1}{4}$ x 300 = 75 Fraction of remainder left: $1 - \frac{1}{3} = \frac{2}{3}$ Number of tarts left: $\frac{2}{3}$ x 75 = 2 x 25 = 50	Number sold: $\frac{3}{4}$ x 300 = 225 Remainder: 300 - 225 = 75 Number given to neighbor: $\frac{1}{3}$ x 75 = 25 Number of tarts left: 75 - 50 = 50

6.

Method 1:	Method 2:
Use diagram. 1 unit = \$300 2 units = \$300 x 2 = \$600 He had \$600 after giving 2 parts to his wife. 3 parts = \$600 1 part = \$$\frac{600}{3}$ = \$200 5 parts = \$200 x 5 = \$1,000 He had **\$1,000** at first.	Use diagram. Subdivide larger bar into 10 units. He has 6 units left after giving some to his wife. Of that, he had 3 units left after spending half of it. 3 units = \$300 1 unit = \$$\frac{300}{3}$ = \$100 10 units = \$100 x 10 = \$1,000
Method 3: $\frac{1}{2}$ of the remainder = \$300 All of the remainder = \$600 Fraction of total remaining: $1 - \frac{2}{5} = \frac{3}{5}$ $\frac{3}{5}$ of his money: \$600 $\frac{1}{5}$ of his money: \$600 ÷ 3 = \$200 $\frac{5}{5}$ of his money: \$200 x 5 = \$1,000	Method 4: Fraction remaining: $1 - \frac{2}{5} = \frac{3}{5}$ $\frac{1}{2}$ of the remainder is left. $\frac{1}{2} \times \frac{3}{5} = \frac{3}{10}$ $\frac{3}{10}$ of his money = \$300 $\frac{1}{10}$ of his money = \$$\frac{300}{3}$ = \$100 $\frac{10}{10}$ of his money = \$100 x 10 = \$1,000

Workbook Exercises 28-29

Practice 3G (p. 60)

Practice 3G, p. 60

Methods can vary. Only two will be shown here. You may want to discuss some of the problems as part of a lesson. If so, try #3 and #8.

1.

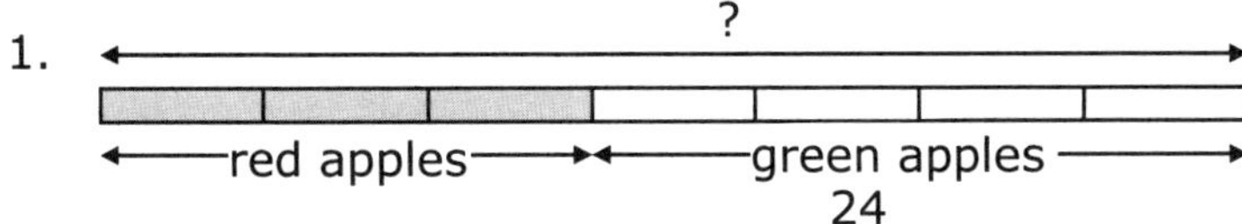

4 units = 24

1 unit = $\frac{24}{4}$ = 6

7 units = 6 x 7 = 42

There are **42** apples altogether.

OR:

$\frac{4}{7}$ of the apples = 24

$\frac{1}{7}$ of the apples = $\frac{24}{4}$ = 6

All of the apples = 6 x 7 = 42

2.

?

toy car | $42

3 units = $42

1 unit = $$\frac{42}{3}$ = $14

5 units = $14 x 5 = $70

He had **$70**.

OR:

$\frac{3}{5}$ of his money = $42

$\frac{1}{5}$ of his money = $$\frac{42}{3}$ = $14

All of his money = $14 x 5 = $70

3.

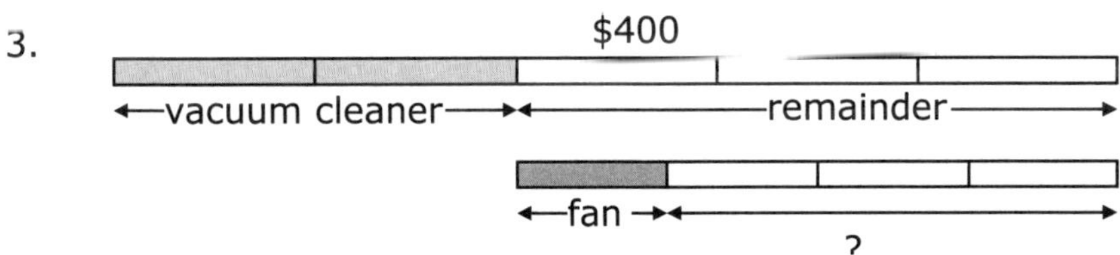

5 parts = $400
1 part = $400 ÷ 5= $80
3 parts = $80 x 3 = $240
4 units = $240
1 unit = $240 ÷ 4 = $60
3 units = $60 x 3 = $180
He had **$180** left.

OR:

The remainder is $\frac{3}{5}$ of his money.

He had $\frac{3}{4}$ of the remainder left.

$\frac{3}{4}$ x $\frac{3}{5}$ x $400 = $180

4. 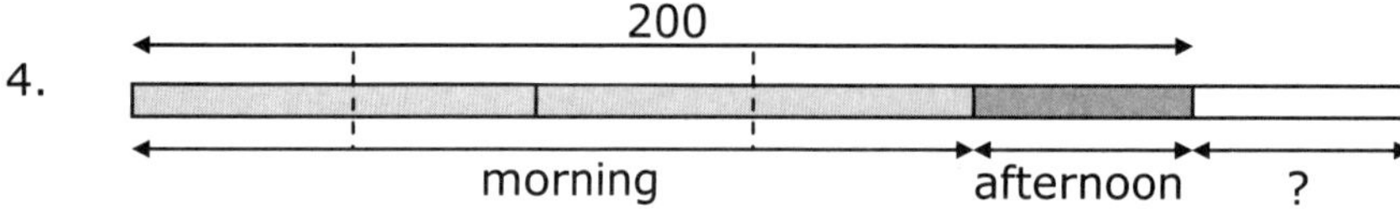

5 units = 200

1 unit $= \frac{200}{5} = 40$

He had **40** items left.

US> items = hot dogs
3d> items = curry puffs

OR:

Fraction sold $= \frac{2}{3} + \frac{1}{6} = \frac{4}{6} + \frac{1}{6} = \frac{5}{6}$

Fraction left $= \frac{1}{6}$

$\frac{5}{6}$ of his items = 200

$\frac{1}{6}$ of his items $= \frac{200}{5} = 40$

5. 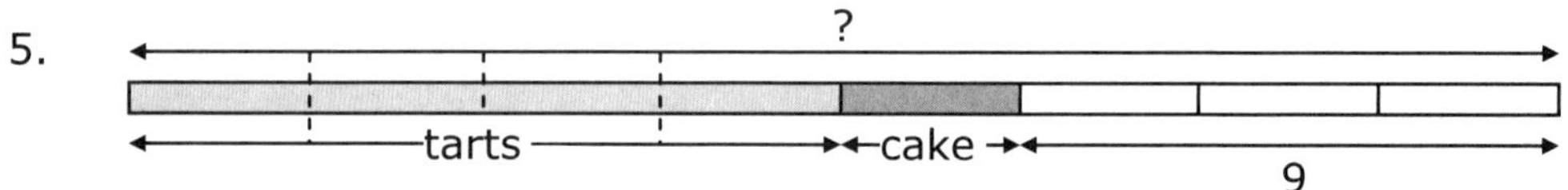

3 units = 9

1 unit $= \frac{9}{3} = 3$

8 units = 3 x 8 = 24

She bought **24** eggs.

OR:

$\frac{3}{4} \times \frac{1}{2}$ of her eggs = 9

$\frac{3}{8}$ of her eggs = 9

$\frac{1}{8}$ of her eggs $= \frac{9}{3} = 3$

All of her eggs = 3 x 8 = 24

6. 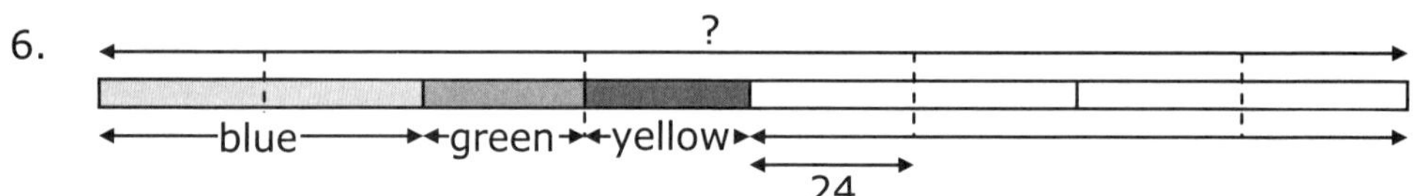

Divide bar into fourths, mark $\frac{1}{4}$ for blue marbles, divide each fourth into half for eighths, mark $\frac{1}{8}$ for green marbles. Remainder is 5 units, so mark 1 unit (one fifth of remainder) for yellow marbles.
There are a total of 8 units.
1 unit = 24.
8 units = 24 x 8 = 192

He bought **192** marbles.

OR:
Remainder:

$1 - \frac{1}{4} - \frac{1}{8} = 1 - \frac{2}{8} - \frac{1}{8} = \frac{5}{8}$

Fraction of marbles that are yellow:

$\frac{1}{5} \times \frac{5}{8}$

$\frac{1}{8}$ of the marbles = 24

All of the marbles = 24 x 8 = 192

7.

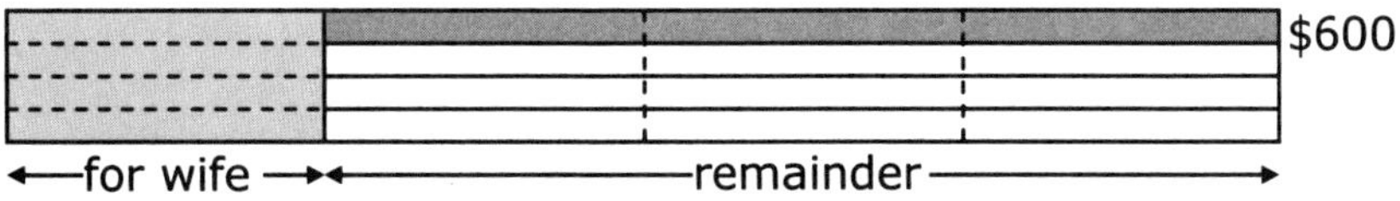

for wife — remainder — $600

(a) Fraction each child receives = $\frac{1}{4} \times \frac{3}{4} = \mathbf{\frac{3}{16}}$

(b) 3 units = $600

1 unit = $\$\frac{600}{3}$ = $200

16 units = $200 x 16 = $3,200

The sum of money was **$3,200**.

OR:

$\frac{3}{16}$ of the money = $600

$\frac{1}{16}$ of the money = $\$\frac{600}{3}$ = $200

All of the money = $200 x 16
= $3,200

8.

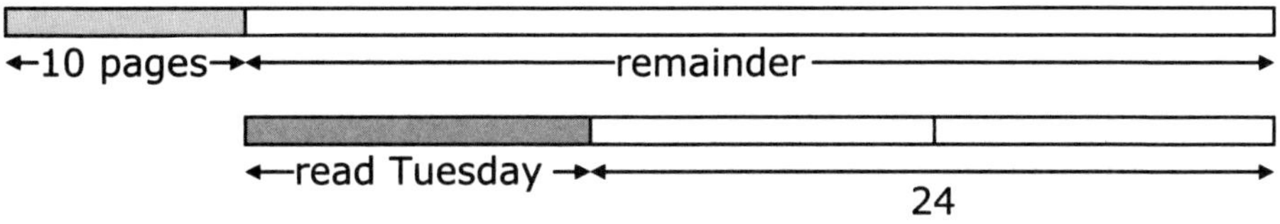

10 pages — remainder

read Tuesday — 24

2 units = 24

1 unit = $\frac{24}{2}$ = 12

3 units = 12 x 3 = 36

Total pages = 3 units + 10
= 36 + 10 = 46

There were **46** pages in the book.

OR:

$\frac{2}{3}$ of the remainder = 24

$\frac{1}{3}$ of the remainder = $\frac{24}{2}$ = 12

All of the remainder = 12 x 3 = 36

Total pages = remainder + 10
= 36 + 10 = 46

Review A (pp. 61-64)

Review A, pp. 61-64

1. (a) **515,407** (b) **4,600,000**
2. (a) **eight hundred seventy-two thousand, five hundred twenty**
   (b) **one million, thirty-four thousand**
   (c) **four million, five hundred thousand**
   (d) **one hundred sixty-two thousand, three**
3. **9,000,000**
4. **5,164,000**
5. (a) **$438,000** (b) **43,000 km**
6. **281,000**
7. **$2,356,000**
8. (a) Factors of 24: 1, 2, 3, 4, 6, 8, 12, 24
   Factors of 32: 1, 2, 4, 8, 16, 32
   Common factors: **1, 2, 4, or 8**

   (b) Multiples of 8: 8, 16, 24, 32, 40, 48 ...
   Multiples of 10: 10, 20, 30, 40, 50...
   Common multiples: **Any multiple of 40** (LCM of 8 and 10)
9. (a) 3,000 + 2,000 = **5,000** (b) 29,000 + 6,000 = **35,000**
   (c) 9,000 – 6,000 = **3,000** (d) 14,000 – 6,000 = **8,000**
10. Numbers increase by 600. **4,200**; **6,000**
11. (a) 3,000 x 7 = **21,000** (b) 5,000 x 60 = **300,000**
    (c) 4,200 ÷ 6 = **700** (d) 7,200 ÷ 80 = **90**
12. (a) **1,590,000** (b) **4,980,000** (c) **2,752,000**
    (d) **16** (e) **16 r10** (f) **12**
13. (a) **1,008** (b) **3,900** (c) **19,680**
    (d) **14** (e) **24** (f) **12 r13**
14. (a) $2 \times (\underline{28 + 36}) - 49$
    $= \underline{2 \times 64} - 49$
    $= \underline{128 - 49}$
    = **79**

    (b) $78 + \underline{21 \div 3} - (\underline{6 + 25})$
    $= \underline{78 + 7} - 31$
    $= \underline{85 - 31}$
    = **54**

    (c) $50 - (\underline{225 \div 15} + 13)$
    $= 50 - (\underline{15 + 13})$
    $= \underline{50 - 28}$
    = **22**

    (d) $29 + (\underline{300 \div 10} - \underline{3 \times 9})$
    $= 29 + (\underline{30 - 27})$
    $= \underline{29 + 3}$
    = **32**

(e) $\underline{28 + 19} - 24$
$= \underline{47 - 24}$
$= \mathbf{23}$

(f) $12 - \underline{9 \times 5} \div 15$
$= 12 - \underline{45 \div 15}$
$= \underline{12 - 3}$
$= \mathbf{9}$

(g) $(\underline{42 + 14}) \div 7 \times 5$
$= \underline{56 \div 7} \times 5$
$= \underline{8 \times 5}$
$= \mathbf{40}$

(h) $(\underline{59 + 13}) \div (\underline{4 \times 2})$
$= \underline{72 \div 8}$
$= \mathbf{9}$

15. (a) $\mathbf{\frac{3}{4}}$ (b) $\mathbf{\frac{3}{5}}$ (c) $\mathbf{\frac{2}{3}}$ (d) $\mathbf{\frac{4}{5}}$

16. (a) $\mathbf{\frac{43}{8}}$ (b) $\mathbf{\frac{40}{11}}$ (c) $\mathbf{\frac{41}{9}}$ (d) $\mathbf{\frac{11}{4}}$

17. (a) $\mathbf{3\frac{1}{3}}$ (b) $\mathbf{4\frac{1}{2}}$ (c) **11** (d) $\mathbf{3\frac{3}{4}}$

18. (a) $\mathbf{\frac{6}{8}, \frac{9}{12}, \frac{12}{16}...}$ (b) $\mathbf{\frac{1}{3}, \frac{4}{12}, \frac{6}{18}...}$

(c) $\mathbf{\frac{10}{18}, \frac{15}{27}, \frac{20}{36}...}$ (d) $\mathbf{\frac{22}{28}, \frac{33}{42}, \frac{44}{56}...}$

19. (a) $\frac{8}{12} = \mathbf{\frac{2}{3}}$ (b) $\frac{15}{54} = \mathbf{\frac{5}{18}}$

(c) $\frac{63}{18} = 3\frac{9}{18} = \mathbf{3\frac{1}{2}}$ (d) $\frac{100}{35} = 2\frac{30}{35} = \mathbf{2\frac{6}{7}}$

20. (a) $\frac{3}{2} = \frac{6}{4}$
$\mathbf{\frac{3}{2}}$ is greater than $\frac{5}{4}$.

(b) $\frac{1}{2}$ is greater than $\frac{1}{7}$, so
$\mathbf{2\frac{1}{2}}$ is greater than $2\frac{1}{7}$.

(c) **4** is greater than $3\frac{8}{9}$.

(d) $\frac{12}{7} = 1\frac{5}{7}$
$\mathbf{1\frac{6}{7}}$ is greater than $\frac{12}{7}$.

(e) $\frac{9}{2} = 4\frac{1}{2}$
$\mathbf{4\frac{2}{3}}$ is greater than $\frac{9}{2}$.

(f) $\frac{16}{5} = 3\frac{1}{5}$
$\mathbf{\frac{16}{5}}$ is greater than $3\frac{1}{6}$.

21. (a) $1\frac{3}{4} = 1\frac{6}{8}$; $\frac{9}{4} = 2\frac{2}{8}$; $1\frac{5}{8}$; $\frac{9}{2} = 4\frac{1}{2}$ Order is $\mathbf{1\frac{5}{8}, 1\frac{3}{4}, \frac{9}{4}, \frac{9}{2}}$

(b) $1\frac{2}{8}$; $\frac{36}{5} = 7\frac{1}{5}$; $1\frac{2}{3}$; $\frac{8}{2} = 4$ Order is $\mathbf{1\frac{2}{8}, 1\frac{2}{3}, \frac{8}{2}, \frac{36}{5}}$

22. $5 - 4\frac{2}{9} = 1 - \frac{2}{9} = \mathbf{\frac{7}{9}}$

23. There are 3 x 4 = 12 quarters in 3, so 13 quarters in $3\frac{1}{4}$.

Or: $3\frac{1}{4} \times 4 = \frac{13}{4} \times 4 = \mathbf{13}$

24. (a) $\frac{5}{6}+\frac{3}{4}=\frac{10}{12}+\frac{9}{12}=\frac{12}{12}+\frac{7}{12}=\mathbf{1\frac{7}{12}}$

(b) $3\frac{3}{8}+\frac{5}{12}=3\frac{9}{24}+\frac{10}{24}=\mathbf{3\frac{19}{24}}$

(c) $2\frac{1}{2}+5\frac{4}{5}=7\frac{5}{10}+\frac{8}{10}=7\frac{3}{10}+\frac{10}{10}=\mathbf{8\frac{3}{10}}$

(d) $6-\frac{6}{7}=\mathbf{5\frac{1}{7}}$

(e) $4\frac{3}{4}-\frac{2}{3}=4\frac{9}{12}-\frac{8}{12}=\mathbf{4\frac{1}{12}}$

(f) $6\frac{1}{3}-2\frac{3}{5}=4\frac{5}{15}-\frac{9}{15}=3\frac{20}{15}-\frac{9}{15}=\mathbf{3\frac{11}{15}}$

25. (a) $\frac{7}{\cancel{20}_5} \times \cancel{4}^1 = \frac{7}{5} = \mathbf{1\frac{2}{5}}$

(b) $\cancel{24}^3 \times \frac{5}{\cancel{8}_1} = \mathbf{15}$

(c) $\cancel{35}^7 \times \frac{2}{\cancel{5}_1} = \mathbf{14}$

(d) $\frac{\cancel{3}^1}{\cancel{4}_1} \times \frac{\cancel{8}^2}{\cancel{9}_3} = \mathbf{\frac{2}{3}}$

(e) $\frac{\cancel{5}^1}{\cancel{8}_4} \times \frac{\cancel{14}^7}{\cancel{15}_3} = \mathbf{\frac{7}{12}}$

(f) $\frac{\cancel{8}^2}{\cancel{12}_3} \times \frac{\cancel{16}^4}{\cancel{20}_5} = \mathbf{\frac{8}{15}}$

(g) $\frac{3}{5} \div 3 = \frac{\cancel{3}^1}{5} \times \frac{1}{\cancel{3}_1} = \mathbf{\frac{1}{5}}$

(h) $\frac{7}{8} \div 2 = \frac{7}{8} \times \frac{1}{2} = \mathbf{\frac{7}{16}}$

(i) $\frac{4}{7} \div 12 = \frac{\cancel{4}^1}{7} \times \frac{1}{\cancel{12}_3} = \mathbf{\frac{1}{21}}$

26. (a) $\frac{3}{5}$ m = $\frac{3}{5}$ x 100 cm = **60 cm**

(b) $\frac{7}{10}$ kg = $\frac{7}{10}$ x 1,000 g = 700 g

$1\frac{7}{10}$ kg = **1 kg 700 g**

US› (c) $\frac{3}{4}$ lb = $\frac{3}{4}$ x 16 oz = 12 oz

$2\frac{3}{4}$ lb = **2** lb **12** oz

27. (a) 1 year = 12 months

$\frac{4}{12} = \frac{1}{3}$

4 months = $\mathbf{\frac{1}{3}}$ of a year

(b) $1\frac{1}{2}$ h = 90 min

$\frac{48}{90} = \frac{8}{15}$

48 min = $\mathbf{\frac{8}{15}}$ of $1\frac{1}{2}$ h

US› (c) $3\frac{1}{2}$ qt = 7 pt

1 pt = $\mathbf{\frac{1}{7}}$ of $3\frac{1}{2}$ qt

28. 600 ÷ 24 = 25. She had **25** packets.

29. Number of boys = 2,204 – 925 = 1,279
Difference between boys and girls = 1,279 – 925 = 354
There are **354** more boys than girls.

30. Amount cut = 3 x 85 cm = 255 cm
3 m = 300 cm
Amount left = 300 – 255 = **45 cm**

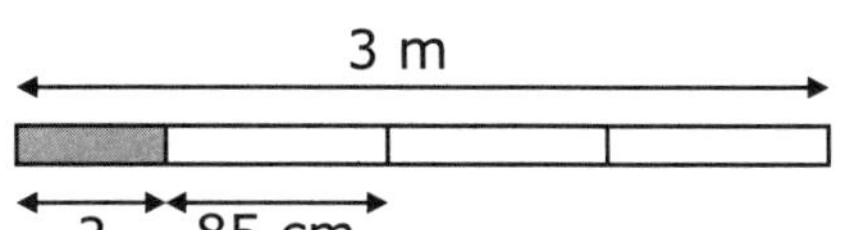

31. Peter's share = \$1,458 ÷ 3 = \$486
Cost of bicycle = \$486 – \$139 = **\$347**

32. Number of oranges in one layer = 6 x 8 = 48
Number of oranges in 4 layers = 48 x 4 = **192**

33. Total money = 1,400 x 80¢ = 112,000¢ = **\$1,120**

34. Fraction answered correctly = $\frac{28}{32} = \mathbf{\frac{7}{8}}$

35. $2\frac{1}{5} - 1\frac{1}{2} = 1\frac{2}{10} - \frac{5}{10} = \frac{12}{10} - \frac{5}{10} = \frac{7}{10}$

She bought $\mathbf{\frac{7}{10}}$ **kg** more potatoes than carrots.

36. Number of students who wear glasses = $\frac{3}{7}$ x 42 = 3 x 6 = **18**

37. Total amount of drink = 6 x $\frac{1}{4}$ ℓ = $\frac{6}{4}$ ℓ = $\frac{3}{2}$ ℓ = $\mathbf{1\frac{1}{2}}$ ℓ

38. Amount used = $\frac{1}{4}$ x $\frac{3}{5}$ kg = $\mathbf{\frac{3}{20}}$ **kg**

39. $\frac{1}{2} \div 4 = \frac{1}{2} \times \frac{1}{4} = \frac{1}{8}$ Each piece is $\mathbf{\frac{1}{8}}$ of the cake.

40.

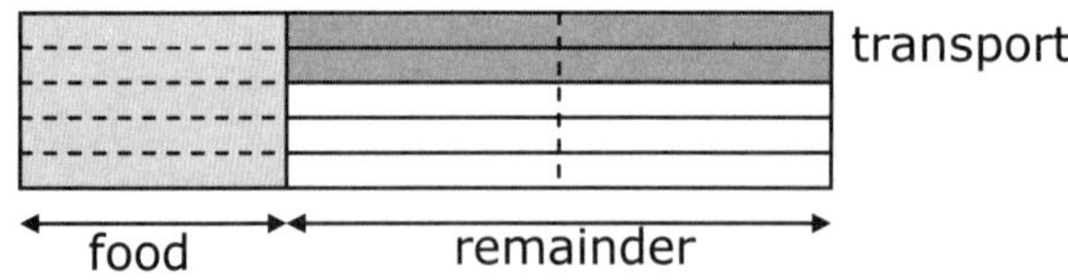

(a) Fraction left = $\frac{3}{5} \times \frac{2}{3} = \frac{6}{15} = \mathbf{\frac{2}{5}}$

(b) 6 units = \$600
1 unit = \$100
15 units = \$1,500

His salary is **\$1,500.**

OR:
$\frac{2}{5}$ of his salary = \$600
$\frac{1}{5}$ of his salary = $\$\frac{600}{2}$ = \$300
All of his salary = \$300 x 5 = \$1,500

41.

6 m
skirt — shirt — ?
$1\frac{3}{4}$ m $\frac{3}{4}$ m

$$6 - 1\frac{3}{4} - \left(3 \times \frac{3}{4}\right) = 5 - \frac{3}{4} - \frac{9}{4} = 5 - \frac{3}{4} - 2\frac{1}{4} = 4\frac{1}{4} - 2\frac{1}{4} = 2$$

She had **2 m** left.

42.

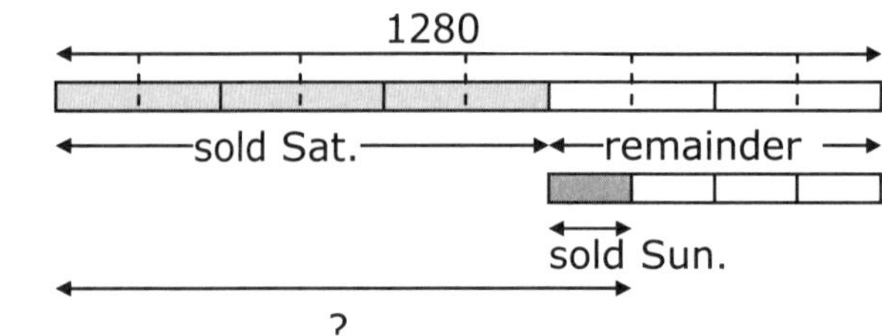

10 units = 1,280
1 unit = 1,280 ÷ 10 = 128
7 units = 7 x 128 = 896
He sold **896** eggs on the two days.

Unit 4 – Area of Triangle

Part 1 – Finding the Area of a Triangle (pp. 65-69)

(1) Area of a Triangle

- Find the area of a triangle drawn on a square grid.
- Understand the terms base and height.
- Find the area of a triangle by using the formula.

This section introduces the concept that the area of a triangle is half the area of a related rectangle. From this we can derive the formula

area of a triangle = $\frac{1}{2}$ x base x height

where base and height are the sides of the related rectangle and are perpendicular to each other.

Initially, the triangles are drawn with the base horizontal (parallel to the bottom of the paper) so that the height is vertical. However, any side of the triangle can be considered the base.

There are three kinds of triangles. Right triangles have one right angle. Acute triangles have all angles less than 90°. Obtuse triangles have one angle greater than 90°.

Have your student draw a triangle that is half of a 6 by 6 square on square grid paper and find the area of the triangle. The area of the triangle is half the area of the square.

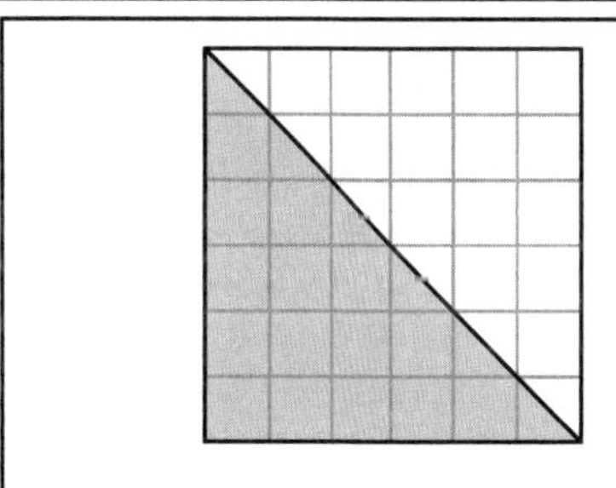

Area of square = 6 x 6 = 36 square units

Area of triangle = $\frac{1}{2}$ x 36 = 18 square units

Repeat with a triangle that is half of a 5 by 6 rectangle. He can find the area by finding the area of the rectangle and then finding half of that. He can cut out the rectangle and fold it in half to see that the triangle is half the area, or count the squares.

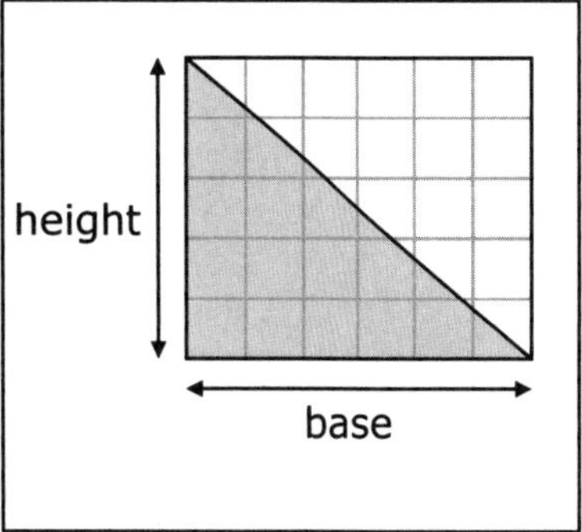

Area of rectangle = 6 x 5 = 30 square units

Area of triangle = $\frac{1}{2}$ x 30 = 15 square units

➤ Tell your student that the **base** of the triangle is one of the sides. For now, we are calling the side parallel with the bottom of the page the base. The **height** is the perpendicular distance to the corner of the triangle that is opposite the base. We draw a line perpendicular with the base that intersects the opposite corner of the triangle. The height is the distance from the base line to this corner along the perpendicular line. For this triangle, it is the other side of the related rectangle. So we can say that the area of the rectangle is half of the base times the height. Have your student use the following formula to find the area.

$$\text{Area of triangle} = \frac{1}{2} \times \text{base} \times \text{height}$$

Point out that since we can do multiplication in any order, we can find the area by multiplying 6 and 5 first (to get the area of the related rectangle) and then multiply by $\frac{1}{2}$ to get half of that. We can also find half the base first (since it is an even number and it is easy to find half of it) and then multiply by the height.

$$\text{Area of triangle} = \frac{1}{2} \times \text{base} \times \text{height}$$
$$= \frac{1}{2} \times 6 \times 5 = \frac{1}{2} \times 30 = 15 \text{ square units}$$
$$= \frac{1}{2} \times 6 \times 5 = 3 \times 5 = 15 \text{ square units}$$

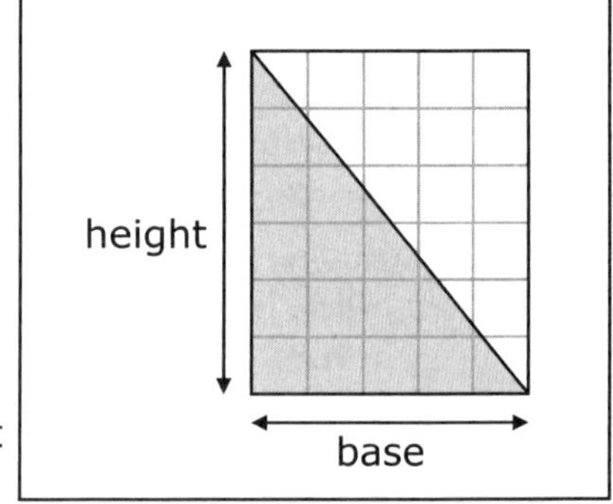

Turn the triangle and show a new base and height. We can find the area by first finding half the height if we want. The area is the same.

➤ Draw an acute triangle (a triangle with all angles less than 90°) on square grid paper and shade it. Show the related rectangle with the two sides of the rectangle the same lengths as the base and height of the triangle. Ask your student to find the area of this triangle. Let her come up with some methods:

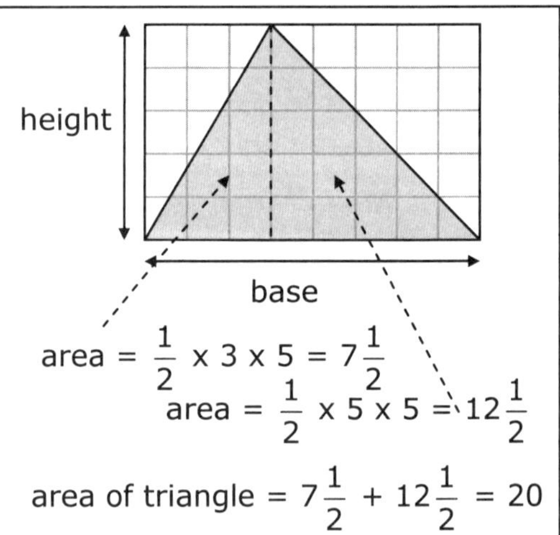

- Count the squares.
- Divide the triangle into two separate right triangles and add the areas of each right triangle.

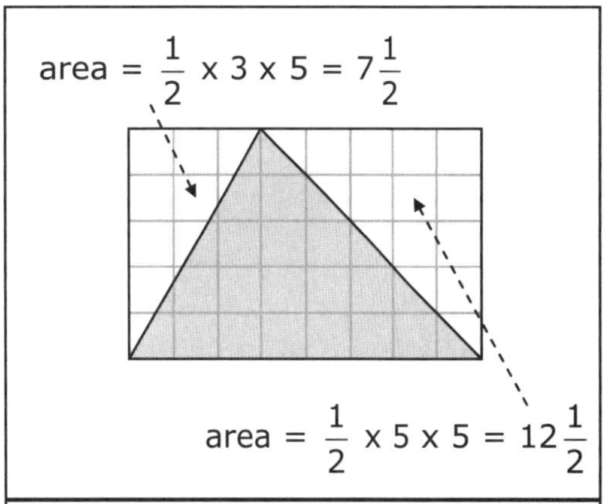

- Find the area of the square and of the two unshaded right triangles, using the formula found for right triangles.

  area of rectangle = 8 x 5
  = 40 square units

  area of triangle = $40 - 7\frac{1}{2} - 12\frac{1}{2}$
  = 20 square units

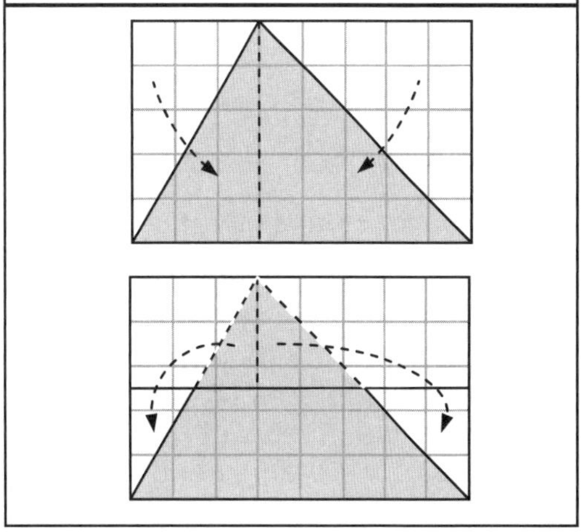

- Cut out the rectangle and the unshaded parts. Rotate the unshaded parts to show that the areas of the unshaded part of the rectangle match the area of the triangle.

- Cut out the triangle and cut it into three pieces as shown and rearrange into a rectangle that is half the original related triangle (this method isn't a very obvious one).

So the area of an acute triangle can also be found using the formula:

Area of triangle = $\frac{1}{2}$ x base x height

➤ Draw an obtuse triangle on square grid paper and have your student find its area using several methods.

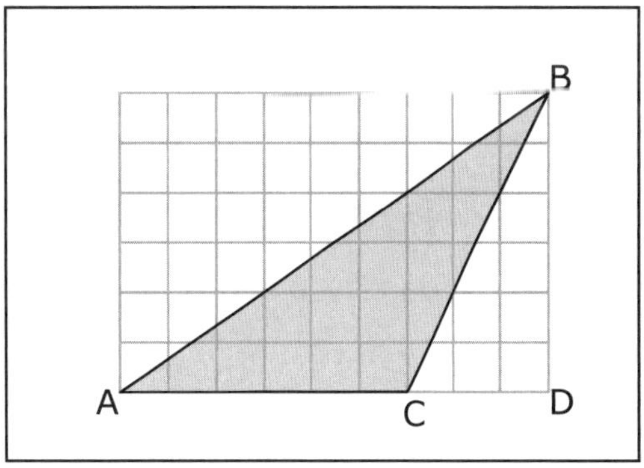

- Count the squares.

- Find the area of the larger right triangle (triangle ABD) and subtract the area of the smaller one (triangle CBD) to get the area of the shaded triangle (triangle ABC).

Area of triangle ABD = $\frac{1}{2}$ x 9 x 6 = 27 square units

Area of triangle CBD = $\frac{1}{2}$ x 3 x 6 = 9 square units

Area of triangle ABC = 27 – 9 = 18 square units

Point out that the rectangle enclosing the entire obtuse triangle is not the related rectangle. The related rectangle has one side the same as the base of the triangle; with the other side the same length as the perpendicular distance from the base line AD to the corner B.

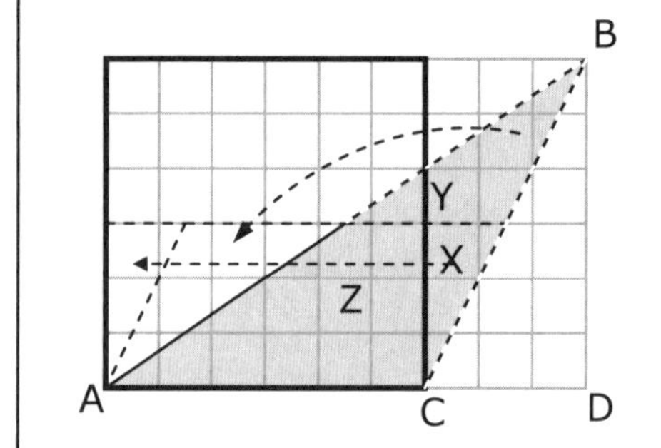

Draw the related rectangle. Show how the triangle can be cut into three pieces and rearranged to form a rectangle that is half of the related rectangle.
(One way to do this is to slide piece X over so that C is at A, rotate and slide piece Y so that B ends up at A.)

Area of triangle = $\frac{1}{2}$ x 6 x 6 = 18 square units.

So the area of an obtuse triangle can also be found using the formula

Area of triangle = $\frac{1}{2}$ x base x height

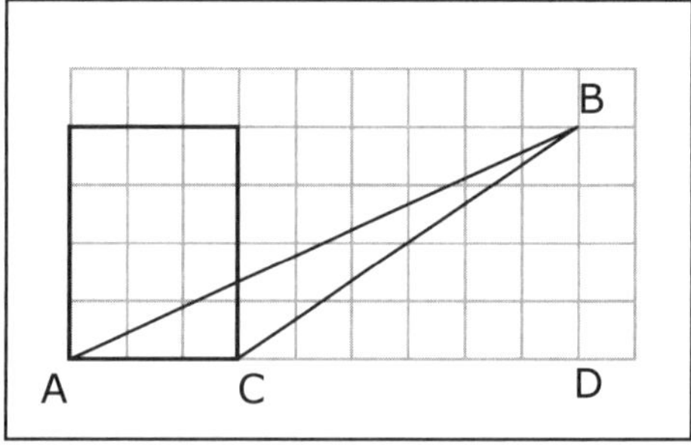

- Show your students one more triangle, an obtuse one which "leans over" farther. Guide them in finding the width, length, and area of the related rectangle. The width is the same as one side of the triangle and the length is the same as the perpendicular distance to the opposite vertex.

For this triangle, it is harder to see how it can be cut up to fit into half the rectangle. But they can still show that the area of the triangle is half the area of the related rectangle by finding the area of right triangles ABD and CBD.

Area of triangle ABD = $\frac{1}{2}$ x 9 x 4 = 18 square units

Area of triangle CBD = $\frac{1}{2}$ x 6 x 4 = 12 square units

Area of triangle ABC = 18 – 12 = 6 square units

Area of triangle ABC = $\frac{1}{2}$ x base x height

= $\frac{1}{2}$ x 3 x 4 = 6 square units

- Draw some other triangles on square grid paper and have your student find and draw the related rectangles, the area of the related rectangles, and the area of the triangles.

➤ Draw several triangles with the same base and height and ask your student to find their area. She should realize that since they all have the same base and height they will all have the same area.

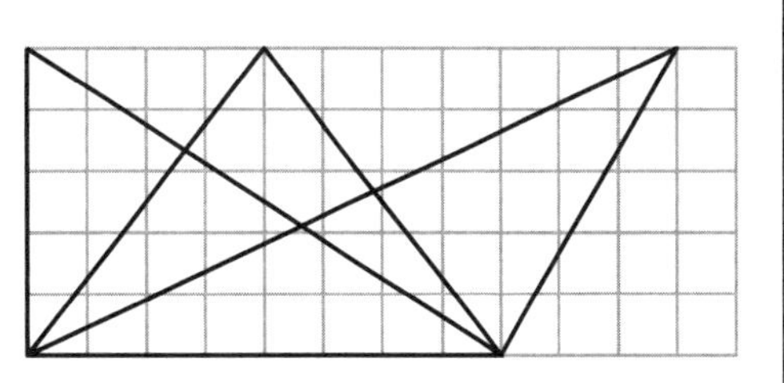

pp. 65-66
Learning Task 1, p. 67

1. (a) **24** (b) **40** (c) **60**

➤ Draw an acute triangle with sides that are not parallel to the sides of the paper. Tell your student that any side can be a base of the triangle. Point to one side and tell your student that is the base. Have your student draw a line showing the height using the indicated base. She can place the edge of a ruler on the base and slide it along until the side of the ruler touches the opposite corner or vertex of the triangle, or use a plastic triangle with a right angle. Do the same with the other sides.

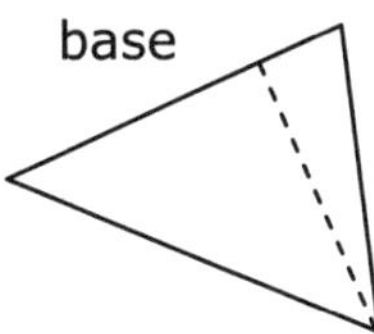

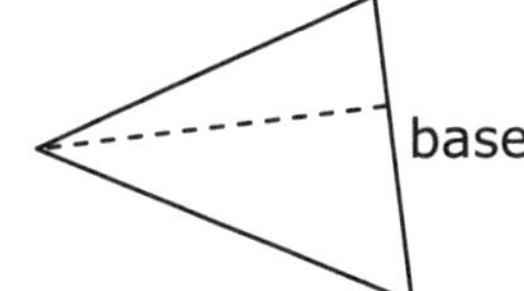

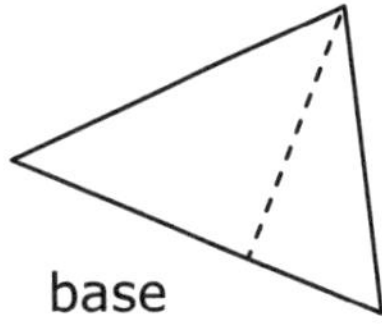

Draw an obtuse triangle and have your student find the height with each side as the base. Note that for two of the sides the base needs to be extended to be able to draw the corresponding heights.

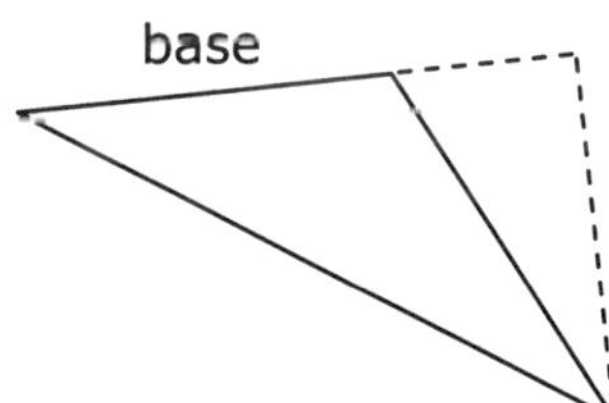

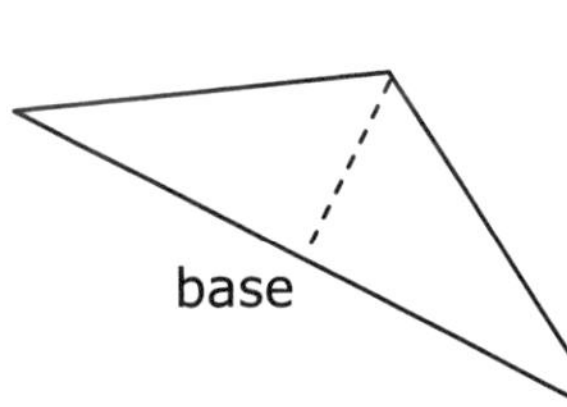

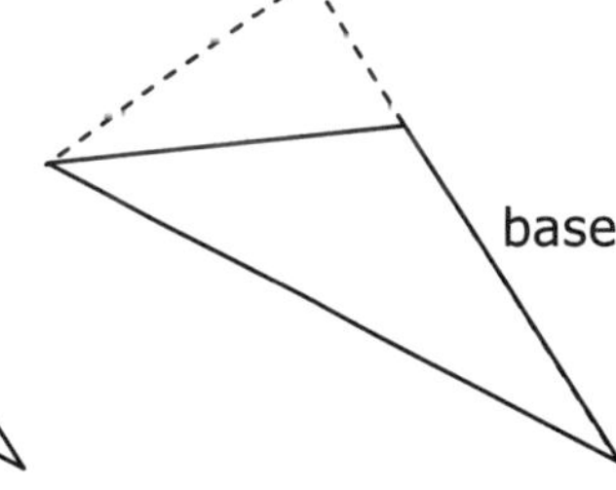

Learning Task 2, p. 68

2. (a) $\frac{1}{2}$ x 10 x 4 = **20 cm²** (b) $\frac{1}{2}$ x 12 x 9 = **54** (**›US** in.^{2} **›3d** cm^2)

   (c) $\frac{1}{2}$ x 7 x 9 = **31$\frac{1}{2}$ m²** (d) $\frac{1}{2}$ x 20 x 22 = **220** (**›US** ft^2, **›3d** m^2)

Workbook Exercises 30-32

(2) Problem Solving

➢ Solve problems involving area of a triangle.

Learning Tasks 3-5, pp. 68-69

3. (a) Base = 48 + 15 = 63 yd
   Height = 20 yd
   Area = $\frac{1}{2}$ x 63 x 20 = **630 yd²**
   (3d› yd ↔ m, yd² ↔ m²)

   (b) Take 16 cm for the base.
   Height is then 12 cm.
   Area = $\frac{1}{2}$ x 16 x 12 = **96 cm²**

   (c) Base = 10 + 4 = 14 m
   Height = 6 m
   Area = $\frac{1}{2}$ x 14 x 6 = **42 m²**

   (d) Base = 6 cm
   Height = 5 cm
   Area = $\frac{1}{2}$ x 6 x 5 = **15 cm²**

4. (a) Base = 20 cm
   Height = 12 cm
   Area = $\frac{1}{2}$ x 20 x 12 = **120 cm²**

   (b) Base = 4 m
   Height = 18 m
   Area = $\frac{1}{2}$ x 4 x 18 = **36 m²**

5. (a) Area of □ = 12 x 8 = 96 cm²
   Area of Δ = $\frac{1}{2}$ x 7 x 8 = 28 cm²
   Shaded area = 96 - 28 = **68 cm²**

   (b) Area of □ = 20 x 16 = 320 m²
   Area of Δ = $\frac{1}{2}$ x 10 x 16 = 80 m²
   Shaded area = 320 – 80
   = **240 m²**

   (c) Area of □ = 14 x 20 = 280 cm²
   Area of Δ = $\frac{1}{2}$ x 14 x 8 = 56 cm²
   Shaded area = 280 – 56
   = **224 cm²**

Workbook Exercise 33

Practice 4A (p. 70)

 **Practice 4A, p. 70**

1. A Base = 14 cm
   Height = 3 cm
   Area = $\frac{1}{2}$ x 14 x 3 = **21 cm²**

   B Base = 4 cm
   Height = 11 cm
   Area = $\frac{1}{2}$ x 4 x 11 = **22 cm²**

   C Base = 9 m
   Height = 8 m
   Area = $\frac{1}{2}$ x 8 x 9 = **36 m²**

   D Base = 14 m
   Height = 7 m
   Area = $\frac{1}{2}$ x 14 x 7 = **49 m²**

2. Base = 60 - 20 - 15 = 25 cm   Height = 12 cm
   Area = $\frac{1}{2}$ x 25 x 12 = **150 cm²**

3. Area of each Δ = $\frac{1}{2}$ x 6 x 6 = 18 cm²
   Area of figure = 8 x 18 = **144 cm²**

4. (a) Find the area of the large triangle formed by a base of 18 cm and height of 5 + 7 = 12 cm and subtract the area of the small triangle with a base of 18 cm and a height of 5 cm to get the area of the shaded figure.
   Area = ($\frac{1}{2}$ x 18 x 12) - ($\frac{1}{2}$ x 18 x 5) = 108 - 45 = **63 cm²**

   (b) Area = area of top triangle + area of bottom triangle
   = ($\frac{1}{2}$ x 110 x 40) + ($\frac{1}{2}$ x 66 x 88) = 2200 + 2904 = **5,104 m²**

Unit 5 – Ratio

Part 1 – Finding Ratio (pp. 71-74)

(1) Ratios

- Compare two quantities using ratio.

Students have learned how to compare two quantities by finding their difference and by finding how many times more one quantity is than another. In this section they will learn to compare two quantities by finding their ratio. In a ratio the relative sizes of two or more quantities are being compared. We can compare the number of objects in two sets or two parts of the same whole. For example if one set has 3 oranges and the other set has 2 apples, the ratio of oranges to apples is 3 : 2. We read 3 : 2 as **3 to 2**. The ratio of oranges to total fruit is 3 : 5. We can also compare two measurements. They must be in the same unit. To find the ratio of a length of 24 inches to 1 foot we need to find the ratio of inches to inches or feet to feet. The ratio of their lengths is 2 : 1 (or 24 : 12). When expressing the ratio, we don't include the units, but we know that the units must be the same.

In a ratio the first and second numbers represent the first and second quantities respectively. In the example above, the ratio of oranges to apples is 3 : 2, but the ratio of apples to oranges is 2 : 3.

p. 71
Learning Task 1, p. 72

Tell your student that we can compare amounts using **ratios**. Discuss these pages. Discuss a few other situations involving ratios, such as the ratio of the number of males to females in the family.

1. 1 : 3

Note that the ratio of white paint to red paint is different than the ratio of red paint to white paint.

➤ Set out 6 counters of one color (such as yellow) and 10 of another color (such as red). (Or use other objects.) Have your student put the counters into groups of 2. Each group is 1 unit.

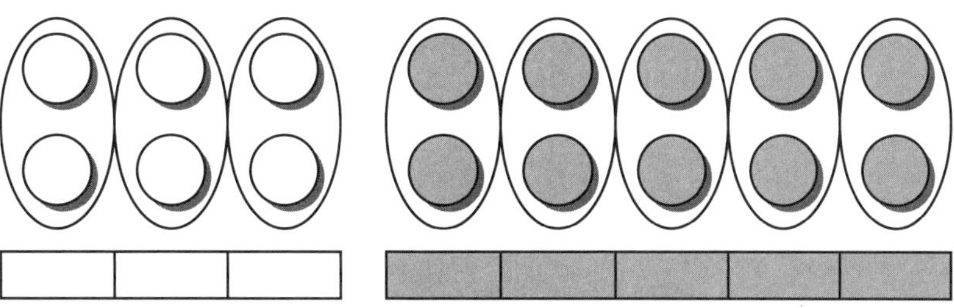

1 unit = 2 counters.
The number of yellow counters = 3 units
The number of red counters = 5 units
The ratio of the number of yellow counters to the number of red counters = 3 : 5.

The ratio 3 : 5 does not mean that there are 3 yellow counters and 5 red counters. It means that there are 3 units of yellow counters and 5 units of red counters and the number of counters in each unit is the same, whether yellow or red counters. For every 3 yellow counters, there are 5 red counters. Here 3 refers to the number of units of yellow counters and 5 to the number of units of red counters.

Ask your student for the ratio of red counters to yellow counters. It is 5 : 3. Point out that 5 : 3 is different from 3 : 5. One is the ratio of red counters to yellow counters, and the other is the ratio of yellow counters to red counters.

 **Learning Tasks 2-9, pp. 72-74**

2. **2 : 3**
3. **2 : 5**; **5 : 2**
4. **3 : 2**
5. **3 : 7**
6. **5 : 4**
7. 4 : 6 = **2 : 3**
8. **3 : 8**
9. **5 : 7**

 **Workbook Exercise 34**

Part 2 – Equivalent Ratios (pp. 75-78)

(1) Equivalent Ratios

- Find equivalent ratios.
- Express a ratio in simplest form.

If each term (each number) of a ratio has a common factor, the ratio can be written in simpler terms.

8 : 4, 4 : 2, and 2 : 1 are **equivalent ratios**.

If there is no common factor for all the terms, then the ratio is in its **simplest form**.

2 : 1 is the simplest form of the ratio 8 : 4.

We simplify a ratio by dividing each term of the ratio by its common factors.

12 : 18 = 2 : 3.

Divide 12 and 18 by the common factor 6. We can show this by cancellation – crossing out the term and writing the quotient.

$\cancel{12}^2 : \cancel{18}^3 = 2 : 3$

Reducing a ratio to its simplest form can be done in several steps.

12 : 18 = 6 : 9 = 2 : 3

In the first step the common factor is 2, and in the second it is 3.

Give your student 6 counters of one color, such as blue, and 12 counters of another color, such as red. Ask for the ratio of the number of blue counters to red counters (6 : 12). For 6 blue counters, there are 12 red counters. Then ask for the ratio of the number of red counters to blue counters (12 : 6).

Ask your student to put the counters into groups of 2.

Ask for the ratio of the number of units of blue counters to units of red counters (3 : 6).

Point out that 1 unit = 2 and 3 : 6 means 3 units to 6 units. For every 3 blue counters, there are 6 red counters.

Repeat, having your student put the counters in groups of 3. The ratio is now 2 : 4, and 1 unit has a value of 3.

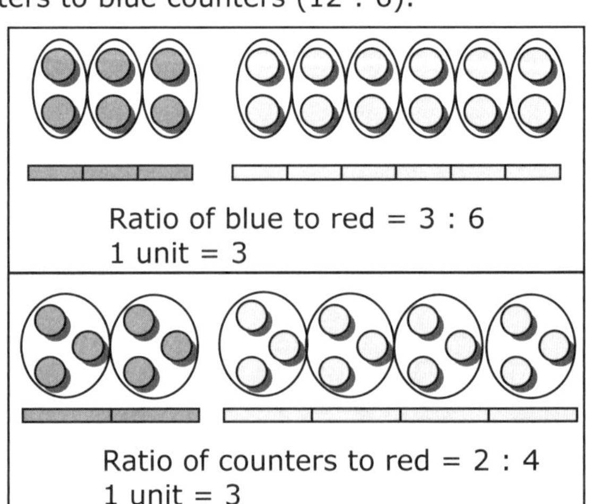

Now have your student put them in groups of 6. Each time discuss the value of one unit.

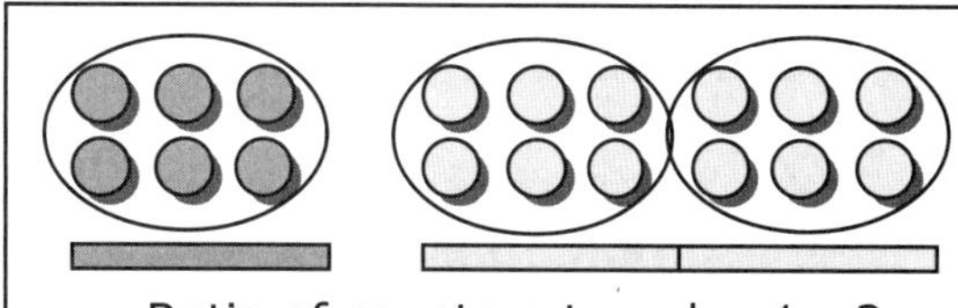

Ratio of counters to red = 1 : 2
1 unit = 6

Tell your student we have found 4 different ratios to compare the number of blue counters and red counters. These are **equivalent ratios**.

$$6 : 12 = 3 : 6 = 2 : 4 = 1 : 2$$

Ask her how we can derive one equivalent ratio from the other. We can divide each term by a common factor to get a simpler ratio. 2 is a common factor of 6 and 12. 6 ÷ 2 = 3 and 12 ÷ 2 = 6

$$\cancel{6}^3 : \cancel{12}^6 = 3 : 6$$

1 : 2 is the **simplest form** of the ratio. The terms do not have a common factor (other than 1). It can be obtained from 6 : 12 by dividing both terms by the common factor 6, or it can be obtained in steps, such as dividing both terms first by the common factor 3, and then by the common factor 2.

$$\cancel{6}^1 : \cancel{12}^2 = 1 : 2 \qquad \text{or} \qquad \cancel{6}^2 : \cancel{12}^4 = \cancel{2}^1 : \cancel{4}^2 = 1 : 2$$

p. 75

Learning Tasks 1-3, p. 76

1. (a) **2 : 5** (b) **2 : 3**
2. (a) **4 : 5** (common factor 2) (b) **5 : 3** (common factor 2)
   (c) **1 : 4** (common factor 6) (d) **3 : 2** (common factor 7)
3. **5 : 4** (common factor 3)

Workbook Exercise 35

(2) Word Problems

- Use the comparison model to represent a ratio of two quantities.
- Solve word problems involving a ratio of two quantities.

Ratios can be diagrammed as unit bars. Since in a ratio two quantities are being compared, we can use a comparison model to illustrate word problems involving ratios. For example, if the ratio of A to B is 5 : 7, this can be diagrammed using 5 units for A and 7 units for B:

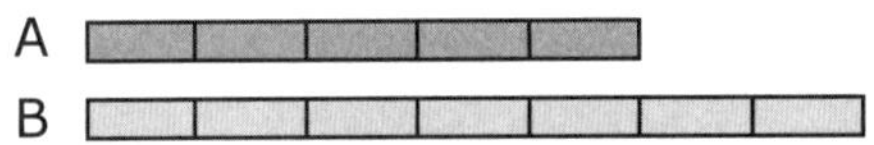

If we are given the value for A, the value for B, the total, or the difference between A and B, we can find the value for 1 unit by division. Once we find the value for 1 unit, we can find other values by multiplication.

Learning Tasks 4-7, pp. 77-78

For tasks 5 – 7 you can ask for additional values, such as the total length of the two ribbons for task 5, or the difference in their lengths.

4. 25 : 15 = **5** : **3**

5. 1 unit = 21 m ÷ 7 = **3** m
   4 units = 3 m x 4 = **12** m
   The length of ribbon B is **12** m.

6. 1 unit = $35 ÷ 7 = $**5**
   4 units = $5 x 4 = $**20**
   Siti received $**20**.

7. 1 unit = 40 kg ÷ 5 = **8** kg
   8 units = 8 kg x 8 = **64** kg
   The total weight is **64** kg.

Workbook Exercise 36

Practice 5A (p. 79)

Practice 5A, p. 79

1. (a) 3 : 6 = **1 : 2** (b) 6 : 4 = **3 : 2**

2. 16 : 12 = **4 : 3**

3. Amount spent = \$50 - \$35 = \$15
   Amount saved : amount spent = 35 : 15 = **7 : 3**

4. 2 units = 4 ℓ

   1 unit = $\frac{4}{2}$ = 2 ℓ

   7 units = 2 x 7 = 14 ℓ
   She used **14 ℓ** of water.

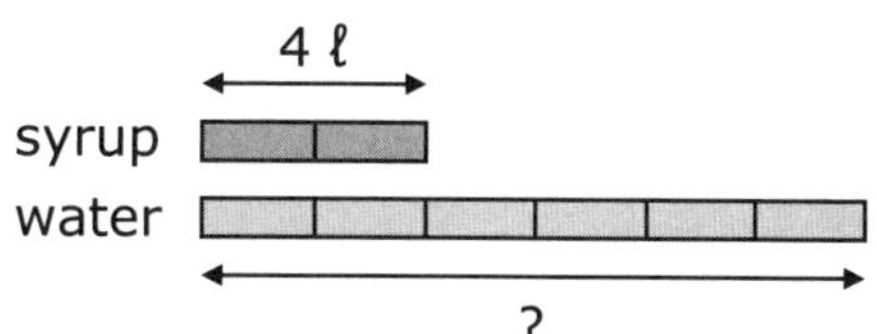

5. 5 units = 60 m

   1 unit = $\frac{60}{5}$ = 12 m

   2 units = 12 x 2 = 24 m
   The shorter piece was **24 m** long.

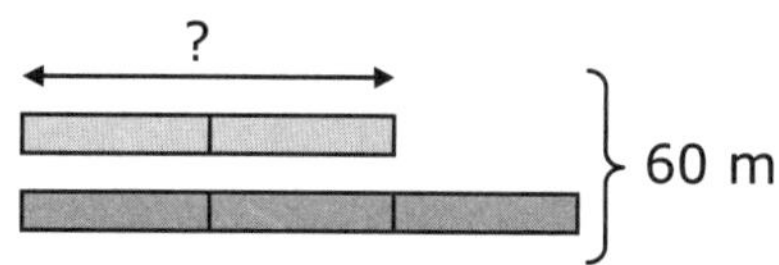

6. 6 units = 48 kg

   1 unit = $\frac{48}{6}$ = 8 kg

   5 units = 8 x 5 = 40 kg
   John weighs **40 kg**.

48 kg
Adam
John
?

7. 2 units = 100

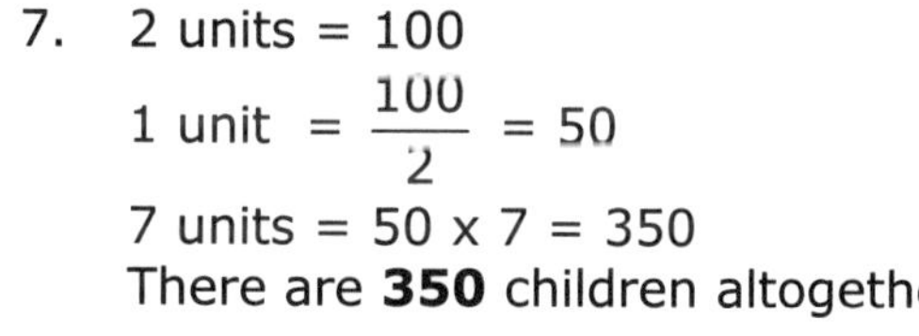

   1 unit = $\frac{100}{2}$ = 50

   7 units = 50 x 7 = 350
   There are **350** children altogether.

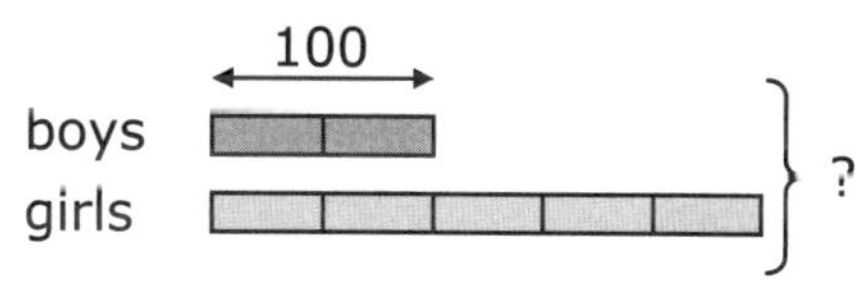

Part 3 – Comparing Three Quantities (pp. 80-81)

(1) Comparing Three Quantities

- Compare three quantities using ratios.
- Express a ratio of three quantities in simplest form.
- Solve 1-step and 2-step word problems involving ratios of three quantities.

The concept of ratios, equivalent ratios, and simplest form is extended to the comparison of three quantities in this section. Word problems involving ratios comparing three quantities can be solved using a comparison model.

Use 3 colors of counters or other similar object, such as red, green, and blue. Use 12 red counters, 24 blue counters, and 18 green counters. Have your student write the ratio of red counters to blue counters to green counters as 12 : 24 : 18. Then have her group the counters in units of 2, 3, and 6 and compare the number of equal units as ratios, as in lesson 1 of part 2 of this unit.

12 : 24 : 18 = 6 : 12 : 9 = 4 : 8 : 6 = 2 : 4 : 3

Discuss how each equivalent ratio can be obtained from 12 : 24 : 18 by dividing each term by a common factor. 2 : 4 : 3 is the equivalent ratio in its simplest form. Its terms do not have a common factor. For every 2 red counters there are 4 blue counters and 3 green counters.

p. 80
Learning Tasks 1-2, p. 81

(a) **2 : 1** (b) **6 : 3 : 2**

1. (a) **6 : 3 : 2** (b) **4 : 2 : 3**

2. 1 unit = 20 ÷ 10 = **2** liters
   5 units = 2 x 5 = **10** liters
   The volume of water in Bucket C is **10** liters.

Workbook Exercises 37-38

Practice 5B (p. 82)

Practice 5B, p. 82

1. 10 : 24 = **5 : 12**

2. 60 : 20 : 35 = **12 : 4 : 7**

3. 3 units = 12 cups
   1 unit = $\frac{12}{3}$ = 4 cups
   She used **4 cups**.
   (**3d›** oatmeal ↔ rice)

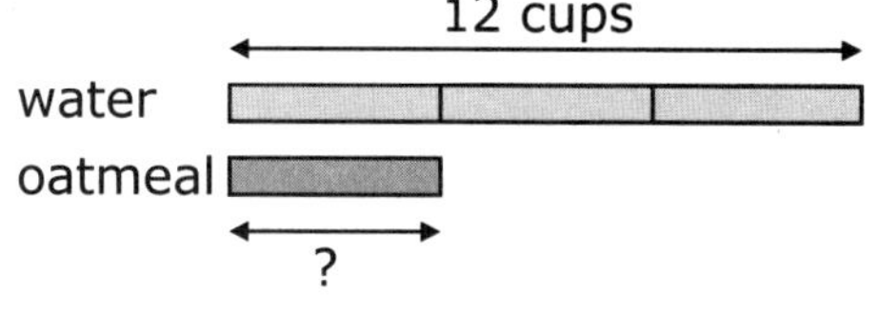

4. 11 units = 121
   7 units = $\frac{121}{11}$ x 7 = 77
   There are **77** boys.

5. Amount of money Steve had = \$120 - \$20 = \$100 (**3d›** Steve ↔ Ahmad)
   Steve's money : William's money = 100 : 120 = **5 : 6**

6. 9 units = 90 cm
   1 unit = 90 ÷ 9 = 10 cm

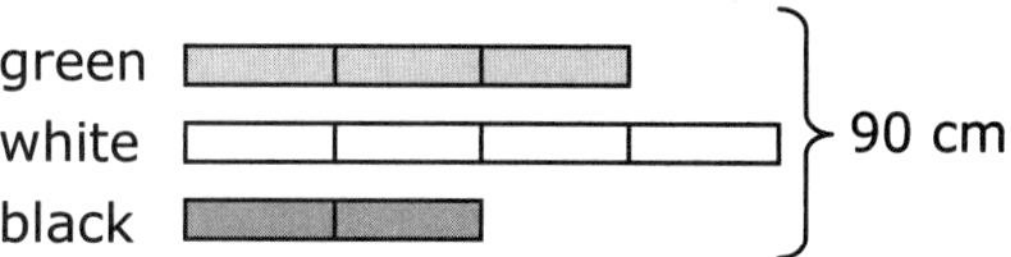

   (a) 3 units = 10 x 3 = 30 cm
   30 cm was painted green.

   (b) 2 units = 10 x 2 = 20 cm
   20 cm was painted black.

7. 6 units = 24 m^3
   1 unit = 24 ÷ 6 = 4 m^3

   (a) 1 unit = 4 m^3
   4 m^3 cement was used.

   (b) 2 units = 4 x 2 = 8 m^3
   8 m^3 sand was used.

8. 5 units = 30 kg
   17 units = $\frac{30}{5}$ x 17 = 102 kg
   Total weight = **102 kg**
   (**3d›** Ryan ↔ Raju)

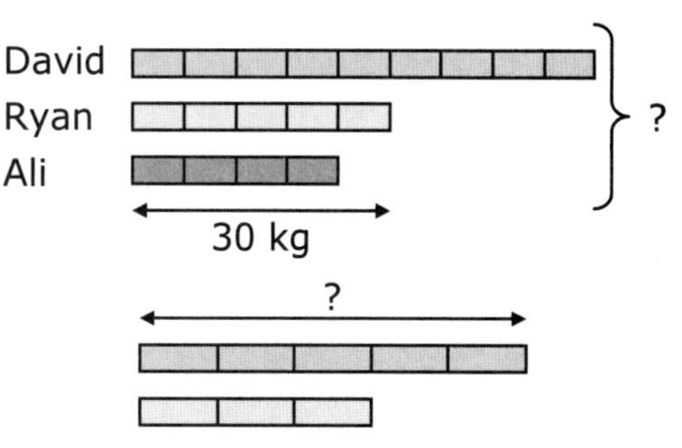

9. 2 units = \$30
   5 units = \$$\frac{30}{2}$ x 5 = \$75
   The biggest share is **\$75.**

Unit 6 – Angles

Part 1 – Measuring Angles (pp. 83-84)

(1) Measuring Angles

- Estimate and measure angles.

Students learned how to measure angles in *Primary Mathematics 4A*. This is reviewed here.

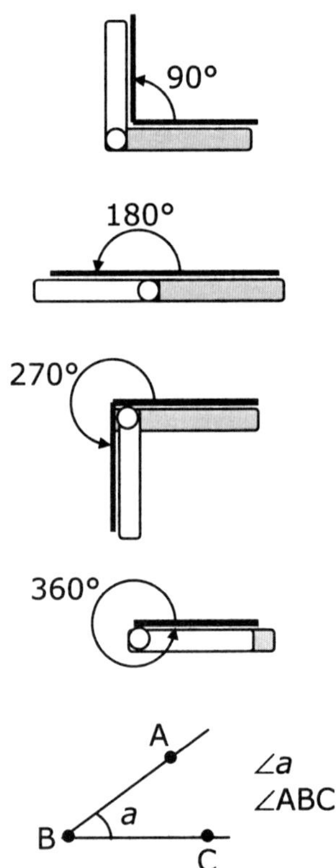

Remind your student that angles are a measure of the amount, or degree, of turning from one line to another line with a common point. The angle does not depend on the length of the lines. You can use two pieces of cardboard connected at one end with a brad to demonstrate the concept of an angle as an amount of turning. Ask your student for the number of degrees in one full turn around a circle (360°). Form a right angle with the strips, a quarter turn, or draw a right angle. Ask for the number of degrees in a right angle (90°). Similarly, make sure your student knows the number of degrees in a half-turn (180°) and a three quarter turn (270°). Have your student tell you the number of right angles in a quarter turn, half turn, three quarter turn, or full turn.

Remind your student that *angle* is abbreviated with ∠. An angle is named with a lowercase letter, or with three points named with uppercase letters, one on each arm and one at the vertex, with the one at the vertex in the middle.

Draw some angles less than 180° and have your student measure them with a protractor. He should be able to estimate whether the angle will be greater than or less than 90°. He should also be able to estimate whether the angle is close to 10°, 30°, 45°, or 60°. Note that 45° is half of a right angle. 30° and 60° are one third and two thirds of a right angle.

p. 83

An angle greater than 180° can be measured either by measuring the amount of turning past 180° and adding that to 180°, or measuring the opposite (smaller) angle formed and subtracting from 360°. Note that $\angle m$ is larger than two right angles. Have your student use both methods to find the measure of $\angle n$. Note that $\angle n$ is larger than three right angles. Ask your student how much larger it is than 3 right angles.

$\angle n = 180° + 130° = 310°$
$\angle n = 360° - 50° = 310°$

Learning Task 1, p. 84

Have your student estimate these angles before measuring.

1. x = **123°**
   y = **240°**
   z = **325°**

Draw some additional angles for your student to estimate and measure.

Have your student draw angles of various sizes with a protractor.

Workbook Exercise 39

(2) Compass Points and Angles

- Tell direction in relation to an 8-point compass.
- Determine the angle between various points on the compass.

Make sure your student understands what it means to turn in a clockwise or in a counterclockwise direction. Use an analog (face) clock to demonstrate.

Give your student a circle and have him fold it into eighths (three folds). He can mark each crease with a line. Have him label them with the eight points of the compass. Ask him for the angle between each line (45°). Discuss the angles between various points of the compass. For example, ask him for the angle between north and southwest, both clockwise and counterclockwise.

Have your student face north and hold his arms out. Ask him to point to different directions ("Where is south-west?") Ask him where he would be facing if he turned 45° clockwise or counterclockwise. Repeat with other multiples of 45°. Ask him to turn to a certain direction and then give you the number angle he turned through. For example, have him face north and turn clockwise to the south-east. He turned 135°. Repeat with different starting position. For example, have him face west and turn counterclockwise to the north-east. Or, have him face south-west and tell him to turn 270° clockwise and give the direction he is facing.

Let your student use a compass and locate points in various directions.

(**3d›** counterclockwise ↔ anticlockwise)

Learning Tasks 2-3, p. 84

2. (a) 45° x 3 = **135°** (b) **45°**

3. (a) **north-east** (b) **north-west**

Workbook Exercise 40

Part 2 - Finding Unknown Angles (pp. 85-88)

(1) Finding Unknown Angles

- Recognize that vertically opposite angles of intersecting lines are equal.
- Recognize that adjacent angles on a straight line add up to 180°.
- Recognize that all angles around the intersection of lines add up to 360°.
- Find unknown angles involving vertically opposite angles, angles formed by lines intersecting at a point on a straight line, and angles formed by lines intersecting at a point.

In *Primary Mathematics* 4A students learned that given a right angle divided into two parts and the angle of one of those parts, they can find the angle for the other part by finding the difference between the known angle and 90°.

Here they will learn some more angle properties that can be used to find unknown angles involving intersecting lines.

Angles that add up to 90° are called complementary angles and those that add up to 180° are called supplementary angles. It is not a requirement of this curriculum that they memorize those terms at this time, but you can use and define them in discussion if you wish.

p. 85

Students should measure the unknown angles.

$\angle a$ = 34°
$\angle b$ = **146°**
$\angle c$ = **34°**
$\angle d$ = **146°** $\angle a = \angle c$ and $\angle b = \angle d$

Also ask your student to find
$\angle a + \angle b$, $\angle b + \angle c$, $\angle c + \angle d$, $\angle d + \angle a$
They all add to 180°.

Each of the two sums are on either side of a line that runs into a straight line, whose angle is 180°.

Draw a few more intersecting angles and have your student measure the angles to see that vertically opposite angles are equal in each case.

p. 86

Students should measure the unknown angles.

$\angle q$ = **85°**
$\angle r$ = **45°**
$\angle p + \angle q + \angle r$ = **180°**

Note that the angles on a straight line divide up a half-turn, which is 180°. Draw some other examples for your student to measure.

$\angle y$ = **150°**
$\angle z$ = **150°**
$\angle x + \angle y + \angle z$ = **360°**

Note that the angles at a point divide up a complete turn, which is 360°. Draw some other examples for your student to measure.

Learning Tasks pp. 87-88

Remind your student that a little square drawn in an angle indicates that the angle is a right angle. Tell your student that these figures are not drawn exactly to scale, so they cannot find the unknown angles by direct measurement. They must use angle properties to find the unknown angles by calculation. As you go through the learning tasks, ask your student to give you the reason for each step orally. Do not require your student to write them down.

1. (a) $\angle p$ = **48°** (b) $\angle q$ = **143°** (c) $\angle r$ = **345°**

2. $\angle x$ = 180° - 46° = **134°**
 $\angle y = \angle w$ = **46°**
 $\angle z = \angle x$ = **134°**

3. $\angle$COB = $\angle$AOD = $\angle$AOE + $\angle$EOD = 105° + 50° = **155°**

4. **90°**

5. **35°**

6. **40°**

7. $\angle a$ = 180° – 75° – 76° = **29°**
 $\angle b$ = 360° – 60° – 90° – 65° = **145°**
 $\angle c$ = 125° – 40° = **85°**

Workbook Exercise 41

Review B (pp. 89-92)

 **Review B, pp. 89-92**

1. **19,000**
2. **$43,000**
3. (a) **6,700** (b) **72,800** (c) **350,000**
   (d) **430** (e) **580** (f) **628**
4. 5 stars = 60
   2 stars = $\frac{60}{5}$ x 2 = **24**
5. 3 ℓ = 3,000 ml
   $\frac{800}{3,000} = \mathbf{\frac{4}{15}}$
6. Fraction sold = $\frac{6}{24} = \mathbf{\frac{1}{4}}$
7. $\frac{1}{4}$ h = $\frac{1}{4}$ x 60 min = 15 min
   $2\frac{1}{4}$ h = **2 h 15 min**
8. $\frac{3}{5}$ m = $\frac{3}{5}$ x 100 cm = 3 x 20 cm = **60 cm**
9. (a) Mary has $25 + $10 = $35
   Amber has 3 x $35 = **$105** (**3d›** Amber ↔ Minah)
   (b) Amber has $105 – $25 = **$80** more than Lily.
   (c) Together they have $25 + $35 + $105 = **$165**.
10. Fraction remaining = $1 - \frac{5}{8} = \frac{3}{8}$
    Amount of string remaining = $\frac{3}{\not{8}_1} \times \not{8}^1$ = **3 m**
11. Length of each piece = $\frac{4}{5} \div 8 = \frac{\not{4}^1}{5} \times \frac{1}{\not{8}_2} = \mathbf{\frac{1}{10}}$ **m**
12. Number sold = $\frac{3}{\not{4}_1} \times \not{64}^{16}$ = **48**
13. Fraction of flour left = $1 - \frac{2}{5} = \frac{3}{5}$
    Amount left = $\frac{3}{5}$ x 2 = $\frac{6}{5} = \mathbf{1\frac{1}{5}}$ **kg**

14. 1500

men

single (**3d›** single ↔ Malaysians)

12 units = 1,500

1 unit $= \frac{1{,}500}{12}$

3 units $= \frac{1{,}500}{12} \times 3 = 375$

There were **375** single men.

Or:

$\frac{3}{10} \times \frac{5}{6} \times 1{,}500 = 375$

15. 3 units = $756

2 unit $= \$\frac{756}{3} \times 2 = \$504$

She had **$504** left.

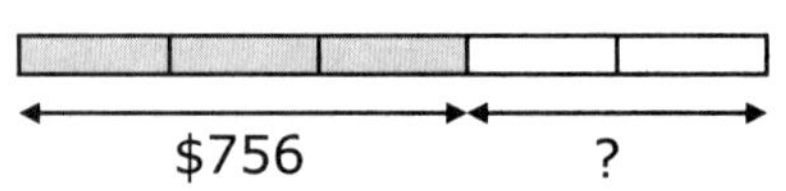

16. 1 unit = Brett's money

Maria's money = 1 unit + $60

4 units = $600 – $60 = $540

1 unit $= \$\frac{540}{4} = \$135$

Maria's money = $135 + $60 = **$195**

(**3d›** Dan ↔ Ali, Brett ↔ Ramat

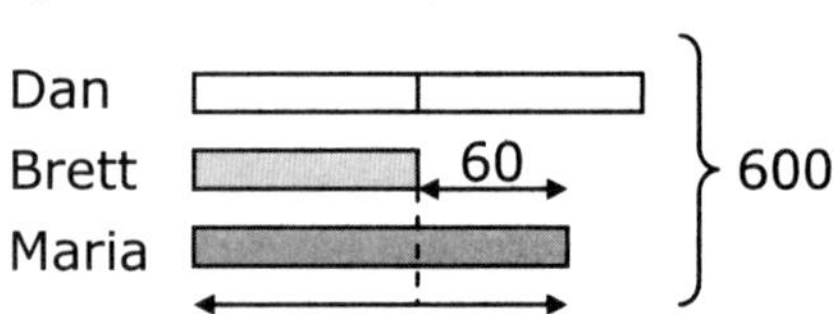

17. Total fruit picked = 257 + 493 = 750

Groups of 50 = 750 ÷ 50 = 15

Money received = 15 x $3 = **$45**

18. Total number of oranges = 40 x 24 = 960

Number of oranges sold = 960 – 15 = 945

Groups of 3 = 945 ÷ 3 = 315

Money received = 315 x $1 = $315

Profit = $315 – $258 = **$57**

19. 5 units = $180

1 unit = $180 ÷ 5 = $36

John received **$36** more.

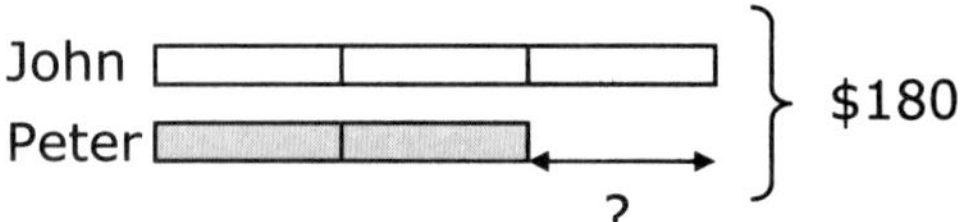

20. Length = 4 units; Width = 3 units

Length = 4 units = 20 m

Width = 3 units $= \frac{20}{4} \times 3 = 15$ m

Area = 15 m x 20 m = **300 m^2**

Perimeter = 2 x (20 + 15) = 2 x 35 = **70 m**

21. 3 units = \$30

$1 \text{ unit} = \$\frac{30}{3} = \$10$

12 units = \$10 x 12 = \$120

Total sum of money = **\$120**

\$30

Sean

Ryan

John

?

(**3d>** Sean ↔ Sumin, Ryan ↔ Raju)

22. Area = **9 cm²** (count the squares, or (3 x 2) + 3)
Perimeter = 2 + 3 + 2 + 1 + 1 + 3 + 1 + 1 = **14 cm**
(Or: Push the sides out; perimeter is 2 x (3 + 4) = 2 x 7 = 14 cm)

23. Methods may vary.
   (a) Perimeter = 2 x (12 + 8) + (2 + 2) = 40 + 4 = **44 m**
   Area = (12 x 8) – (6 x 2) = 96 – 12 = **84 m²**

   (b) Perimeter = 2 x (15 + 14) = 2 x 29 = **58 cm**
   Area = (15 x 14) – (10 x 5) – (5 x 4) = 210 - 50 – 20 = **140 cm²**

24. (a) $\angle a$ = **160°** (b) $\angle b$ = **205°**

25. (a) x = 360° – 63° – 90° = **207°** (b) $\angle x$ = 90° – 43° = **47°**

26. (a) Area = $\frac{1}{2}$ x 10 x 15 = **75 cm²** (b) Area = $\frac{1}{2}$ x 12 x 7 = **42 cm²** (c) Area = $\frac{1}{2}$ x 6 x 6 = **18 cm²**

27. base = 36 – 9 – 15 = 12 m
area = $\frac{1}{2}$ x 12 x 9 = **54 m²**

28. (a) Base = 20 – 10 – 4 = 6 cm
   Height = 8 cm
   Area = $\frac{1}{2}$ x 6 x 8 = **24 cm²**

   (b) Base = 10 cm
   Height = 5 cm
   Area = $\frac{1}{2}$ x 10 x 5 = **25 cm²**

   (c) Area of = 12 x 24 = 288 cm²
   Base of unshaded Δ = 4 cm
   Area of Δ = $\frac{1}{2}$ x 4 x 24
   = 48 cm²
   Shaded area = 288 - 48
   = **240 cm²**

   (d) Base = 2 cm
   Height = 10 cm
   Area = $\frac{1}{2}$ x 2 x 10 = **10 cm²**

US› Review C (pp. 93-96)

 **Review C, pp. 93-96**

1. **5800 mi**

2. David's weight = $\frac{1}{2}(259 - 17)$
   = **121 lb**

3. Total cups = 5 c x 4 = 20 c   Total quarts = 20 x $\frac{1}{4}$ qt = **5 qt**

4. Length for each napkin = 5 yd ÷ 12 = $\frac{5}{12}$ yd = $\frac{5}{12}$ x 3 ft = $\frac{5}{4}$ ft = $\mathbf{1\frac{1}{4}}$ ft

5. Amount in each jug = $\mathbf{\frac{4}{5}}$ **qt** (or 0.8 qt)

6. Weight of each share = $\frac{8}{12}$ lb = $\frac{2}{3}$ lb
   $\frac{2}{3}$ x 16 oz = $\frac{32}{3}$ oz = $\mathbf{10\frac{2}{3}}$ **oz**

7. 12 in. x 12 in. x 12 in. = **1728 in.^{3}**

8. (a) 3 lb = 48 oz $\frac{8}{48} = \frac{1}{6}$ 8 oz is $\mathbf{\frac{1}{6}}$ of 3 lb
   (b) 2 gal = 8 qt 3 qt is $\mathbf{\frac{3}{8}}$ of 2 gal
   (c) 2 qt = 8 c $\frac{4}{8} = \frac{1}{2}$ 4 c is $\mathbf{\frac{1}{2}}$ of 2 qt
   (or, if there are 4 c in 1 qt, then 4 c is half of 2 qt)

9. $\frac{3}{4}$ ft = $\frac{3}{4}$ x 12 in. = **9 in.**

10. Amount left $\frac{4}{5}$ x 6 lb = $\frac{24}{5}$ lb = $\mathbf{4\frac{4}{5}}$ **lb**

11. length = 5 units = 30 yd
    1 unit = 30 ÷ 5 = 6 yd
    width = 2 units = 6 yd x 2 = 12 yd
    perimeter = 2 x (30 yd + 12 yd) = 2 x 42 yd = **84 yd**
    area = 30 yd x 12 yd = **360 yd^2**

12. (a) Perimeter = **42 ft** Area = **68 ft^2**
(b) Perimeter = **40 in.** Area = **69 in.^{2}**

13. 1 gal = 16 c
$\frac{1}{4}$ gal = $\frac{1}{4}$ x 16 c = 4 c
$2\frac{1}{4}$ gal = **2 gal 4 c**

14. Length for each case = 8.7 ft ÷ 5 = **1.74 ft**

15. side x side = 81 in.^{2}
side = 9 in.
perimeter = 9 in. x 4 = **36 in.**

16. 1 lb 11 oz – 15 oz = 1 oz + 11 oz = **12 oz**

17. (a) 18 in. = 12 in. + 6 in. = **1 ft 6 in.**
(b) 28 in. = 24 in. + 4 in. = **2 ft 4 in.**
(c) 57 in. = 48 in. + 9 in. = **4 ft 9 in.**

18. Volume = 6 in. x 6 in. x 6 in. = **216 in.^{3}**

19. Volume = 12 ft x 6 ft x 7 ft = **504 ft^3**

20. $\frac{2}{3} \rightarrow$ 6 c
$\frac{1}{3} \rightarrow$ 6 c ÷ 2 = 3 c
$\frac{3}{3} \rightarrow$ 3 c x 3 = **9 c**

Or:

6 c

2 units = 6 c
1 unit = 3 c
3 units = 3 c x 3 = 9 c

21. Amount drunk in 3 weeks = 3 x 7 x 2 c = 42 c = 40 c + 2 c = **10 qt 2 c**

22. (a) 3 yd 2 ft x 7
= 21 yd 14 ft
= 21 yd + 12 ft + 2 ft
= 21 yd + 4 yd + 2 ft
= **25 yd 2 ft**

(b) 5 lb 14 oz x 3
= 15 lb 42 oz
= 15 lb + 32 oz + 10 oz
= 15 lb + 2 lb + 10 oz
= **17 lb 10 oz**

(c) 4 gal 3 qt x 5
= 20 gal 15 qt
= 20 gal + 12 qt + 3 qt
= 20 gal + 3 gal + 3 qt
= **23 gal 3 qt**

(d) 2 ft 11 in. x 2
= 4 ft 22 in.
= 4 ft + 12 in. + 10 in.
= 4 ft + 1 ft + 10 in.
= **5 ft 10 in.**

23. (a) 3 yd 1 ft ÷ 2 = (2 yd + 3 ft + 1 ft) ÷ 2 = (2 yd + 4 ft) ÷ 2 = **1 yd 2 ft**
   (b) 2 lb 10 oz ÷ 6 = (32 oz + 10 oz) ÷ 6 = 42 oz ÷ 6 = **7 oz**
   (c) 6 gal 3 qt ÷ 3 = (6 gal ÷ 3) + (3 qt ÷ 3) = **2 gal 1 qt**
   (d) 2 ft 8 in. ÷ 4 = (24 in. + 8 in.) ÷ 4 = 32 in. ÷ 4 = **8 in.**

24. Length of rope = 1 ft 6 in. x 3 = 3 ft 18 in. = 3 ft + 12 in. + 6 in. = **4 ft 6 in.**

25. (a) $\frac{1}{3}$ x 24 yd = 1 x 8 yd = **8 yd**
   (b) $\frac{4}{5}$ x 35 in. = 4 x 7 in. = 28 in. = **2 ft 4 in.**
   (c) $1\frac{1}{2}$ x 14 oz = 14 oz + 7 oz = 21 oz = **1 lb 5 oz**
   (d) $\frac{5}{6}$ x 12 gal = 5 x 2 gal = **10 gal**

26. 7 lb 9 oz + 12 oz = 7 lb + 5 oz + 4 oz + 12 oz
   = 7 lb + 5 oz + 1 lb
   = **8 lb 5 oz**

27. Distance jogged on Sat. = 2.2 mi – 0.7 mi = 1.5 mi
   Total distance = 1.5 mi + 2.2 mi = **3.7 mi**

28. Weight of 5 bars = 3.4 lb – 1.1 lb = 2.3 lb
   Weight of 1 bar = 2.3 lb ÷ 5 = **0.46 lb**

29. Total spent = ($\frac{1}{2}$ x \$3.50) + (2 x \$1.95) = \$1.75 x \$3.90 = **\$5.65**

30. 258.8 lb

31. 2.5 ft = 24 in. + 6 in. = 30 in.
   2.25 ft = 24 in. + 3 in. = 27 in.
   0.5 yd = 1.5 ft = 12 in. + 6 in. = 18 in.
   37 in. is greatest.

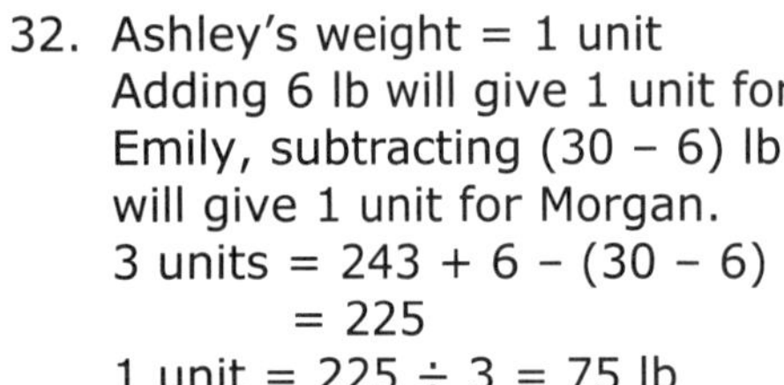
32. Ashley's weight = 1 unit
   Adding 6 lb will give 1 unit for Emily, subtracting (30 – 6) lb will give 1 unit for Morgan.
   3 units = 243 + 6 – (30 – 6)
   = 225
   1 unit = 225 ÷ 3 = 75 lb
   Ashley weighs **75 lb**

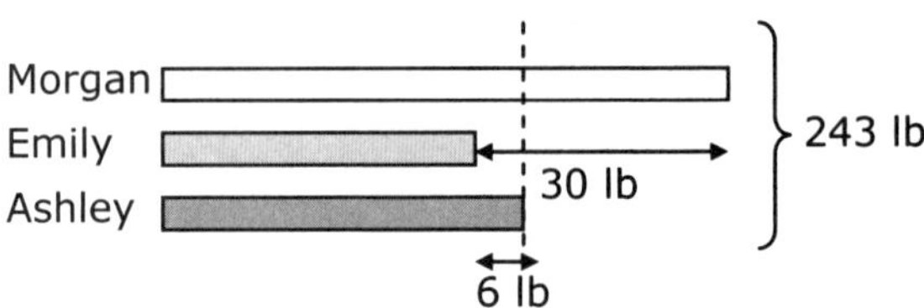

Workbook Answers and Solutions

Exercise 1

1. (a) **24,608** (b) **16,011** (c) **99,009** (d) **312,460**
   (e) **802,003** (f) **540,014** (g) **900,909**

2. (a) **Fifty thousand, two hundred thirty-four**
   (b) **Twenty-six thousand, eight**
   (c) **Seventy-three thousand, five hundred six**
   (d) **Three hundred sixty-seven thousand, four hundred fifty**
   (e) **Five hundred six thousand, nine**
   (f) **Four hundred thirty thousand, sixteen**
   (g) **Eight hundred thousand, five hundred fifty**

3. (a) **7,000** (b) **6; 60,000** (c) **hundreds** (d) **40**

4. (a) **42,108** (b) **562,032** (c) **770,077** (d) **900,214**

5. (a) **800** (b) **300,000** (c) **3,000** (d) **8**

6. (a) **36,552**
   37,552
   (b) **71,880**
   72,080
   (c) **30,361**
   31,361

7. (a) **31,862** (b) **42,650** (c) **33,856** (d) **65,703**

8. For the greatest number, arrange the digits in order from greatest to smallest. For the smallest number, arrange the digits in order from smallest to greatest.

	Greatest number	Smallest number
9, 6, 4, 1, 3	**96,431**	**13,469**
1, 1, 6, 8, 7	**87,611**	**11,678**

Exercise 2

1. (a) **3,000,000** (b) **4,150,000** (c) **6,031,000** (d) **7,208,000**
   (e) **5,005,000** (f) **9,909,000** (g) **10,000,000**

2. (a) **Four million**
   (b) **Three million, forty thousand**
   (c) **Six million, three hundred fifty thousand**
   (d) **Five million, six thousand**
   (e) **Seven million, seven hundred three thousand**
   (f) **Nine million, ninety-nine thousand**
   (g) **Eight million, five hundred sixty-seven thousand**

3. **$2,003,705** **Two million, three thousand, seven hundred five dollars**

4. **$2,400,000** **Two million, four hundred thousand dollars**

Exercise 3

1. (a) **300** (b) **1,320**
2. (a) **6,000** (b) **36,300**
3. (a) **46,000** (b) **236,000**
4. (a) **245,000** (b) **248,000**
5. (a) **43,190** (b) **14,600**
   (c) **83,000** (d) **196,000**
6. (a) **$4,400** (b) **$5,300**
   (c) **$26,100** (d) **$39,700**
   (e) **$59,900** (f) **$62,300**
7. (a) **$3,000** (b) **$6,000**
   (c) **$18,000** (d) **$25,000**
   (e) **$44,000** (f) **$49,000**
   (g) **$329,000** (h) **$693,000**

Exercise 4

1. (a) **36,000** (b) **13,000** (c) **40,000**
2. (a) **49,000** (b) **4,000** (c) **39,000**
3. (a) **1,600** (b) **2,000** (c) **12,000**
4. (a) **300** (b) **300** (c) **800**
5. (a) 3,064 + 5,604 ≈ 3,000 + 6,000 = **9,000**
   (b) 4,831 + 8,205 ≈ 5,000 + 8,000 = **13,000**
   (c) 25,468 + 6,925 ≈ 25,000 + 7,000 = **32,000**
   (d) 86,723 + 9,207 ≈ 87,000 + 9,000 = **96,000**
   (e) 7,356 − 3,988 ≈ 7,000 − 4,000 = **3,000**
   (f) 9,306 − 4,568 ≈ 9,000 − 5,000 = **4,000**
   (g) 36,547 − 8,865 ≈ 37,000 − 9,000 = **28,000**
   (h) 63,006 − 1008 ≈ 63,000 − 1000 = **62,000**
6. (a) 3,306 x 2 ≈ 3,000 x 2 = **6,000**
   (b) 4,811 x 4 ≈ 5,000 x 4 = **20,000**
   (c) 8,286 x 6 ≈ 8,000 x 6 = **48,000**
   (d) 9,560 x 5 ≈ 10,000 x 5 = **50,000**
   (e) 6,146 ÷ 3 ≈ 6,000 ÷ 3 = **2,000**
   (f) 4,759 ÷ 6 ≈ 4,800 ÷ 6 = **800**
   (g) 5,268 ÷ 5 ≈ 5,000 ÷ 5 = **1,000**
   (h) 6,398 ÷ 9 ≈ 6,300 ÷ 9 = **700**

Exercise 5

1. (a) **2,540** (b) **60,200**
   (c) **3,720** (d) **57,000**
   (e) **25,800** (f) **313,600**
   (g) **360,000** (h) **2,415,000**

   Answers in questions 2, 3 and 4 may differ according to the method used.

2. (a) $326 \times 47 \approx 300 \times 50$
   $= \mathbf{15{,}000}$

   (b) $78 \times 586 \approx 80 \times 600$
   $= \mathbf{48{,}000}$

   (c) $32 \times 705 \approx 30 \times 700$
   $= \mathbf{21{,}000}$

   (d) $4{,}165 \times 53 \approx 4{,}000 \times 50$
   $= \mathbf{200{,}000}$

3. 28 x \$229 ≈ 30 x \$200 = **\$6,000**

4. 114 in. x 92 in. ≈ 100 in. x 92 in. = **9,200 in.^{2}** **<US**
   114 cm x 92 cm ≈ 100 cm x 92 cm = **9,200 cm^2** **<3d**

Exercise 6

1. (a) $36\cancel{0} \div 1\cancel{0} = \mathbf{36}$ (b) $4{,}2\cancel{00} \div 1\cancel{00} = \mathbf{42}$
   (c) $25\cancel{0} \div 5\cancel{0} = \mathbf{5}$ (d) $5{,}6\cancel{00} \div 8\cancel{00} = \mathbf{7}$
   (e) $1{,}05\cancel{0} \div 7\cancel{0} = \mathbf{15}$ (f) $6{,}0\cancel{00} \div 4\cancel{00} = \mathbf{15}$
   (g) $63{,}0\cancel{00} \div 9{,}0\cancel{00} = \mathbf{7}$ (h) $96{,}\cancel{000} \div 6{,}\cancel{000} = \mathbf{16}$

   Answers in questions 2, 3 and 4 may differ according to the method used.

2. (a) $282 \div 52 \approx 300 \div 50 = \mathbf{6}$ (b) $324 \div 42 \approx 320 \div 40 = \mathbf{8}$
   (c) $4{,}406 \div 49 \approx 4{,}500 \div 50 = \mathbf{90}$ (d) $1{,}705 \div 31 \approx 1{,}800 \div 30 = \mathbf{60}$

3. \$805 ÷ 28 ≈ \$900 ÷ 30 = **\$30**

4. 1,044 m^2 ÷ 36 m ≈ 1,200 ÷ 40 = **30 m**

Exercise 7

1. (a) $\underline{48 + 12} + 37$
   $= \underline{60 + 37}$
   $= \mathbf{97}$

   (b) $\underline{40 - 14} - 9$
   $= \underline{26 - 9}$
   $= \mathbf{17}$

   (c) $\underline{36 + 18} - 19$
   $= \underline{54 - 19}$
   $= \mathbf{35}$

   (d) $\underline{51 - 35} + 18$
   $= \underline{16 + 18}$
   $= \mathbf{34}$

   (e) $\underline{7 \times 5} \times 8$
   $= \underline{35 \times 8}$
   $= \mathbf{280}$

   (f) $\underline{96 \div 3} \div 4$
   $= \underline{32 \div 4}$
   $= \mathbf{8}$

(g) 14 x 9 ÷ 3
= 126 ÷ 3
= **42**

(h) 64 ÷ 8 x 5
= 8 x 5
= **40**

2. (a) 84 + 6 x 8
= 84 + 48
= **132**

(b) 140 – 40 x 3
= 140 – 120
= **20**

(c) 46 + 32 ÷ 8
= 46 + 4
= **50**

(d) 100 – 60 ÷ 4
= 100 – 15
= **85**

(e) 8 x 6 + 14
= 48 + 14
= **62**

(f) 80 + 18 ÷ 6
= 80 + 3
= **83**

(g) 12 x 10 – 5
= 120 – 5
= **115**

(h) 72 + 6 x 6
= 72 + 36
= **108**

3. (a) 70 + 24 ÷ 6 – 4
= 70 + 4 – 4
= 74 – 4
= **70**

(b) 125 ÷ 5 – 12 x 2
= 25 – 12 x 2
= 25 – 24
= **1**

(c) 160 – 60 ÷ 4 x 3
= 160 – 15 x 3
= 160 – 45
= **115**

(d) 32 + 8 + 30 x 2
= 32 + 8 + 60
= 40 + 60
= **100**

(e) 52 – 35 ÷ 7 – 7 x 2
= 52 – 5 – 14
= 47 – 14
= **33**

(f) 9 x 8 – 6 x 10
= 72 – 60
= **12**

(g) 7 x 8 + 24 ÷ 8
= 56 + 3
= **59**

(h) 63 ÷ 9 + 20 ÷ 10
= 7 + 2
= **9**

Exercise 8

1. (a) 69 + (46 – 15)
= 69 + 31
= **100**

(b) 90 – (24 + 36)
= 90 – 60
= **30**

(c) 52 – (40 – 22)
= 52 – 18
= **34**

(d) (31 – 20) – 8
= 11 – 8
= **3**

(e) 8 x (3 x 2)
= 8 x 6
= **48**

(f) 84 ÷ (4 ÷ 2)
= 84 ÷ 2
= **42**

(g) 9 x (20 ÷ 5)
= 9 x 4
= **36**

(h) 45 ÷ (15 x 3)
= 45 ÷ 45
= **1**

2. (a) (19 + 16) ÷ 5
= 35 ÷ 5
= **7**

(b) 12 x (9 – 4)
= 12 x 5
= **60**

(c) 64 ÷ (8 – 6)
= 64 ÷ 2
= **32**

(d) (14 + 6) x 5
= 20 x 5
= **100**

(e) 10 x (15 ÷ 5)
= 10 x 3
= **30**

(f) (100 – 44) ÷ 7
= 56 ÷ 7
= **8**

(g) 72 ÷ (9 – 3)
= 72 ÷ 6
= **12**

(h) (28 – 18) x 10
= 10 x 10
= **100**

3. (a) 20 + (8 + 4) ÷ 3
= 20 + 12 ÷ 3
= 20 + 4
= **24**

(b) 16 + (9 – 3) x 5
= 16 + 6 x 5
= 16 + 30
= **46**

(c) 7 x (4 + 2) x 8
= 7 x 6 x 8
= 42 x 8
= **336**

(d) 7 x (13 – 6) – 19
= 7 x 7 – 19
= 49 – 19
= **30**

(e) 60 + (18 + 7) ÷ 5
= 60 + 25 ÷ 5
= 60 + 5
= **65**

(f) 8 x (11 - 8) ÷ 6
= 8 x 3 ÷ 6
= 24 ÷ 6
= **4**

(g) 24 ÷ 6 + 3 x (6 – 4)
= 4 + 3 x 2
= 4 + 6
= **10**

(h) 30 + (28 – 8) ÷ 5 x 2
= 30 + 20 ÷ 5 x 2
= 30 + 4 x 2
= 30 + 8
= **38**

Exercise 9

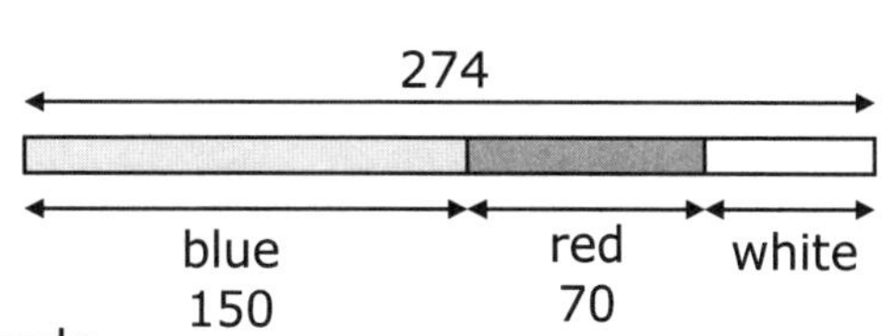

1. Number of white beads
= 274 – 150 – 70 = 54
Red beads – white beads = 70 – 54 = 16
There are **16** more red beads than white beads.

2. Cost of tickets for adults = \$15 x 4 = \$60
Cost of tickets for children = \$8 x 5 = \$40
Total cost of tickets = \$60 + \$40 = \$100
He spends **\$100** altogether.

3. 2 units = 314 – 66 = 248
1 unit = 248 ÷ 2 = 124
She sold **124** bottles in the morning.

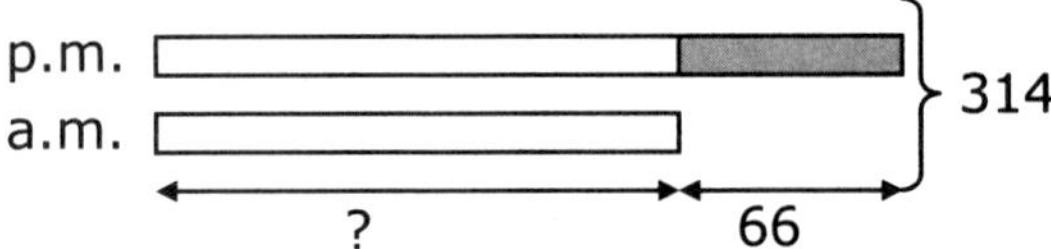

4. Cost of pen is 1 unit. Cost of book is 3 units. Total cost is 4 units.
4 units = \$112
1 unit = \$112 ÷ 4 = \$28
3 units = \$28 x 3 = \$84
The book costs **\$84**.

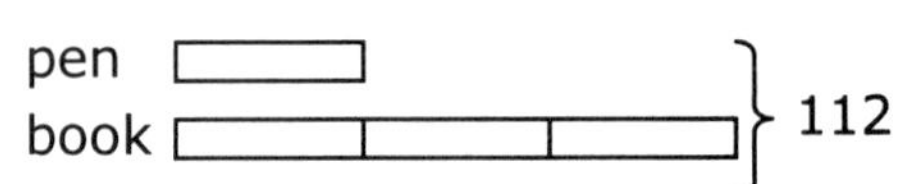

Exercise 10

1. Since a T-shirt costs 3 times as much as a tank top, we can make the cost of a tank-top one unit and the cost of T-shirt 3 units. The cost of 2 T-shirts would then be 6 units.
9 units = \$36
1 unit = \$36 ÷ 9 = \$4
6 units = \$4 x 6 = \$24
He spent **\$24** on the T-shirts.

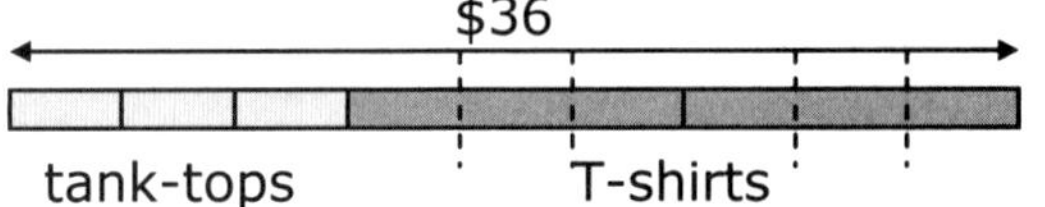

2. We need to find cost price and selling price. How much he made is the difference. To find cost price, find the cost of 45 cards. Since 3 cards cost \$2, divide the 45 cards up into units of 3 to find the number of units of 3:
45 ÷ 3 = 15
Each of the 15 units cost \$2. So
Cost price = 15 x \$2 = \$30
He sold them in units of 5. Find how many units he sold.
45 ÷ 5 = 9
He sold each of these 9 units of 5 cards for \$4. So
Selling price = 9 x \$4 = \$36
Profit = Selling Price – Cost price = \$36 – \$30 = **\$6**

Or, find the cost price and selling price of each card:

Purchase:	Sale:
3 cards cost \$2	5 cards for \$4
1 card cost $\$\frac{2}{3}$	1 card for $\$\frac{4}{5}$
45 cards cost $\$\frac{2}{3} \times 45 = \$30$	45 cards for $\$\frac{4}{5} \times 45 = \$36$

Profit = Selling Price – Cost price = \$36 – \$30 = \$6

3. Cost of 2 boxes of cookies = 2 x $6 = $12 (**3d›** tins of biscuits)
Cost of 6 bottles of milk = 6 x $2 = $12
Amount she spent = $12 + $12 = $24
She had $30 left.
She started with what she spent + what she had left.
Amount she started with = $24 + $30 = **$54**

4. Since we are told that Lily ends up with twice as many as Sara, we can draw units to show this. Since we know they started with the same amount, we can add a part to bring both out to the same amount.
From the diagram, we can find 1 unit subtracting 18 from 25.
1 unit = $25 – $18 = $7
Money before = $7 + $25 = $32
They each had **$32** at first.

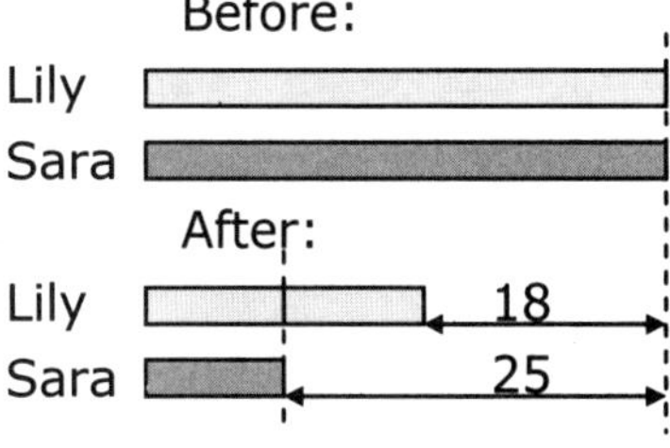

(**3d›** Sara ↔ Sufen)

Exercise 11

1. (a) **3,120** (b) **2,300**
(c) **1,272** (d) **5,785**
(e) **17,220** (f) **18,540**
(g) **16,256** (h) **66,120**

2. (a) **37,710** (b) **280,560**
(c) **37,400** (d) **80,977**
(e) **85,600** (f) **63,189**
(g) **78,475** (h) **377,522**

Exercise 12

1. (a) **3** (b) **3 r4**
(c) **9 r70** (d) **6 r37**
(e) **3 r2** (f) **1 r39**
(g) **9 r4** (h) **5 r34**

2. (a) **5 r7** (b) **3 r19**
(c) **3 r2** (d) **2 r28**
(e) **5 r51** (f) **8 r21**
(g) **7 r47** (h) **5 r2**

Exercise 13

1. (a) **17 r18** (b) **20 r20**
(c) **15 r7** (d) **13**
(e) **32 r5** (f) **33 r7**
(g) **19 r22** (h) **16 r12**

2. (a) **243** (b) **517 r10**
(c) **120** (d) **318 r7**
(e) **82** (f) **92 r25**
(g) **162 r25** (h) **120 r8**

Review 1

1. (a) **Two thousand, forty-four**
(b) **Fifteen thousand, five hundred eight**
(c) **Three hundred seventy-six thousand, nine hundred twenty**
(d) **Six million, four hundred thousand**

2. (a) **4,008** (b) **27,300**
(c) **60,011** (d) **2,904,000**

3. (a) **58,030** (b) **6,042,500**

4. (a) **4** (b) **10,000**

5. (a) **7,206** (b) **63,440**
(c) **40** (d) **800**

6. (a) **45,832** (b) **30,012**

7. **87,660; 76,435; 64,748; 60,083**

8. (a) **1, 2, 3, 4, 6, 8, 12, 24**
(b) **6, 12, 18, 24, 30, 36, 42, 48, 54, 60, 66, 72**

9. **80,999**

10. (a) 145 − 25 x 4
= 145 − 100
= **45**

(b) 228 ÷ 6 x 2
= 38 x 2
= **76**

(c) 306 − 45 ÷ 9
= 306 − 5
= **301**

(d) 440 − 64 + 36 ÷ 6
= 440 − 64 + 6
= 376 + 6
= **382**

11. (a) 4 h 54 min = (4 x 60) min + 54 min = 240 min + 54 min = **294** min
(b) 3 m 5 cm = (3 x 100) cm + 5 cm = 300 cm + 5 cm = **305** cm
(c) 5 kg 500 g = (5 x 1,000) g + 500 g = 5,000 g + 500 g = **5,500** g
(d) 2,050 g = 2,000 g + 50 g = **2** kg **50** g
(e) 30 months = 24 months + 6 months = **2** years **6** months

12. (a) **49,500** (b) **50,000**

13. (a) 12,099 + 900 = **12,999** (b) 2,100 – 79 = **2,021**
(c) 540 x 28 = **15,120** (d) 127 ÷ 40 = **3 r7**

14. 1 unit = number of boys
4 units = number of girls
5 units = total

boys
girls
200

(a) 5 units = 200
1 unit = 200 ÷ 5 = 40
4 units = 40 x 4 = 160
There are **160** girls.

(b) There are 3 units more girls than boys. Or: 160 – 40 = 120
3 units = 40 x 3 = 120
There are **120** more girls than boys.

15. Solutions can vary; the figure can be divided in different ways.
One way is to divide it into two rectangles by a vertical line.
Area of one rectangle = 12 cm x (5 + 5) cm = 12 cm x 10 cm = 120 cm^2
Area of other rectangle = 8 cm x (5 + 5) cm = 8 cm x 10 cm = 80 cm^2
Total area = 120 cm^2 + 80 cm^2 = **200 cm^2**

16. (a) Area of 1 square = 2 cm x 2 cm
= 4 cm^2
There are 16 squares.
16 x 4 cm^2 = 64 cm^2
The area is **64 cm^2**.

(b) There are 18 edges exposed; each edge is 2 cm.
18 x 2 cm = 36 cm
The perimeter is **36 cm**.

17.

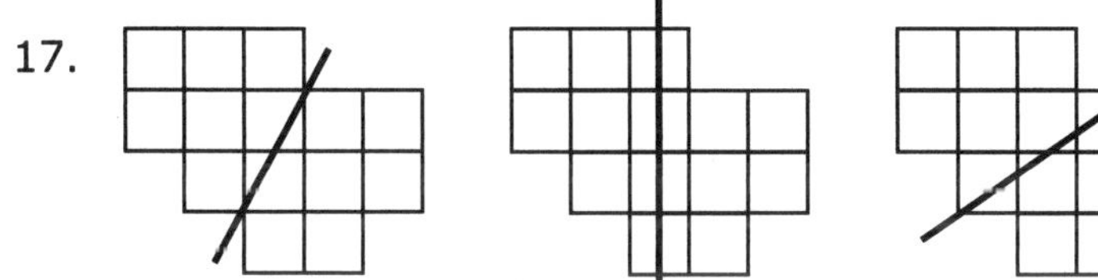

18. (a) Area = (3 in. x 3 in.) + (2 in. x 3 in.) = 9 $in.^2$ + 6 $in.^2$ = **15 $in.^2$**
(b) Starting with the left edge and moving to the right:
Perimeter = (3 x 3 in.) + (2 x 1 in.) + (2 x 2 in.) + 3 in.
= 9 in. + 2 in. + 4 in. + 3 in.
= **18 in.**
(**3d›** in. ↔ cm)

19. Money for 25 melons = 25 x \$6 = \$150
Remaining melons = 45 – 25 = 20
Money for remaining melons = 20 x \$4 = \$80
Total money = \$150 + \$80 = **\$230**

20.

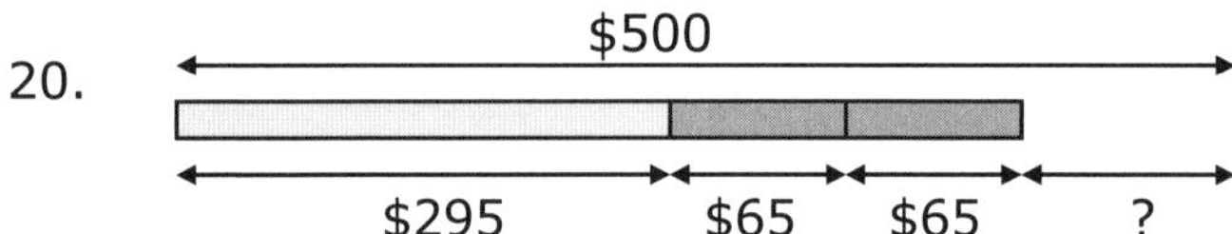

Total money spent = $295 + $65 + $65 = $425
Change = $500 – $425 = **$75**

21.

278
Brandy 64
Jane 500
Sam

(**3d›** Brandy ↔ Lihua, Sam ↔ Samy)

Number of stamps Jane has = 278 + 64 = 342
Sam's stamps = 500 – Jane's stamps = 500 – 342 = **158**

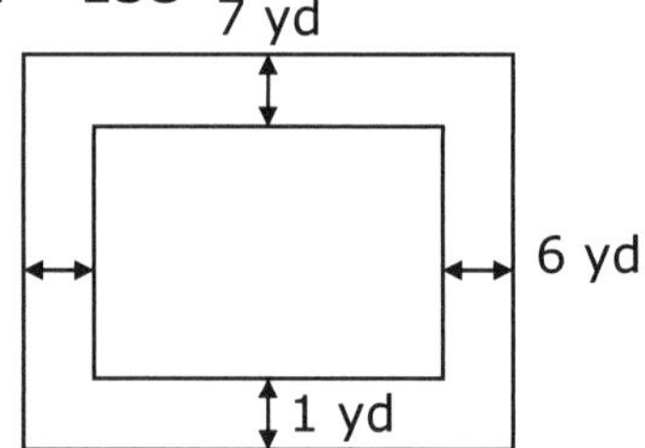

22. Length of carpet = 7 yd – 2 yd = 5 yd
Width of carpet = 6 yd – 2 yd = 4 yd
Area of carpet = 5 yd x 4 yd = 20 yd^2
1 yd^2 → $75
20 yd^2 → 20 x $75 = $1,500
The carpet costs $**1,500**.

(**3d›** yd ↔ m, yd^2 ↔ m^2)

Exercise 14

1. (a) $\mathbf{\frac{3}{2}}$ (b) $\mathbf{\frac{5}{3}}$ (c) $\mathbf{\frac{7}{4}}$

2. $\mathbf{2\frac{2}{3}}$ $\mathbf{3\frac{1}{3}}$ $\mathbf{2\frac{2}{5}}$

   $\mathbf{2\frac{3}{4}}$ $\mathbf{4\frac{3}{5}}$ $\mathbf{6\frac{2}{3}}$

3. (a) **4** (b) $\mathbf{2\frac{1}{5}}$ (c) $\mathbf{2\frac{1}{8}}$ (d) **9**

Exercise 15

1. (a) $\frac{7}{8}+\frac{3}{4}=\frac{7}{8}+\frac{\mathbf{6}}{8}$
$=\frac{8}{8}+\frac{5}{8}$
$=\mathbf{1\frac{5}{8}}$

(b) $\frac{2}{3}+\frac{4}{9}=\frac{\mathbf{6}}{9}+\frac{4}{9}$
$=\frac{9}{9}+\frac{1}{9}$
$=\mathbf{1\frac{1}{9}}$

(c) $\frac{4}{5}+\frac{3}{10}=\frac{8}{10}+\frac{3}{10}$
$=\frac{10}{10}+\frac{1}{10}$
$=\mathbf{1\frac{1}{10}}$

(d) $\frac{3}{4}+\frac{7}{12}=\frac{9}{12}+\frac{7}{12}$
$=\frac{12}{12}+\frac{4}{12}$
$=\mathbf{1\frac{1}{3}}$

(e) $\frac{5}{6}+\frac{2}{3}=\frac{5}{6}+\frac{4}{6}$
$=\frac{6}{6}+\frac{3}{6}$
$=\mathbf{1\frac{1}{2}}$

(f) $\frac{1}{2}+\frac{9}{10}=\frac{5}{10}+\frac{9}{10}$
$=\frac{4}{10}+\frac{10}{10}$
$=\mathbf{1\frac{2}{5}}$

2. (a) $\frac{1}{6}+\frac{3}{4}=\frac{\mathbf{2}}{12}+\frac{\mathbf{9}}{12}$
$=\mathbf{\frac{11}{12}}$

(b) $\frac{5}{9}+\frac{1}{2}=\frac{\mathbf{10}}{18}+\frac{\mathbf{9}}{18}$
$=\frac{18}{18}+\frac{1}{18}$
$=\mathbf{1\frac{1}{18}}$

(c) $\frac{1}{2}+\frac{3}{5}=\frac{5}{10}+\frac{6}{10}$
$=\frac{10}{10}+\frac{1}{10}$
$=\mathbf{1\frac{1}{10}}$

(d) $\frac{2}{5}+\frac{3}{4}=\frac{8}{20}+\frac{15}{20}$
$=\frac{3}{20}+\frac{20}{20}$
$=\mathbf{1\frac{3}{20}}$

(e) $\frac{9}{10}+\frac{1}{6}=\frac{27}{30}+\frac{5}{30}$
$=\frac{30}{30}+\frac{2}{30}$
$=\mathbf{1\frac{1}{15}}$

(f) $\frac{3}{10}+\frac{5}{6}=\frac{9}{30}+\frac{25}{30}$
$=\frac{4}{30}+\frac{30}{30}$
$=\mathbf{1\frac{2}{15}}$

Exercise 16

1. (a) $\frac{7}{8} - \frac{3}{4} = \frac{7}{8} - \frac{\mathbf{6}}{\mathbf{8}}$

$= \frac{\mathbf{1}}{\mathbf{8}}$

(b) $\frac{5}{6} - \frac{1}{12} = \frac{\mathbf{10}}{\mathbf{12}} - \frac{1}{12}$

$= \frac{9}{12}$

$= \frac{\mathbf{3}}{\mathbf{4}}$

(c) $\frac{9}{10} - \frac{1}{2} = \frac{9}{10} - \frac{5}{10}$

$= \frac{4}{10}$

$= \frac{\mathbf{2}}{\mathbf{5}}$

(d) $\frac{11}{12} - \frac{2}{3} = \frac{11}{12} - \frac{8}{12}$

$= \frac{3}{12}$

$= \frac{\mathbf{1}}{\mathbf{4}}$

(e) $1\frac{1}{2} - \frac{3}{4} = 1\frac{2}{4} - \frac{3}{4}$

$= \frac{6}{4} - \frac{3}{4}$

$= \frac{\mathbf{3}}{\mathbf{4}}$

Or:

$1\frac{1}{2} - \frac{3}{4} = 1\frac{2}{4} - \frac{3}{4}$

$= 1 - \frac{3}{4} + \frac{2}{4}$

$= \frac{1}{4} + \frac{2}{4}$

$= \frac{3}{4}$

(f) $1\frac{1}{10} - \frac{3}{5} = 1\frac{1}{10} - \frac{6}{10}$

$= \frac{11}{10} - \frac{6}{10}$

$= \frac{5}{10}$

$= \frac{\mathbf{1}}{\mathbf{2}}$

Or:

$1\frac{1}{10} - \frac{3}{5} = 1\frac{1}{10} - \frac{6}{10}$

$= 1 - \frac{6}{10} + \frac{1}{10}$

$= \frac{4}{10} + \frac{1}{10}$

$= \frac{1}{2}$

2. (a) $\frac{1}{2} - \frac{1}{5} = \frac{\mathbf{5}}{\mathbf{10}} - \frac{\mathbf{2}}{\mathbf{10}} = \frac{\mathbf{3}}{\mathbf{10}}$

(b) $\frac{7}{12} - \frac{3}{8} = \frac{\mathbf{14}}{\mathbf{24}} - \frac{\mathbf{9}}{\mathbf{24}} = \frac{\mathbf{5}}{\mathbf{24}}$

(c) $\frac{3}{4} - \frac{3}{10} = \frac{15}{20} - \frac{6}{20} = \frac{\mathbf{9}}{\mathbf{20}}$

(d) $\frac{9}{10} - \frac{3}{4} = \frac{18}{20} - \frac{15}{20} = \frac{\mathbf{3}}{\mathbf{20}}$

(e) $1\frac{1}{5} - \frac{2}{3} = 1\frac{3}{15} - \frac{10}{15}$

$= \frac{18}{15} - \frac{10}{15}$

$= \mathbf{\frac{8}{15}}$

Or:

$1\frac{1}{5} - \frac{2}{3} = 1\frac{3}{15} - \frac{10}{15}$

$= 1 - \frac{10}{15} + \frac{3}{15}$

$= \frac{5}{15} + \frac{3}{15}$

$= \frac{8}{15}$

(f) $1\frac{1}{10} - \frac{1}{6} = 1\frac{3}{30} - \frac{5}{30}$

$= \frac{33}{30} - \frac{5}{30}$

$= \frac{28}{30}$

$= \mathbf{\frac{14}{15}}$

Or:

$1\frac{1}{10} - \frac{1}{6} = 1\frac{3}{30} - \frac{5}{30}$

$= 1 - \frac{5}{30} + \frac{3}{30}$

$= \frac{25}{30} + \frac{3}{30}$

$= \frac{28}{30}$

$= \frac{14}{15}$

Exercise 17

1. (a) $2\frac{3}{4} + 1\frac{1}{8} = 3\frac{3}{4} + \frac{1}{8}$

$= 3\frac{\mathbf{6}}{8} + \frac{1}{8}$

$= \mathbf{3\frac{7}{8}}$

(b) $1\frac{5}{12} + 3\frac{1}{3} = 4\frac{5}{12} + \frac{1}{3}$

$= 4\frac{5}{12} + \frac{\mathbf{4}}{12}$

$= 4\frac{9}{12}$

$= \mathbf{4\frac{3}{4}}$

(c) $3\frac{7}{10} + 2\frac{2}{5} = 5\frac{7}{10} + \frac{4}{10}$

$= 5\frac{11}{10}$

$= \mathbf{6\frac{1}{10}}$

(d) $2\frac{2}{3} + 2\frac{5}{12} = 4\frac{8}{12} + \frac{5}{12}$

$= 4\frac{13}{12}$

$= \mathbf{5\frac{1}{12}}$

(e) $3\frac{7}{12}+1\frac{3}{4}=4\frac{7}{12}+\frac{9}{12}$
$=4\frac{16}{12}$
$=5\frac{4}{12}$
$=\mathbf{5\frac{1}{3}}$

(f) $1\frac{4}{5}+2\frac{7}{10}=3\frac{8}{10}+\frac{7}{10}$
$=3\frac{15}{10}$
$=4\frac{5}{10}$
$=\mathbf{4\frac{1}{2}}$

2. (a) $2\frac{1}{5}+1\frac{2}{3}=3\frac{1}{5}+\frac{2}{3}$
$=3\frac{\mathbf{3}}{15}+\frac{\mathbf{10}}{15}$
$=\mathbf{3\frac{13}{15}}$

(b) $2\frac{3}{8}+2\frac{1}{6}=4\frac{3}{8}+\frac{1}{6}$
$=4\frac{\mathbf{9}}{24}+\frac{\mathbf{4}}{24}$
$=\mathbf{4\frac{13}{24}}$

(c) $1\frac{2}{5}+5\frac{3}{4}=6\frac{8}{20}+\frac{15}{20}$
$=6\frac{3}{20}+\frac{20}{20}$
$=\mathbf{7\frac{3}{20}}$

(d) $3\frac{1}{2}+2\frac{7}{9}=5\frac{9}{18}+\frac{14}{18}$
$=5\frac{5}{18}+\frac{18}{18}$
$=\mathbf{6\frac{5}{18}}$

(e) $2\frac{3}{10}+2\frac{1}{6}=4\frac{9}{30}+\frac{5}{30}$
$=4\frac{14}{30}$
$=\mathbf{4\frac{7}{15}}$

(f) $2\frac{5}{6}+2\frac{9}{10}=4\frac{25}{30}+\frac{27}{30}$
$=4\frac{30}{30}+\frac{22}{30}$
$=\mathbf{5\frac{11}{15}}$

Exercise 18

1. (a) $3\frac{7}{8}-1\frac{1}{2}=2\frac{7}{8}-\frac{1}{2}$
$=2\frac{7}{8}-\frac{\mathbf{4}}{8}$
$=\mathbf{2\frac{3}{8}}$

(b) $5\frac{4}{5}-2\frac{1}{10}=3\frac{4}{5}-\frac{1}{10}$
$=3\frac{\mathbf{8}}{10}-\frac{\mathbf{1}}{10}$
$=\mathbf{3\frac{7}{10}}$

(c) $4\frac{5}{6} - 2\frac{7}{12} = 2\frac{10}{12} - \frac{7}{12}$

$= 2\frac{3}{12}$

$= \mathbf{2\frac{1}{4}}$

(d) $5\frac{11}{12} - 1\frac{3}{4} = 4\frac{11}{12} - \frac{9}{12}$

$= 4\frac{2}{12}$

$= \mathbf{4\frac{1}{6}}$

(e) $4\frac{1}{9} - 2\frac{2}{3} = 2\frac{1}{9} - \frac{6}{9}$

$= 1\frac{10}{9} - \frac{6}{9}$

$= \mathbf{1\frac{4}{9}}$

(f) $4\frac{1}{4} - 1\frac{5}{12} = 3\frac{3}{12} - \frac{5}{12}$

$= 2\frac{15}{12} - \frac{5}{12}$

$= 2\frac{10}{12}$

$= \mathbf{2\frac{5}{6}}$

2. (a) $4\frac{1}{2} - 1\frac{2}{9} = 3\frac{1}{2} - \frac{2}{9}$

$= 3\frac{\mathbf{9}}{18} - \frac{\mathbf{4}}{18}$

$= \mathbf{3\frac{5}{18}}$

(b) $3\frac{3}{4} - 1\frac{2}{3} = 2\frac{3}{4} - \frac{2}{3}$

$= 2\frac{\mathbf{9}}{12} - \frac{\mathbf{8}}{12}$

$= \mathbf{2\frac{1}{12}}$

(c) $3\frac{5}{9} - 1\frac{1}{2} = 2\frac{10}{18} - \frac{9}{18}$

$= \mathbf{2\frac{1}{18}}$

(d) $4\frac{7}{8} - 2\frac{5}{12} = 2\frac{21}{24} - \frac{10}{24}$

$= \mathbf{2\frac{11}{24}}$

(c) $4\frac{1}{4} - 2\frac{5}{6} - 2\frac{3}{12} - \frac{10}{12}$

$= 1\frac{15}{12} - \frac{10}{12}$

$= \mathbf{1\frac{5}{12}}$

(f) $4\frac{3}{10} - 3\frac{5}{6} = 1\frac{9}{30} - \frac{25}{30}$

$= \frac{39}{30} - \frac{25}{30}$

$= \frac{14}{30}$

$= \mathbf{\frac{7}{15}}$

Exercise 19

1. (a) $\frac{5}{8}$ day = $\frac{5}{8}$ x 24 h
= 5 x 3 h
= **15** h

(b) $\frac{7}{10}$ m = $\frac{7}{10}$ x 100 cm
= 7 x 10 cm
= **70** cm

(c) $\frac{9}{20}$ min = $\frac{9}{20}$ x 60 s
= 9 x 3 s
= **27** s

US› (d) $\frac{3}{4}$ gal = $\frac{3}{4}$ x 4 qt
= **3** qt

3d› (d) $\frac{3}{4}$ ℓ = $\frac{3}{4}$ x 1,000 ml
= 3 x 250 ml
= **750** ml

3d› (e) $\frac{3}{4}$ year = $\frac{3}{4}$ x 12 months
= 3 x 3 months
= **9** months

US› (e) $\frac{3}{4}$ ft = $\frac{3}{4}$ x 12 in.
= 3 x 3 in.
= **9** in.

(f) $\frac{9}{10}$ kg = $\frac{9}{10}$ x 1,000 g
= 9 x 100 g
= **900** g

(g) $\frac{3}{5}$ km = $\frac{3}{5}$ x 1,000 m
= 3 x 200 m
= **600** m

(f) $\frac{5}{6}$ h = $\frac{5}{6}$ x 60 min
= 5 x 10 min
= **50** min

2. (a) $\frac{3}{5}$ m = $\frac{3}{5}$ x 100 cm
= 3 x 20 cm
= 60 cm

$2\frac{3}{5}$ m = 2 m **60** cm

(b) $\frac{7}{10}$ ℓ = $\frac{7}{10}$ x 1,000 ml
= 7 x 100 ml
= 700 ml

$4\frac{7}{10}$ ℓ = 4 ℓ **700** ml

(c) $\frac{1}{4}$ h = $\frac{1}{4}$ x 60 min
= 15 min

$3\frac{1}{4}$ h = **3** h **15** min

(d) $\frac{1}{2}$ days = $\frac{1}{2}$ x 24 h
= 12 h

$2\frac{1}{2}$ days = **2** days **12** h

(e) $\frac{2}{5}$ ℓ = $\frac{2}{5}$ x 1,000 ml
= 2 x 200 ml
= 400 ml

$2\frac{2}{5}$ ℓ = **2** ℓ **400** ml

(f) $\frac{1}{4}$ kg = $\frac{1}{4}$ x 1,000 g
= 250 g

$5\frac{1}{4}$ kg = **5** kg **250** g

US› (g) $\frac{3}{4}$ lb = $\frac{3}{4}$ x 16 oz
= 3 x 4 oz
= 12 oz

$4\frac{3}{4}$ lb = **4** lb **12** oz

(h) $\frac{7}{8}$ km = $\frac{7}{8}$ x 1,000 m
= 7 x 125 m
= 875 m

$3\frac{7}{8}$ km = **3** km **875** m

3d› (g) $\frac{3}{4}$ kg = $\frac{3}{4}$ x 1,000 g
= 3 x 250 g
= 750 g

$4\frac{3}{4}$ kg = **4** kg **750** g

Exercise 20

1. (a) 2 kg = 2,000 g
$\frac{1}{10}$ kg = $\frac{1}{10}$ x 1,000 g
= 100 g

$2\frac{1}{10}$ kg = **2,100** g

(b) 1 h = 60 min
$\frac{1}{6}$ h = $\frac{1}{6}$ x 60 min
= 10 min

$1\frac{1}{6}$ h = **70** min

(c) 2 years = 24 months
$\frac{2}{3}$ years = $\frac{2}{3}$ x 12 months
= 2 x 4 months
= 8 months

$2\frac{2}{3}$ years = **32** months

(d) 3 kg = 3,000 g
$\frac{1}{2}$ kg = $\frac{1}{2}$ x 1,000 g
= 500 g

$3\frac{1}{2}$ kg = **3,500** g

(e) 2 ℓ = 2,000 ml
$\frac{1}{5}$ ℓ = $\frac{1}{5}$ x 1,000 ml
= 200 ml

$2\frac{1}{5}$ ℓ = **2,200** ml

(f) 2 min = 120 s
$\frac{5}{6}$ min = $\frac{5}{6}$ x 60 s
= 5 x 10 s
= 50 s

$2\frac{5}{6}$ min = 120 + 50 = **170** s

(g) 4 m = 400 cm
$\frac{3}{5}$ m = $\frac{3}{5}$ x 100 cm
= 3 x 20 cm
= 60 cm

$4\frac{3}{5}$ m = **460** cm

(h) 3 km = 3,000 m
$\frac{4}{5}$ km = $\frac{4}{5}$ x 1,000 m
= 4 x 200 m
= 800 m

$3\frac{4}{5}$ km = **3,800** m

2. 3 km = 3,000 m

$\frac{1}{8}$ km = $\frac{1}{8}$ x 1,000 m = 125 m

$3\frac{1}{8}$ km = **3,125** m

3. 1 h = 60 min

$\frac{3}{4}$ h = $\frac{3}{4}$ x 60 min = 3 x 15 min = 45 min

$1\frac{3}{4}$ h = 60 min + 45 min = 105 min

Peter practices for 105 min.
125 min – 105 min = 20 min

US› **Pablo** practices for **20** min longer than Peter.
3d› **Hassan** practices for **20** min longer than Peter.

4. (a) $1\frac{1}{2}$ ℓ = 1,500 ml

$1\frac{1}{2}$ ℓ is more than 1,050 ml.

(b) $1\frac{2}{3}$ h = 60 + 40 min = 100 min

105 min is longer than $1\frac{2}{3}$ h.

some **US›** printings:

100 min is **equal** to $1\frac{2}{3}$ h

(c) $2\frac{1}{4}$ km = 2,250 m

2,500 m is longer than $2\frac{1}{4}$ km.

(d) $1\frac{1}{20}$ m = 105 cm

120 cm is longer than $1\frac{1}{20}$ m.

US› (e) $1\frac{3}{4}$ ft = 12 in. + 9 in. = 21 in.

$1\frac{3}{4}$ ft is longer than 20 in.

5. (a) $1\frac{1}{4}$ ℓ = 1,250 ml

$1\frac{1}{4}$ ℓ is less than 1,500 ml.

(b) $1\frac{1}{3}$ days = 24 + 8 = 32 h

30 h is shorter than $1\frac{1}{3}$ days.

(c) $1\frac{2}{3}$ years = 12 + 8 = 20 mths

18 mths is shorter than $1\frac{2}{3}$ y.

some **US›** printings:

20 mths is **equal** to $1\frac{2}{3}$ y.

(d) $1\frac{4}{5}$ kg = 1,800 g

1,400 g is lighter than $1\frac{4}{5}$ kg.

US› (e) $2\frac{1}{4}$ qt = 8 c + 1 c = 9 c

$\mathbf{2\frac{1}{4}}$ qt is less than 10 c.

Exercise 21

1. $\frac{8}{12} = \mathbf{\frac{2}{3}}$

2. 1 m = 100 cm
$\frac{95}{100} = \mathbf{\frac{19}{20}}$

3. 1 h = 60 min
$\frac{45}{60} = \mathbf{\frac{3}{4}}$

4. \$1 = 100 ¢
$\frac{15}{100} = \mathbf{\frac{3}{20}}$

5. 1 kg = 1,000 g
$\frac{650}{1,000} = \frac{65}{100} = \mathbf{\frac{13}{20}}$

6. 2 h = 2 x 60 min = 120 min
$\frac{40}{120} = \frac{4}{12} = \mathbf{\frac{1}{3}}$

7. **US›** 3 ft = 36 in.
$\frac{8}{36} = \mathbf{\frac{2}{9}}$

3d› 3 m = 300 cm
$\frac{75}{300} = \mathbf{\frac{1}{4}}$

8. \$3 = 300 ¢
$\frac{90}{300} = \frac{9}{30} = \mathbf{\frac{3}{10}}$

9. (a) 2 kg = 2,000 g
$\frac{750}{2,000} = \frac{3}{8}$
She used $\mathbf{\frac{3}{8}}$ of the flour.

(b) $1 - \frac{3}{8} = \frac{5}{8}$
$\mathbf{\frac{5}{8}}$ of the flour was left.

Exercise 22

1. (a) $\frac{1}{5} \times \frac{1}{2} = \frac{1 \times 1}{5 \times 2} = \mathbf{\frac{1}{10}}$

   (b) $\frac{3}{4} \times \frac{1}{2} = \frac{3 \times 1}{4 \times 2} = \mathbf{\frac{3}{8}}$

   (c) $\frac{\cancel{2}^{1}}{3} \times \frac{1}{\cancel{2}_{1}} = \frac{1 \times 1}{3 \times 1} = \mathbf{\frac{1}{3}}$

   (d) $\frac{2}{3} \times \frac{2}{3} = \frac{2 \times 2}{3 \times 3} = \mathbf{\frac{4}{9}}$

2. (a) $\frac{\cancel{4}^{2}}{9} \times \frac{1}{\cancel{2}_{1}} = \mathbf{\frac{2}{9}}$

   (b) $\frac{1}{4} \times \frac{3}{8} = \mathbf{\frac{3}{32}}$

   (c) $\frac{1}{5} \times \frac{3}{4} = \mathbf{\frac{3}{20}}$

   (d) $\frac{5}{\cancel{6}_{3}} \times \frac{\cancel{2}^{1}}{3} = \mathbf{\frac{5}{9}}$

   (e) $\frac{\cancel{4}^{1}}{\cancel{5}_{1}} \times \frac{\cancel{5}^{1}}{\cancel{8}_{2}} = \mathbf{\frac{1}{2}}$

   (f) $\frac{\cancel{4}^{2}}{\cancel{9}_{3}} \times \frac{\cancel{3}^{1}}{\cancel{10}_{5}} = \mathbf{\frac{2}{15}}$

   (g) $\frac{\cancel{9}^{3}}{\cancel{10}_{2}} \times \frac{\cancel{5}^{1}}{\cancel{6}_{2}} = \mathbf{\frac{3}{4}}$

   (h) $\frac{3}{\cancel{8}_{4}} \times \frac{\cancel{6}^{3}}{7} = \mathbf{\frac{9}{28}}$

Exercise 23

1. $2 \xrightarrow{\times \frac{5}{12}} \mathbf{\frac{5}{6}} \xrightarrow{\times \frac{2}{15}} \mathbf{\frac{1}{9}}$

   $\mathbf{\frac{1}{9}} \xrightarrow{\times 6} \frac{2}{3}$

   $\frac{2}{3} \xrightarrow{\times \frac{9}{16}} \mathbf{\frac{3}{8}} \xrightarrow{\times \frac{2}{9}} \mathbf{\frac{1}{12}}$

   $\mathbf{\frac{1}{12}} \xrightarrow{\times \frac{9}{10}} \mathbf{\frac{3}{40}}$

   $\mathbf{\frac{3}{40}} \xrightarrow{\times 10} \frac{3}{4} \xrightarrow{\times \frac{8}{9}} \mathbf{\frac{2}{3}}$

   $\mathbf{\frac{2}{3}} \xrightarrow{\times \frac{3}{4}} \mathbf{\frac{1}{2}}$

   $\mathbf{\frac{1}{2}} \xrightarrow{\times \frac{4}{5}} \mathbf{\frac{2}{5}} \xrightarrow{\times 5} 2$

2. Amount cooked = $\frac{\cancel{2}^{1}}{3} \times \frac{5}{\cancel{6}_{3}} = \mathbf{\frac{5}{9}}$ (**US›** lb, **3d›** kg)

3. **US›** Area = $\frac{3}{\cancel{4}_{2}}$ yd $\times$ $\frac{\cancel{2}^{1}}{5}$ yd = $\mathbf{\frac{3}{10}}$ yd^2

3d› Area = $\frac{3}{\cancel{4}_{2}}$ m $\times$ $\frac{\cancel{2}^{1}}{5}$ m = $\mathbf{\frac{3}{10}}$ m^2

4. $\frac{2}{3}$ of remainder

← calculator →← remainder →

Remainder = $1 - \frac{3}{5} = \frac{2}{5}$

Fraction of remainder left = $1 - \frac{2}{3} = \frac{1}{3}$

Fraction of total money left = $\frac{1}{3}$ of $\frac{2}{5} = \frac{1}{3} \times \frac{2}{5} = \mathbf{\frac{2}{15}}$

Exercise 24

1. (a) $\mathbf{\frac{1}{8}}$ (b) $\mathbf{\frac{1}{6}}$

(c) $\mathbf{\frac{2}{9}}$ (d) $\mathbf{\frac{1}{10}}$

2. (a) $\frac{3}{4} \div 2 = \frac{3}{4} \times \frac{1}{2} = \mathbf{\frac{3}{8}}$

(b) $\frac{8}{9} \div 4 = \frac{\cancel{8}^{2}}{9} \times \frac{1}{\cancel{4}_{1}} = \mathbf{\frac{2}{9}}$

(c) $\frac{5}{6} \div 5 = \frac{\cancel{5}^{1}}{6} \times \frac{1}{\cancel{5}_{1}} = \mathbf{\frac{1}{6}}$

(d) $\frac{3}{5} \div 9 = \frac{\cancel{3}^{1}}{5} \times \frac{1}{\cancel{9}_{3}} = \mathbf{\frac{1}{15}}$

(e) $\frac{4}{5} \div 2 = \frac{\cancel{4}^{2}}{5} \times \frac{1}{\cancel{2}_{1}} = \mathbf{\frac{2}{5}}$

(f) $\frac{5}{7} \div 6 = \frac{5}{7} \times \frac{1}{6} = \mathbf{\frac{5}{42}}$

(g) $\frac{5}{8} \div 3 = \frac{5}{8} \times \frac{1}{3} = \mathbf{\frac{5}{24}}$

(h) $\frac{4}{9} \div 10 = \frac{\cancel{4}^{2}}{9} \times \frac{1}{\cancel{10}_{5}} = \mathbf{\frac{2}{45}}$

Exercise 25

1. (a)

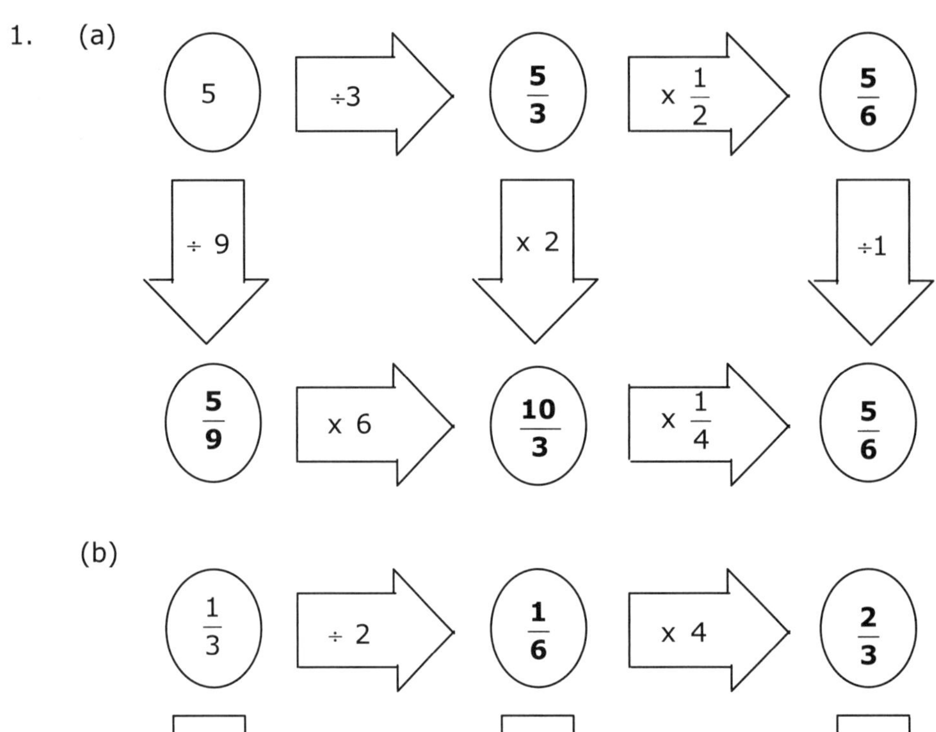

(b)

$\frac{1}{3}$ → ÷ 2 → $\mathbf{\frac{1}{6}}$ → x 4 → $\mathbf{\frac{2}{3}}$

$\frac{1}{3}$ ↓ ÷ 3; $\mathbf{\frac{1}{6}}$ ↓ ÷ 2; $\mathbf{\frac{2}{3}}$ ↓ ÷ 8

$\mathbf{\frac{1}{9}}$ → x $\frac{3}{4}$ → $\mathbf{\frac{1}{12}}$ → ÷ 1 → $\mathbf{\frac{1}{12}}$

2. In 6 days she used $\frac{3}{5}$ (**US›** lb, **3d›** kg)

   In 1 day she used $\frac{3}{5} \div 6 = \frac{3}{5} \times \frac{1}{6} = \mathbf{\frac{1}{10}}$ (**US› lb, 3d› kg**)

3. Length of each piece = $\frac{1}{2} \div 5 = \frac{1}{2} \times \frac{1}{5} = \mathbf{\frac{1}{10}}$ (**US› yd, 3d› m**)

4. The remainder is $\frac{2}{3}$. Each one of his children gets $\frac{1}{4}$ of $\frac{2}{3} = \frac{1}{4} \times \frac{2}{3} = \mathbf{\frac{1}{6}}$

Exercise 26

Methods may vary. Only one method involving modeling will be shown here.

1. 50

?

1 unit = $\frac{1}{10}$ of the oranges

3 units are rotten. 10 – 3 = 7 units are not rotten.
10 units = 50 oranges
1 unit = 50 ÷ 10 = 5 oranges
7 units = 5 x 7 = 35
35 oranges are not rotten.

2. ?

$60

1 unit = $\frac{1}{5}$ of the money

She spent 2 units. 5 – 2 = 3 units are left.
3 units = $60
1 unit = $60 ÷ 3 = $20
5 units = $20 x 5 = $100
She had **$100** at first.

3 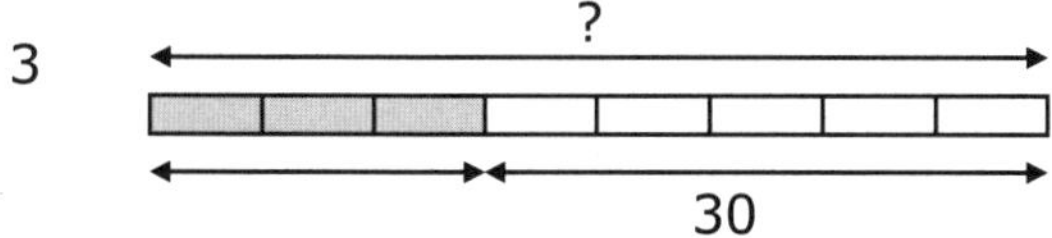

1 unit = $\frac{1}{8}$ of her money

She had 3 units left, so spent 5 units.

5 units = $30
1 unit = $30 ÷ 5 = $6
8 units = $6 x 8 = $48
She had **$48** at first.

4. 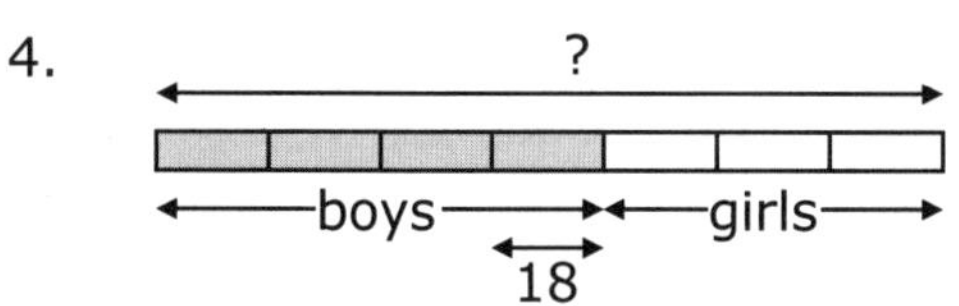

1 unit = $\frac{1}{7}$ of the children
4 units = boys
3 units = girls
There is 1 more unit of boys than girls.

1 unit = 18
7 units = 18 x 7 = 126
There are **126** children altogether.

Exercise 27

Methods may vary.

1. The capacity is how much the tank can hold.

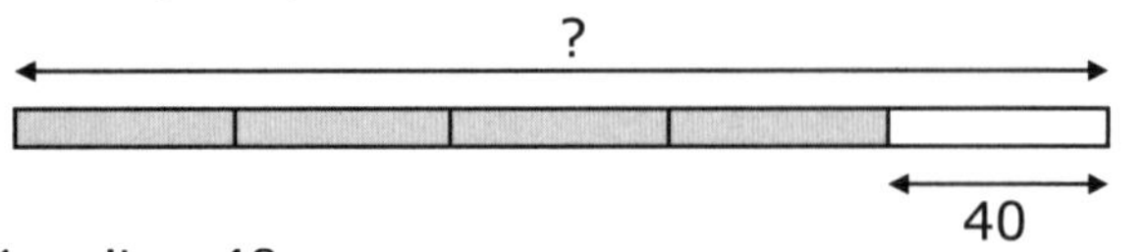

1 unit = $\frac{1}{5}$ of the tank
4 units = amount in tank
1 unit = amount needed

1 unit = 40
5 units = 5 x 40 = 200
The capacity of the tank is **200 (US› gal, 3d› ℓ).**

2. 1400

?

1 unit = $\frac{1}{4}$ of the students

Students who wear glasses = 1 unit = 1400 ÷ 4 = 350
Boys who wear glasses = 2 smaller units.
7 smaller units = 350
1 smaller unit = 350 ÷ 7 = 50
2 smaller units = 50 x 2 = 100

Or: Number of boys who wear glasses = $\frac{2}{7}$ x ($\frac{1}{4}$ x 1400) = 100

100 boys wear glasses.

3.

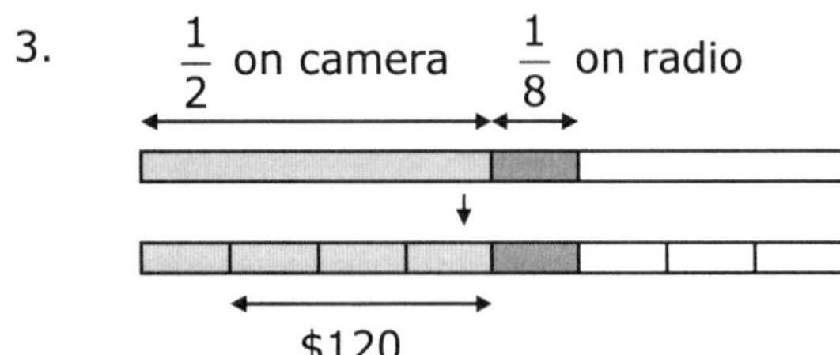

$\frac{1}{2} = \frac{4}{8}$ Bar should have 8 units.
4 units = cost of camera
1 unit = cost of radio
Camera costs 3 more units than radio.
3 units = $120
1 unit = $120 ÷ 3 = $40
8 units = $40 x 8 = $320
He had **$320** at first.

4. $480

$60 ?

1 unit = $\frac{1}{3}$ of her money

Money left = 1 unit – $60

3 units = $480
1 unit = $480 ÷ 3 = $160
Money left = $160 – $60 = **$100**

Exercise 28

Methods may vary.

1. Remainder is 1 part out of 3.
3 parts = 120
1 part = 120 ÷ 3 = 40
She had 3 units out of 4 left.
4 units = 40
1 unit = 40 ÷ 4 = 10
3 units = 10 x 3 = 30

Or:
Subdivide the bar into 3 x 4 = 12 units.
She had 3 units out of a total of 12 left.
12 units = 120
1 unit = 120 ÷ 12 = 10
3 units = 10 x 3 = 30
She had **30** eggs left.

Or:
The remainder after baking cakes is $1-\frac{2}{3}=\frac{1}{3}$
Fraction of remaining eggs not used is $1-\frac{1}{4}=\frac{3}{4}$
She had $\frac{3}{4}$ of the remainder left.
$\frac{3}{4} \times \frac{1}{3}=\frac{1}{4}$
$\frac{1}{4} \times 120 = 30$
She had 30 eggs left.

2. Remainder is 2 parts out of 5.
5 parts = $600
1 part = $\$\frac{600}{5} = \$120$
2 parts = $120 x 2 = $240
He spent 3 units out of 8.
8 units = $240
1 unit = $\$\frac{240}{8} = \$30$
3 units = $30 x 3 = $90
He spent **$90**.

Or: The remainder is $1-\frac{3}{5}=\frac{2}{5}$
He spent $\frac{3}{8}$ of that.
$\frac{3}{8} \times \frac{2}{5}=\frac{3}{20}$.
He spent $\frac{3}{20}$ of his money.
$\frac{3}{20} \times \$600 = 3 \times \$30 = \$90$

3. Remainder = 2 larger parts
1 unit = $\frac{1}{4}$ of 2 parts = $\frac{1}{2}$ of 1 part
There are 10 units.
She sold 1 unit in the afternoon.
10 units = 400
1 unit = 40
She sold **40** tarts in the afternoon.

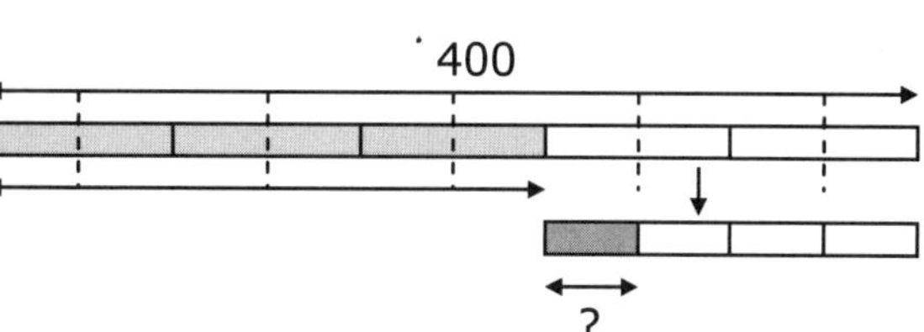

Or: Remainder = $\frac{2}{5} \times 400 = 160$

Amount sold = $\frac{1}{4} \times 160 = 40$

4.

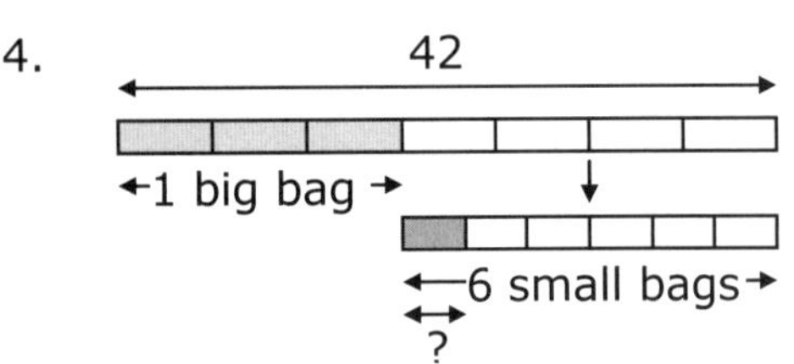

1 part = $\frac{1}{7}$ of the rice

4 parts were put into small bags.

7 parts = 42 kg
1 part = 42 ÷ 7 = 6 kg
4 parts = 6 x 4 = 24 kg
6 units = 24 kg
1 unit = 24 ÷ 6 = 4 kg

He put **4 kg** in each smaller bag.

Or:
The amount put in smaller bags is

$$\frac{1}{6} \times \frac{4}{7} \times 42 = \frac{1 \times \cancel{4}^{2} \times \cancel{42}^{\cancel{6}^{2}}}{\cancel{6}_{\cancel{3}_{1}} \times \cancel{7}_{1}} = 4$$

Exercise 29

Methods may vary.

1. 1 part = $\frac{1}{5}$ of the tarts

2 parts were left in the afternoon. Divide these to get 4 units since $\frac{1}{4}$ of them were sold in the afternoon. Divide the rest of the parts also. The whole bar has 10 units.

?

300

3 units = 300

1 unit = $\frac{300}{3}$ = 100

10 units = 1,000
She made **1,000** tarts.

Or:

$\frac{3}{4} \times \frac{2}{5}$ of total = 300

$\frac{3}{10}$ of total = 300

$\frac{1}{10}$ of total = 300 ÷ 3 = 100

$\frac{10}{10}$ of total = 100 x 10 = 1,000

2. Divide bar into 10 units as with #1. 6 units were sold in the morning and 1 in the afternoon. 5 units more were sold in the morning than in the afternoon.
5 units = 200
1 unit = 200 ÷ 5 = 40
10 units = 40 x 10 =400
She made **400** tarts.

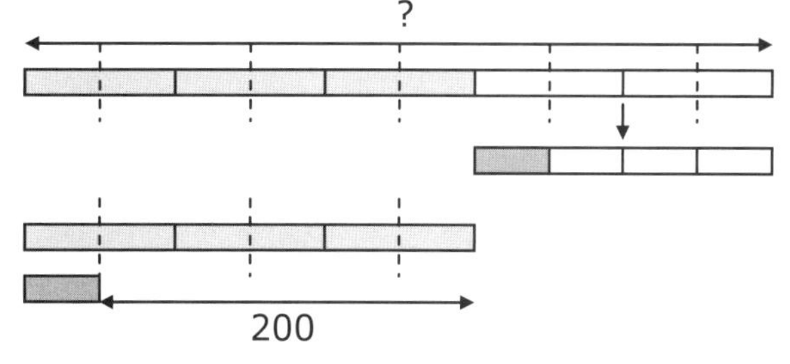

3. 1 part = $\frac{1}{3}$ of his money.

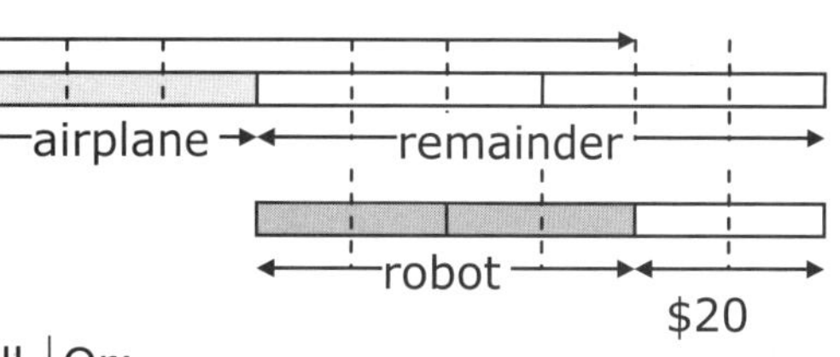

2 parts are left. These are made into 3 parts. If each of these parts is subdivided into 2 units, and each of the original parts is subdivided into 3, there will be 9 parts in the whole bar, and 6 equal parts in the remainder bar. He spent 7 units and had 2 units left.
2 units = $20
1 unit = $$\frac{20}{2}$ = $10
7 units = $10 x 7 = $70
He spent **$70**.

Or:
Fraction he spent is
$\frac{1}{3} + \left(\frac{2}{3} \times \frac{2}{3}\right) = \frac{3}{9} + \frac{4}{9} = \frac{7}{9}$
Fraction left = $1 - \frac{7}{9} = \frac{2}{9}$
$\frac{2}{9}$ of his money = $20
$\frac{1}{9}$ of his money = $$\frac{20}{2}$ = $10
$\frac{7}{9}$ of his money = $10 x 7 = $70

4. Divide $\frac{2}{3}$ of his money into 4 parts since the calculator costs 3 times as much as the pen. This divides each third into 2 units. He had 2 units left.

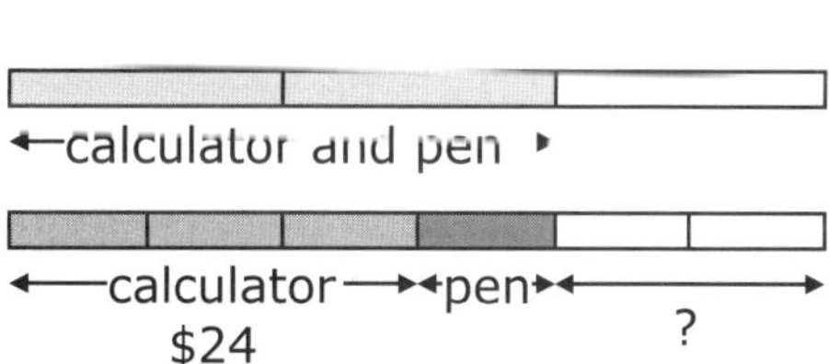

3 units = $24
1 unit = $$\frac{24}{3}$ = $8
2 units = $8 x 2 = $16
He had **$16** left.

Or:
Cost of calculator = $\frac{3}{4} \times \frac{2}{3} = \frac{1}{2}$ of his money
$\frac{1}{2}$ of his money = $24
All of his money = $24 x 2 = $48
He has $\frac{1}{3}$ of his money left.
$\frac{1}{3}$ x $48 = $16

Exercise 30

1.

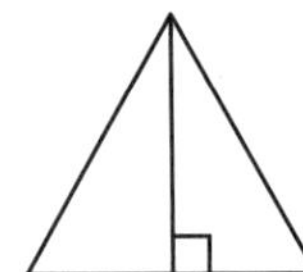
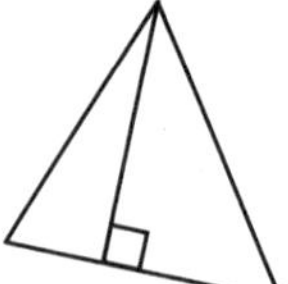

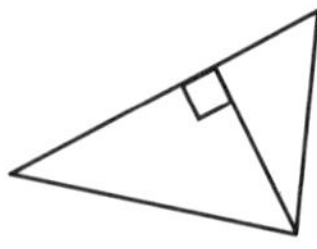
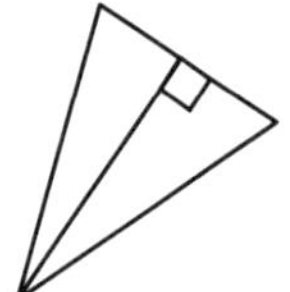

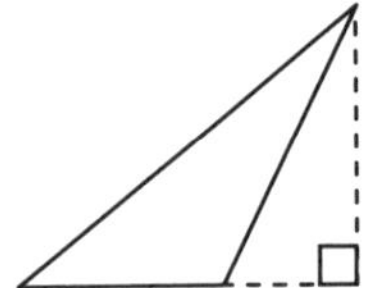

2. (a) **BC** (b) **DF** (c) **QR** (d) **YZ** (e) **LN** (f) **RT**

Exercise 31

1. (a) $\frac{1}{2}$ x 12 x 11 = **66 cm²** (b) $\frac{1}{2}$ x 11 x 8 = **44 m²**
   (c) $\frac{1}{2}$ x 10 x 14 = **70 cm²** (d) $\frac{1}{2}$ x 10 x 10 = **50 m²**

2. (a) $\frac{1}{2}$ x 5 x 6 = **15 cm²** (b) $\frac{1}{2}$ x 10 x 6 = **30 m²**
   (c) $\frac{1}{2}$ x 18 x 15 = **135 cm²** (d) $\frac{1}{2}$ x 12 x 25 = **150 cm²**

Exercise 32

US› 1. (a) $\frac{1}{2}$ x 9 x 8 = **36 in.^{2}** (b) $\frac{1}{2}$ x 15 x 12 = **90 in.^{2}**

(c) $\frac{1}{2}$ x 14 x 16 = **112 yd^2** (d) $\frac{1}{2}$ x 18 x 20 = **180 yd^2**

3d› 1. (a) $\frac{1}{2}$ x 9 x 8 = **36 cm^2** (b) $\frac{1}{2}$ x 15 x 12 = **90 cm^2**

(c) $\frac{1}{2}$ x 14 x 16 = **112 m^2** (d) $\frac{1}{2}$ x 18 x 20 = **180 m^2**

US› 2. (a) $\frac{1}{2}$ x 20 x 12 = **120 in.^{2}** (b) $\frac{1}{2}$ x 14 x 10 = **70 in.^{2}**

(c) $\frac{1}{2}$ x 14 x 13 = **91 ft^2** (d) $\frac{1}{2}$ x 22 x 20 = **220 ft^2**

3d› 2. (a) $\frac{1}{2}$ x 20 x 12 = **120 cm^2** (b) $\frac{1}{2}$ x 14 x 10 = **70 cm^2**

(c) $\frac{1}{2}$ x 14 x 13 = **91 m^2** (d) $\frac{1}{2}$ x 22 x 20 = **220 m^2**

3.

Triangle	A	B	C	D	E
Area	**18 cm^2**	**36 cm^2**	**15 cm^2**	**45 cm^2**	**18 cm^2**

(a) **D** (b) **C** (c) 45 - 15 = **30 cm^2**
(d) **B** (e) **A & E**

Exercise 33

1. (a) Base = 16 cm
Height = 12 cm
Area = $\frac{1}{2}$ x 16 x 12 = **96 cm^2**

(b) Base = 12 cm
Height = 5 cm
Area = $\frac{1}{2}$ x 12 x 5 = **30 cm^2**

(c) Base = 6 + 6 = 12 m
Height = 8 m
Area = $\frac{1}{2}$ x 12 x 8 = **48 m^2**

(d) Base = 6 m
Height = 9 m
Area = $\frac{1}{2}$ x 6 x 9 = **27 m^2**

2. (a) Base = 8 + 4 = 12 cm
Height = 7 cm
Area = $\frac{1}{2}$ x 12 x 7 = **42 cm^2**

(b) Base = 20 – 12 = 8 cm
Height = 12 cm
Area = $\frac{1}{2}$ x 8 x 12 = **48 cm^2**

(c) Area of □ = 30 x 21 = 630 m^2
Area of Δ = $\frac{1}{2}$ x 30 x 14
= 210 m^2
Shaded area = 630 − 210
= **420 m^2**

(d) Area of □ = 20 x 16 = 320 m^2
Area of Δ = $\frac{1}{2}$ x 20 x 8
= 80 m^2
Shaded area = 320 − 80
= **240 m^2**

Exercise 34

1. (a) **3 : 4** (b) **4 : 3**
2. (a) **5 : 3** (b) **3 : 5**
3. (a) **2 : 3** (b) **3 : 2**
4. (a) **5 : 3** (b) **3 : 5**
5. (a) **3 : 7** (b) **7 : 3**
6. (a) **6 : 5** (b) **5 : 6**

Exercise 35

1. (a) 12 : 30 = **2 : 5** (b) 9 : 15 = **3 : 5**

2. **2 : 3** **3 : 1**
1 : 4 **3 : 5**
5 : 3 **2 : 1**
5 : 6 **4 : 5**
1 : 2 **5 : 4**

3. (a) **5**
(b) **32**
(c) **36**
(d) **28**
(e) **1**
(f) **2**
(g) **1**
(h) **12**
(i) **4**
(j) **15**
(k) **1** (some **US›** printings: **1.25**)
(l) **4**

4. 60 : 48 = **5 : 4** (common factor 12)

5. Length of second piece = 40 − 16 = 24 cm
24 : 16 = **3 : 2** (common factor 8)

6. Amount Sumin saves = \$52 + \$20 = \$72
52 : 72 = **13 : 18** (common factor 4)

Exercise 36

1. 4 units = 60

   1 unit = $\frac{60}{4}$ = 15

   7 units = 15 x 7 = 105
   There are **105** apples.

2. 3 units = 42 cm

   1 unit = $\frac{42}{3}$ = 14 cm

   8 units = 14 x 8 = 112 cm
   The length of the original ribbon was **112 cm**.

3. 3 units = $24

   5 units = $$\frac{24}{3}$ x 5 = $40

   The blouse cost **$40**.

4. 10 units = $280

   4 units = $$\frac{280}{10}$ x 4 = $112

   John received **$112** more than Peter.

Exercise 37

1. **2 : 4 : 3**
2. **3 : 2 : 4**
3. **3 : 1 : 4**
4. **6 : 5 : 4**
5. **4 : 3 : 5**
6. **3 : 3 : 2**

Exercise 38

1. 5 units = 90

   1 unit = $\frac{90}{5}$ = 18

   10 units = 18 x 10 = 180
   There are **180** beads altogether.

2. 9 units = 45 cm

   1 unit = $\frac{45}{9}$ = 5

   4 units = 5 x 4 = 20 cm
   The length of the longest side is **20 cm**.

Exercise 39

1. a = **38°** b = **65°** c = **90°** d = **121°**
   e = **160°** f = **180°** g = **202°** h = **245°**
   i = **270°** j = **307°** k = **338°** l = **360°**

2. a = **66°** b = **230°** c = **128°** d = **335°**

3. 

4. 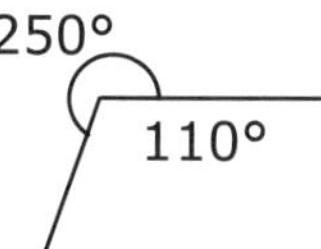

5. 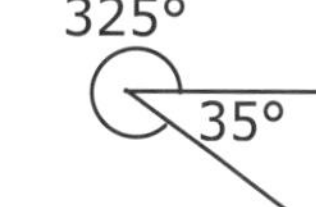

Exercise 40

1. **south**
north-east
south-east
west
north-west
east
south-west

2. **north-east**
east
south-east
north-west
45°
90°
135°
45°

Exercise 41

1. $\angle a = 180° - 135° = \mathbf{45°}$
$\angle b = 90° - 32° = \mathbf{58°}$
$\angle c = \mathbf{48°}$
$\angle d = 360° - 24° = \mathbf{336°}$
$\angle e = 360° - 250° = \mathbf{110°}$
$\angle f = 180° - 90° = \mathbf{90°}$
$\angle g = 180° - 28° = \mathbf{152°}$
$\angle h = \mathbf{145°}$

2. $\angle q = 180° - 72° - 80° = \mathbf{28°}$
$\angle r = 180° - 35° - 28° = \mathbf{117°}$
$\angle s = 360° - 108° - 85° - 90° = \mathbf{77°}$
$\angle t = 360° - 135° - 124° = \mathbf{101°}$
$\angle u = 360° - 92° - 78° - 140° = \mathbf{50°}$

Review 2

1. (a) $4\frac{1}{2} = \frac{9}{2} = \frac{18}{4}$ or $\frac{42}{4} = 10\frac{1}{2}$
$4\frac{1}{2} \mathbf{<} \frac{42}{4}$

(b) $3\frac{1}{7} = \frac{22}{7}$ or $\frac{31}{7} = 4\frac{3}{7}$
$3\frac{1}{7} \mathbf{<} \frac{31}{7}$

(c) $\frac{34}{8} = 4\frac{2}{8} = 4\frac{1}{4}$ or $4\frac{1}{4} = \frac{17}{4} = \frac{34}{8}$
$\frac{34}{8} \mathbf{=} 4\frac{1}{4}$

(d) $10\frac{1}{3} = \frac{31}{3}$ or $\frac{10}{3} = 3\frac{1}{3}$
$10\frac{1}{3} \mathbf{>} \frac{10}{3}$

2. (a) $2\frac{3}{8} + \frac{7}{12} = 2\frac{9}{24} + \frac{14}{24}$
$= \mathbf{2\frac{23}{24}}$

(b) $4\frac{1}{3} - 1\frac{8}{9} = 3\frac{3}{9} - \frac{8}{9}$
$= 2\frac{12}{9} - \frac{8}{9}$
$= \mathbf{2\frac{4}{9}}$

(c) $\frac{7}{\cancel{9}_3} \times \frac{\cancel{3}^1}{4} = \mathbf{\frac{7}{12}}$

(d) $\cancel{36}^4 \times \frac{5}{\cancel{9}_1} = \mathbf{20}$

3. (a) $\frac{1}{2}$ h = $\frac{1}{2}$ x 60 min = 30 min

$4\frac{1}{2}$ h = **4** h **30** min

(b) $\frac{1}{4}$ y = $\frac{1}{4}$ x 12 mths = 3 mths

$2\frac{1}{4}$ y = **2** years **3** months

(c) $\frac{9}{10}$ m = $\frac{9}{10}$ x 100 cm = 90 cm

$3\frac{9}{10}$ = **3** m **90** cm

(d) $\frac{3}{10}$ kg = $\frac{3}{10}$ x 1,000 g = 300 g

$5\frac{3}{10}$ kg = **5** kg **300** g

4. (a) $\frac{4}{5}$ m = $\frac{4}{5}$ x 100 cm = 80 cm

85 cm is longer than $\frac{4}{5}$ m.

(b) $\frac{2}{3}$ y = $\frac{2}{3}$ x 12 mths = 8 mths

$1\frac{2}{3}$ y = 12 + 8 = 20 mths

$\mathbf{1\frac{2}{3}}$ y is longer than 17 months.

(c) $\frac{1}{10}$ kg = $\frac{1}{10}$ x 1,000 g = 100 g

$2\frac{1}{10}$ kg = 2,100 g

$\mathbf{2\frac{1}{10}}$ kg is heavier than 2,001 g.

(d) 3 ℓ = 3,000 ml
3 ℓ 50 ml = 3,050 ml
3 ℓ 50 ml is more than 350 ml.

5. Fraction shaded = $\frac{1}{2}$ of $\frac{3}{4}$ = $\frac{1}{2}$ x $\frac{3}{4}$ = $\mathbf{\frac{3}{8}}$

6.**US›** Perimeter of rectangle = 2 x (12 + 6) = 36 yd
Perimeter of square = 36 yd
One side of square = 36 ÷ 4 = 9 yd
Area of square = 9 x 9 = **81 yd^2**

3d› Perimeter of rectangle = 2 x (12 + 6) = 36 m
Perimeter of square = 36 m
One side of square = 36 ÷ 4 = 9 m
Area of square = 9 x 9 = **81 m^2**

7. 2 ℓ weighs 600 g.
1 ℓ weighs 600 ÷ 2 = 300 g
3 ℓ weighs 300 x 3 = **900** g

8. Total number of packets = 5 + 3 = 8
Total number of envelopes = 8 x 112 = **896**

9. Number of packets = 1,320 ÷ 22 = 60
Amount of money made = 60 x $2 = **$120**

10. $6\frac{1}{4} - 2\frac{1}{2} = 4\frac{1}{4} - \frac{2}{4} = 3\frac{5}{4} - \frac{2}{4} = 3\frac{3}{4}$

$\frac{3}{4}$ year = $\frac{3}{4}$ x 12 months = 9 months

$3\frac{3}{4}$ years = **3** years **9** months

11.

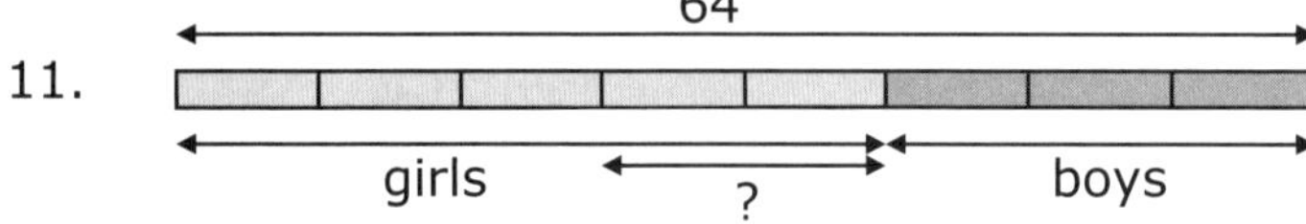

8 units = 64

1 unit = $\frac{64}{8}$ = 8

2 units = 8 x 2 = 16

There are **16** more girls than boys.

Or: There are $\frac{5}{8}$ girls and $\frac{3}{8}$ boys

Fraction more girls = $\frac{5}{8} - \frac{3}{8} = \frac{2}{8}$

$\frac{2}{8}$ x 64 = 16

12.**US›** (a) 5 units = 20 in.

3 units = $\frac{20}{5}$ x 3 = 12 in.

The width is **12 in.**

20 in.
length
width

(b) Area = 20 x 12
= **240 in.^{2}**

(c) Perimeter = 2 x (12 + 20)
= **64 in.**

3d› (a) 5 units = 20 cm

3 units = $\frac{20}{5}$ x 3 = 12 cm

The width is **12** cm

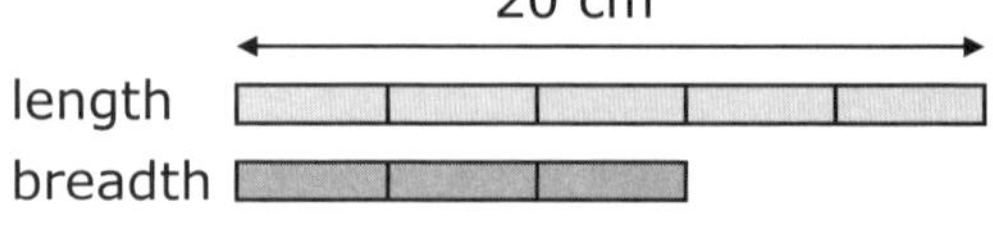

(b) Area = 20 x 12
= **240 cm^2**

(c) Perimeter = 2 x (12 + 20)
= **64 cm**

13. 5 units = 15 cm

1 unit = $\frac{15}{3}$ = 3 cm

15 cm

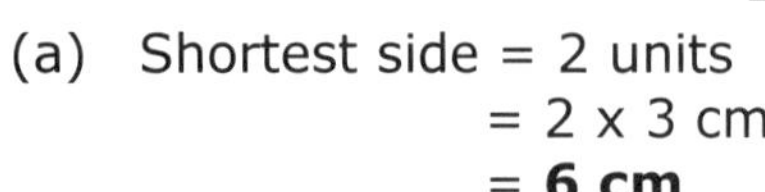

(a) Shortest side = 2 units
= 2 x 3 cm
= **6 cm**

(b) Perimeter = 11 units
= 11 x 3 cm
= **33 cm**

14. (a) $x + 90° = 55° + 103°$
$x = (55° + 103°) - 90°$
$= 158° - 90°$
$=$ **68°**

(b) $x = 360° - 90° - 90° - 38°$
$=$ **142°**

15. Shaded area is a triangle with a base of 14 m and corresponding height of 12 m.

Shaded area = $\frac{1}{2}$ x 14 x 12 = 84 m^2

Area of rectangle = 21 x 12 = 252 m^2

Fraction shaded = $\frac{84}{252}$ = $\mathbf{\frac{1}{3}}$

16. 9 units = 117 kg

1 unit = $\frac{117}{9}$ = 13 kg

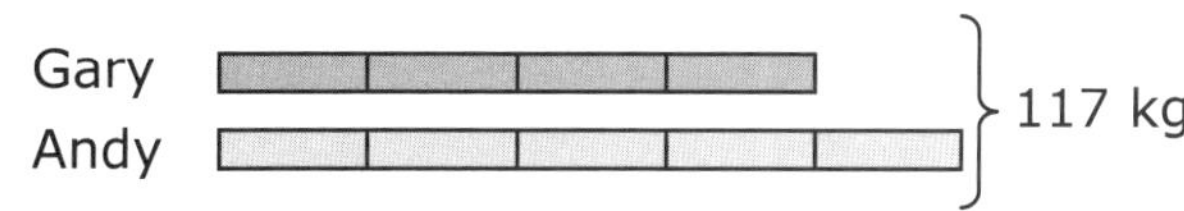

(**3d›** Gary ↔ Gomez, Andy ↔ Ali)

(a) Andy's weight = 5 units
= 5 x 13 kg
= **65 kg**

(b) Gary's weight = 4 units
= 4 x 13 kg
= **52 kg**
(Or: 117 kg - 65 kg = 52 kg)

17. 3 units = 15 m

2 units = $\frac{15}{3}$ x 2 = 10 m

The length of the shadow is **10 m**.

15 m
tree
shadow

18. $\frac{9}{4} = 2\frac{1}{4}$. $\frac{12}{11}$ is less than 2. The others are greater than 2 by $\frac{1}{4}$, $\frac{1}{12}$, and $\frac{1}{2}$. The numerators are the same, so the one with the smallest denominator is the largest. Order from largest is $\mathbf{2\frac{1}{2}, \frac{9}{4}, 2\frac{1}{12}, \frac{12}{11}}$.

19. $3\frac{1}{8}$ is $\frac{7}{8}$ from 4; $3\frac{11}{12}$ is $\frac{1}{12}$ from 4; the last two are closer to 5 than 4.

$\frac{1}{12}$ is smaller than $\frac{7}{8}$, so $\mathbf{3\frac{11}{12}}$ is nearest to 4.

20. (a) (**3d›** in. ↔ cm, in.^{2} ↔ cm^2)
Shaded area is a triangle with base 14 in. and height 10 – 4 = 6 in.

Area = $\frac{1}{2}$ x 14 x 6 = **42 in.^{2}**

(b) (**3d›** ft ↔ m, ft^2 ↔ m^2)
The shaded area is the area of the rectangle with length 10 + 5 = 15 ft and width 12 ft minus the two unshaded triangles, one with base 5 ft and height 12 – 3 = 9 ft and the other with base 10 ft and height 12 ft.

Area = (15 x 12) – ($\frac{1}{2}$ x 5 x 9) – ($\frac{1}{2}$ x 10 x 12)

= 180 – $22\frac{1}{2}$ – 60 = $\mathbf{97\frac{1}{2}}$ **ft^2**

Or: The shaded area can be split up into a small rectangle of length 5 ft and width 3 ft, a triangle of base 5 ft and height 12 – 3 = 9 ft, and a triangle of base 10 ft and height 12 ft.

Area = $(3 \times 5) + (\frac{1}{2} \times 5 \times 9) + (\frac{1}{2} \times 10 \times 12)$

$= 15 + 22\frac{1}{2} + 60 = 97\frac{1}{2}$ ft^2

21. Area of shaded part = $\frac{1}{2} \times 16 \times 18 = 144$ m^2

Area of rectangle = 3 x 144 m^2 = **432 m^2**

22.

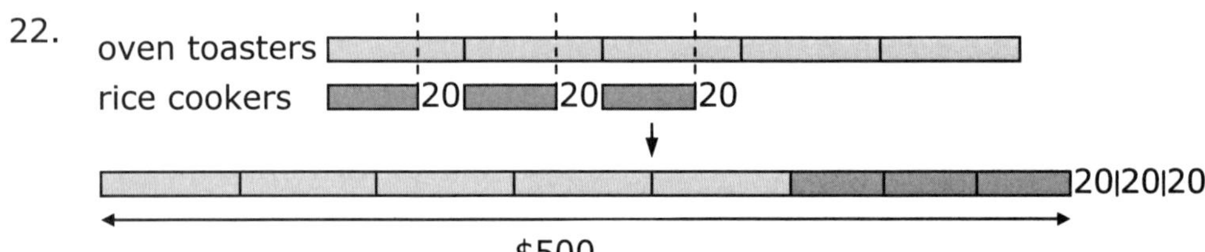

1 unit is cost of oven toaster.
8 units = \$500 + (3 x \$20) = \$500 + \$60 = \$560

1 unit = $\$\frac{560}{8} = \$70$

Cost of rice cooker = \$70 – \$20 = \$50

Or: 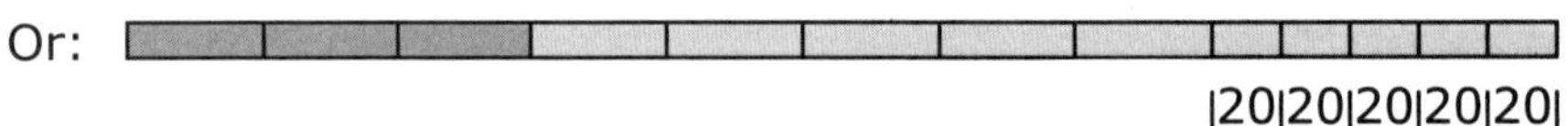

1 unit is cost of rice cooker.
8 units = \$500 – (5 x \$20) = \$500 - \$100 = \$400

1 unit = $\$\frac{400}{8} = \$50$

Cost of rice cooker = **\$50**.

23. 2 units = \$800

1 unit = $\$\frac{800}{2} = \$400$

6 units = \$400 x 6 = \$2,400
Henry had \$**2,400**.

(**3d›** Bill ↔ Mr Lin, Henry ↔ Mr Ho)

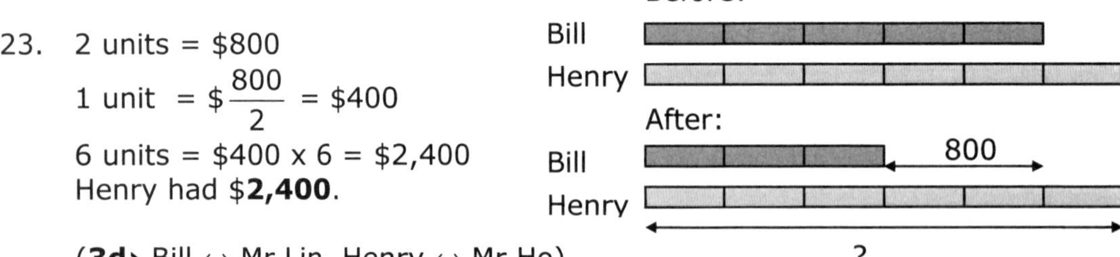

24. (**3d›** in. ↔ cm, in.^{2} ↔ cm^2)

Area of triangle = $\frac{1}{2} \times 10 \times 5 = 25$ in.^{2}

Area of square = 25 in.^{2}
Side of square = 5 in. (5 x 5 = 25)
Perimeter of square = 4 x 5 cm = **20 in.**

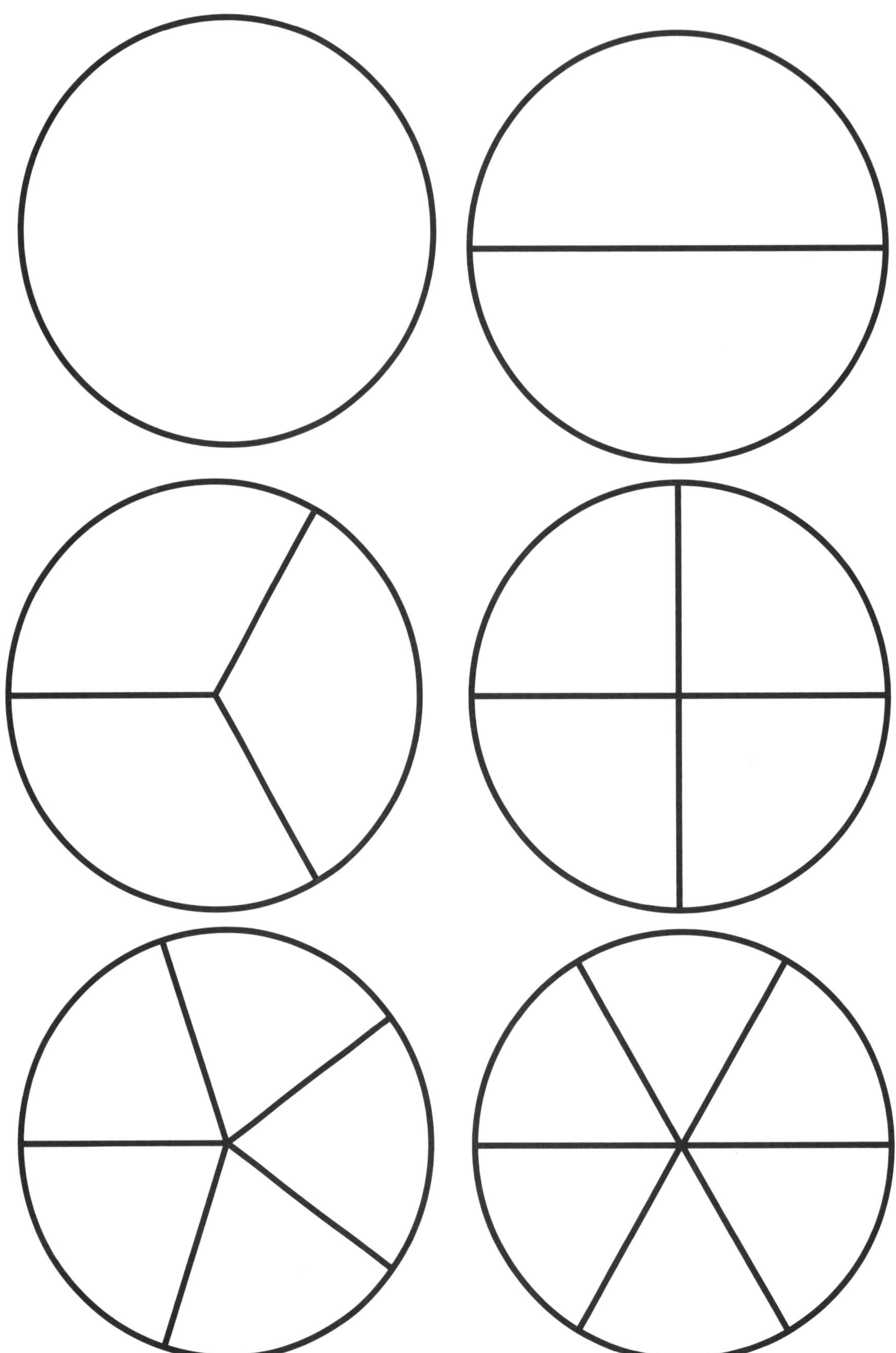

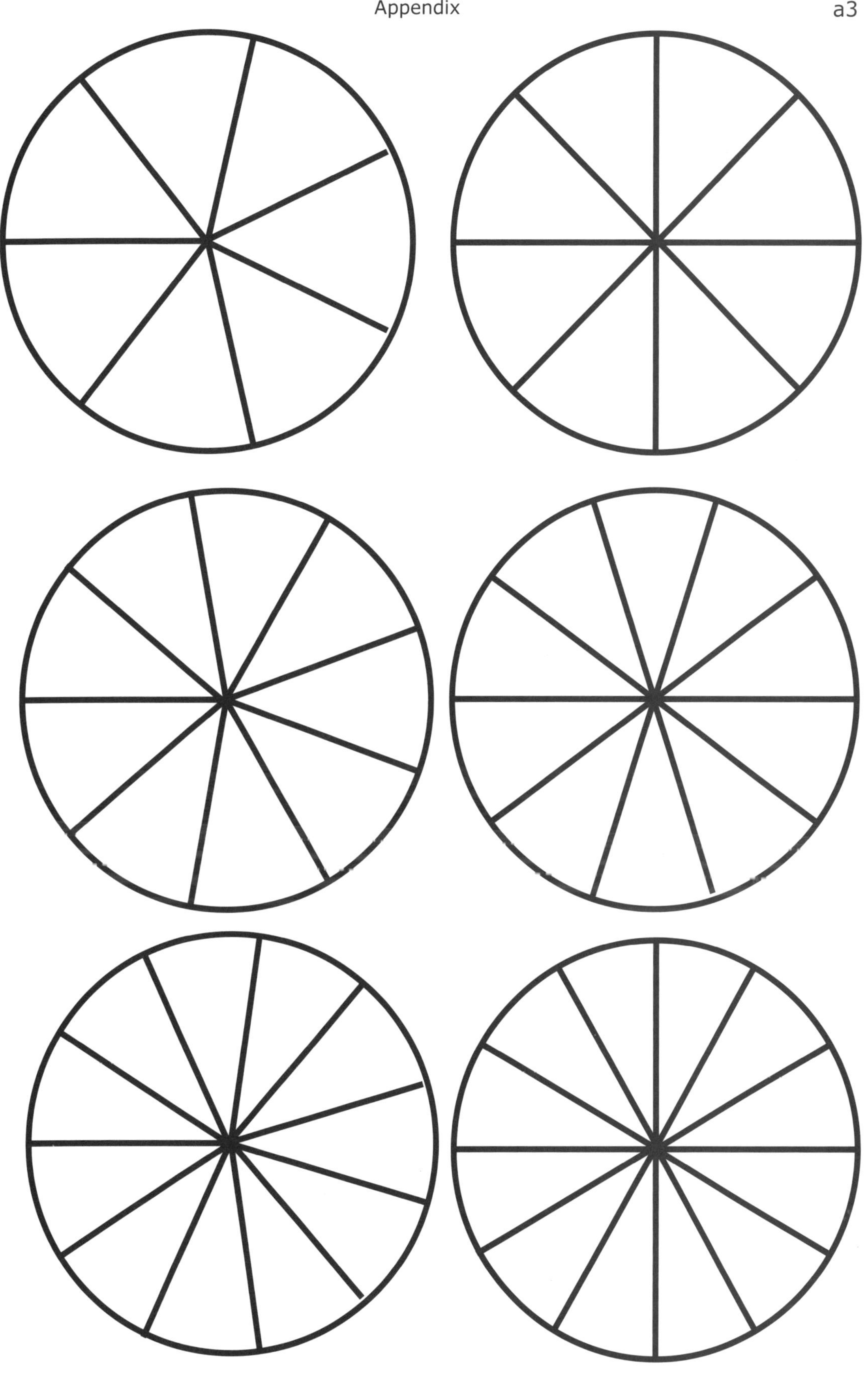